The Biblical Seminar
84

Gospel Images
in Fiction and Film

Gospel Images

in Fiction and Film

On Reversing the Hermeneutical Flow

Larry J. Kreitzer

SHEFFIELD ACADEMIC PRESS
A Continuum imprint
LONDON • NEW YORK

Published by Sheffield Academic Press Ltd
The Tower Building, 11 York Road, London SE1 7NX
370 Lexington Avenue, New York NY 10017-6550

www.SheffieldAcademicPress.com
www.continuumbooks.com

British Library Cataloguing-in-Publication Data

A catalogue record for this book is available from the British Library

Typeset by Sheffield Academic Press
Printed on acid-free paper in Great Britain The Cromwell Press,
Trowbridge, Wiltshire

ISBN   1-84127-343-0 (hardback)
       1-84127-266-3 (paperback)

CONTENTS

In the movie *Conan the Barbarian*,[1] the mighty hero Conan is captured by his arch-enemy, the sorcerer Thulsa Doom, who then crucifies him. Tied to a wonderfully gnarled, surrealistic tree, Conan (played by Arnold Schwarzenegger) strikes cruciform body-building poses composed of equal parts venerable European traditions of religious art and the popular 'pulp' magazine fantasy art of Frank Frazetta. Conan is eventually raised up, although not by the gods. His three companions, two thieves and a wizard, use a combination of magical incantations (including spells written on his body) and violent struggles with the gods of the underworld who arrive to claim Conan's spirit.

Nevertheless, Conan is no Christ, and not even a Christ-figure. He is a thief and adventurer, a wild, ignorant and often brutal (and brutish) hero of the 'sword and sorcery' sub-genre of fantasy. He lives some 12,000 years ago (according to his creator, Robert E. Howard) in a world that only slightly resembles our own. Conan comes from the fictional land of Cimmeria, he worships the earth god Crom, and he seeks the 'mystery of steel'. He does not offer the mystery of the kingdom of God. His crucifixion comes not at the end of his earthly story but rather nearer to its beginning, and the kingdom that he eventually wins is very much one of this world.

What then does Conan's crucifixion story have to do with the crucifixion stories in the Gospels? If you hold that the meaning of a story is locked into its text at the moment of its formation, and that it derives from the intention of an author or even from some actual historical event, then the meaning of the Gospel stories remains untouched by Conan's story. Conan's crucifixion is nothing more than an incidental by-product, an allusion (probably blasphemous, certainly humorous) designed to titillate

---

1.   Dir. John Milius (MCA/Universal Pictures and Dino de Laurentiis Corporation, 1981). Starring Arnold Schwarzenegger and James Earl Jones (as Thulsa Doom). The screenplay was co-written by John Milius and Oliver Stone and draws loosely on several of Robert E. Howard's Conan stories (see Howard 1967).

the movie-going masses. It is a product not of faith but of marketing, of 'the work of art in the age of mechanical reproduction' (Benjamin 1968). Conan's crucifixion is but one further development, and a relatively minor one at that, in a two-millennium-long trajectory. As such it says something about the cinematic tastes of contemporary viewers, but it says nothing about the Gospel stories themselves. It offers no hermeneutical insight into the life or death of Jesus.

However, if you hold that the meaning of a text is not some invisible substance inserted in it at the moment of its origin (rather like the immortal soul that mysteriously appears in a human foetus), but rather that the meaning of a text must be negotiated and continually re-negotiated between that text and its reader, then Conan's crucifixion becomes more interesting. Then meaning does not lie 'in' the text at all. Instead, meaning lies between texts, in intertextual configurations of texts that intersect one another in a wide variety of ways. These configurations are made by the texts' readers, and no two readers will configure the texts in the same arrangement, for no two readers draw on exactly the same combination of texts. The meaning that is produced by this intertextual process is fluid and shifting, and it plays out differently from one reader to the next.

If that is the case, then not only do the stories of Christ interpret Conan, but Conan's stories also interpret Christ. The hermeneutical flow is 'reversed'. Conan's crucifixion invites a reading of Jesus as a Conan-like hero of tales of sword and sorcery. That Jesus and other Gospel characters live in a narrative world in which magic is very real cannot be denied (Mk 5.28-30; 8.23-25), and it is also evident that Jesus has at least some association with the sword (Mt. 10.34; Mk 14.47). He may even be a thief (Mk 3.27; 14.48) and a wanderer, not unlike Conan. Nevertheless, Conan 'fleshes out' Jesus, filling narrative gaps in the Gospel accounts in ways that will be new and perhaps unsettling to many.

One measure of the lasting power of biblical texts is that they continue to be recycled again and again in the cultural forms and available media of each age. Even in non-religious milieux, biblical texts are resurrected in 'afterlives' (see Sherwood 2000) in which they have been re-read and rewritten in countless ways, and they often reappear, like Jesus on the road to Emmaus, in unexpected forms. These texts cannot be killed, it seems, and they proliferate and mutate far beyond any control. If meaning really is not neatly packaged in the texts themselves but rather flows in many different directions at once, intertextually, then the study of these prolif-erations and mutations is an important way to trace the flow of meaning, to bring the relevant semiotic processes to light, and to understand the construction of biblical meaning.

Larry Kreitzer has become one of the foremost explorers of this hermeneutical dynamics, and he has done so in numerous recent writings on the Bible and modern culture, especially in what are now four volumes on the reappearance of biblical phrases, images and themes in works of contemporary literary fiction and film (Kreitzer 1993, 1994, 1999, 2000). 'Intertextuality' is not a word that Kreitzer uses often, but the concept lurks everywhere in his writings. In these four books, his interest ranges from relatively blatant intertextual relationships (such as my example from the Conan movie) to connections that are far more subtle and even fragile, but no less important for all that. In fact, often non-obvious intertextuality works more powerfully than the more apparent variety, just because it is subliminal. The message that the reader (or viewer) derives from the texts seems all the more 'natural' when its ideological formation is invisible.

In the present book, Kreitzer's interest is usually in less than obvious instances of intertextuality. In every case, he uncovers connections between the texts—often more than two texts, for the traces of meaning are sometimes quite complex—in ways that illuminate each of them. As he makes the connections between the texts more apparent, the meaning attached to them become less natural and obvious, and more thought-provoking. The fictional and cinematic rewritings of biblical materials serve as lenses through which we recognize the arbitrary and artificial character of every reading. Every reading attaches to the texts some hermeneutical baggage, often quite surreptitiously. Kreitzer's approach makes evident just what that baggage is and how it operates in any reading.

Kreitzer does not discuss the Conan stories in this book, although his third chapter does address images associated with Jesus's crucifixion. His earlier book, *The New Testament in Fiction and Film* (1993), also devotes several chapters to the crucifixion, but without mentioning Howard's fantasy hero. However, this is not a problem, because it is neither necessary nor possible to survey the full range of relevant texts completely. The field of intertextual possibilities is simply too huge, too fluid, and constantly growing. As Kreitzer himself says in the conclusion to this book, 'There remains so much more to do along these lines; the door is wide open for such interdisciplinary approaches to be developed and refined'.

Nor would a survey of textual proliferations or mutations be particularly valuable. For one thing, such a survey would be instantaneously out of date! What is valuable, and what Kreitzer does offer both here and in his previous writings, are the beginnings of what might be called a semio-dynamics of interpretation, an outline of ways in which the hermeneutical flow reverses. In addition, Kreitzer demonstrates an array of tools through which this sort of reading can be conducted, so that his readers can not only profit from his insights into specific texts, but also reconsider their own readings and better understand their own construction of meaning. Thus he both contributes to the understanding of these texts, and invites the reader to join with him in the larger endeavour. I hope that many readers will accept his invitation.

George Aichele

ABBREVIATIONS

ABD	David Noel Freedman (ed.), *The Anchor Bible Dictionary* (New York: Doubleday, 1992)
ANTC	Abingdon New Testament Commentary
AV	Authorized Version
BETL	Bibliotheca ephemeridum theologicarum lovaniensium
Bib	*Biblica*
BS	Biblical Seminar
BST	Bible Speaks Today
BZNW	Beihefte zur *ZNW*
CBQ	*Catholic Biblical Quarterly*
DSB	Daily Study Bible
EC	Epworth Commentaries
EstBib	*Estudios bíblicos*
ExpTim	*Expository Times*
GNS	Good News Studies
HC	Hermeneia Commentary
IBT	Interpreting Biblical Texts
ICC	International Critical Commentary
IVPNTCS	Intervarsity Press New Testament Commentary Series
JAAR	*Journal of the American Academy of Religion*
JBL	*Journal of Biblical Literature*
JRS	*Journal of Roman Studies*
JSNT	*Journal for the Study of the New Testament*
JSNTSup	*Journal for the Study of the New Testament*, Supplement Series
JSOT	*Journal for the Study of the Old Testament*
JSOTSup	*Journal for the Study of the Old Testament*, Supplement Series
JSPSup	*Journal for the Study of the Pseudepigrapha*, Supplement Series
JTS	*Journal of Theological Studies*
KPG	Knox Preaching Guides
NCB	New Century Bible
NCF	*Nineteenth-Century Fiction*
NIBC	New International Bible Commentary
NICNT	New International Commentary on the New Testament
NIGTC	The New International Greek Testament Commentary

NIV	New International Version
NovT	*Novum Testamentum*
NovTSup	*Novum Testamentum*, Supplements
NTG	New Testament Guides
NTS	*New Testament Studies*
PEQ	*Palestine Exploration Quarterly*
PMLA	*Proceedings of the Modern Language Association*
RB	*Revue biblique*
SNTSMS	Society for New Testament Studies Monograph Series
TDNT	Gerhard Kittel and Gerhard Friedrich (eds.), *Theological Dictionary of the New Testament* (trans. Geoffrey W. Bromiley; 10 vols.; Grand Rapids: Eerdmans, 1964–1976)
TNTC	Tyndale New Testament Commentaries
TZ	*Theologische Zeitschrift*
VT	*Vetus Testamentum*
WBC	Word Biblical Commentary
WUNT	Wissenschaftliche Untersuchungen zum Neuen Testament
ZKT	*Zeitschrift für katholische Theologie*
ZNW	*Zeitschrift für die neutestamentliche Wissenschaft*

When watching films the viewer may occasionally discover the Bible making a surprising guest appearance. Some films even use biblical texts to help set the stage for the drama that is to be unfolded, perhaps using a biblical phrase as the title for the film or a controlling theme. A good example of this is Clint Eastwood's *Pale Rider*, a Western which uses the image contained in Rev. 6.8 about a pale horse being ridden by the figure of death to convey the image of retribution and judgment central to the film's story-line. In this case Clint Eastwood, who plays a solitary gunfighter knowns simply as the Preacher, rides a suitably coloured mount throughout the film; the point is further illustrated by one of the minor characters reading Rev. 6.4-8 as the mysterious Preacher enters the mining community for which he serves as justice personified. The promotional tag-line from the film is even drawn from Rev. 6.8b: 'And Hell followed him'.

Another fine example is Oliver Stone's Oscar-winning film about the Vietnam war, *Platoon* (1986). The film opens with a pre-title graphic of a phrase from Eccl. 11.9: 'Rejoice O young man in thy youth…', accompanied by the evocatively mournful sound of Samuel Barber's *Adagio for Strings*. The text seems to have been inserted in order to remind us of how often it is the young who are called upon to sacrifice the most in war and suggests that the story which follows is an explication of the fragility of life in the midst of such armed conflict. An even more intriguing example of such use of a biblical text involves a familiar saying of Jesus to introduce a film. This is the controversial *Caligula* (1980), directed by Tinto Brass and Bob Guccione and produced in association with the men's soft-porn magazine *Penthouse*. This film includes within its opening pre-title sequence a graphic of the text of Mk 8.34: 'What shall it profit a man if he should gain the whole world and lose his own soul?', suggesting that the story of the Roman Emperor, visualized with all of the decadence and sexual depravity one might expect, is an illustration of the truth of Jesus' words. In other words, this is a story of a man who reached the height of Roman imperial power, and lost his own soul.

At the same time, few would deny the fact that the cinematic world also contains countless images which invoke thoughts of biblical texts, even if those texts are not explicitly cited. Examples of such texts are numerous passages from the Gospels recounting the life and words of Jesus of Nazareth. At times resultant cinematic images bring the words and personality of Jesus storming into the modern world from unexpected quarters, enabling them to cross two millennia with startling ease, and often making their impact all the more startling as a result. For example, Andrei Tarkovsky's allegorical film *The Sacrifice* (1986) is perhaps best viewed as a way of illustrating Jesus mishearing the apocalyptic call of God, an interpretation of the Gospels perhaps best exemplified in Albert Schweitzer's *The Quest of the Historical Jesus* (1906). In this instance the central character Alexander (played by Arland Josephson), discovers that bombers have gone on their way to unleash World War III. He offers his own life as a sacrifice, if only his family can be spared. What the film presents us with is an uncompromising exploration of the nature of human sacrifice, particularly as motivated by a religious mania.

Alternatively, it is possible to cite another example, one which builds upon a saying of Jesus which has worked its way into the common consciousness of Western peoples and become something of a byword for Christian tolerance and acceptance of others. I recently had occasion to see Richard Attenborough's *Cry Freedom!* (1987) again and was struck by the way in which the film could be taken to illustrate Jesus' cryptic words about 'turning the other cheek' (Mt. 5.39b/Lk. 6.29a), but doing so with fresh power and a surprising perspective.

The film includes a powerful scene depicting the black activist Steve Biko in police custody following his arrest by white South African police for violation of his banning orders. Biko is in the office of Captain De Wet, seated at a table and flanked by two police 'heavies' who threaten ominously. Captain De Wet, who obviously detests Biko and all that he represents, strides threateningly towards Biko, making a move to strike him. Biko, although held in his seat by the two police thugs who pin him down, blocks the fist of De Wet and shouts 'Don't!' De Wet moves back momentarily, and then comes forward to strike Biko on the face with the back of his hand, all under the protection afforded by the two men who hold Biko in position. Biko flares for a moment, and then relaxes, the moment of a violent retaliation seemingly having passed. De Wet is then seen to nod, almost imperceptibly, to his two colleagues, signalling them to relax their hold on the man. An instant passes and then Biko springs out of his seat like a coiled spring, striking De Wet in the same manner that the Captain had struck him. The Captain reels backwards, and Biko is grabbed by the two other policemen. De Wet barks instructions to his subordinates to leave the activist alone and not inflict any further bodily harm on the man since he will have to appear before the court shortly. De Wet then moves to confront Biko face-to-face and the following words are exchanged between the two:

De Wet: You're lucky Biko! Lucky!
Biko: I just expect to be treated like you expect to be treated!
De Wet: You and your big-headed ideas!
Biko: Well, if you're afraid of ideas you had better quit now!
De Wet: *[with a slight mocking laugh]* We'll never quit.
Biko: Come on! What are you so afraid of? Once you try, you will see that there is nothing to fear. We are just as weak and human as you are!

What is intriguing about this scene is the way in which it visualizes the basic image of 'turning the other cheek' when struck by an adversary, but does so in a surprising and unexpected way. Far from simply having Biko passively turn the other cheek and thereby encourage the hate-filled De Wet to have another go on the other side of his face, we are given an alternative vision, or at least a glimpse of one. This comes in the form of Biko's allusion to the so-called Golden Rule of Jesus, 'Whatever you wish that men should do to you, so do to them' (Mt. 7.12/Lk. 6.31). In other words, the fact that Biko does not literally follow the exhortation of Jesus about 'turning the other cheek' is not necessarily a denial of the ethics of the Lord in this particular situation. In fact, the way in which Biko responds to the actions of Captain De Wet could be taken as a literal following of Jesus' exhortation in the 'Golden Rule'. The not-too-subtle message of the sequence is that there may come a time in human relationships when striking another being (in response to being struck) is the only way in which that person can be brought to face the reality of Jesus' words about 'doing unto others'.

This volume is the fourth that I have written within the Biblical Seminar series, and like the three previous volumes the aim is to encourage a multi-disciplinary approach to biblical studies. At its heart is the suggestion that the three worlds of biblical studies, literature and cinema have overlapping territory and that this territory is ripe for fresh exploration and mapping. Thus, in keeping with my earlier efforts, I continue my attempt to 'reverse the hermeneutical flow' and plot some of the ways in which our understanding of the diversity of meaning inherent in biblical texts can be brought out in the open by examining key works of literature and their cinematic adaptations. The various studies in this volume have a common denominator. Each chapter takes a key phrase or image from the Gospel accounts of the life and ministry of Jesus and examines some of the ways in which these have been taken up in literature and film.

The story recorded in Mt. 2.1-12 about the visitation of the Magi to the place of Jesus' birth in Bethlehem has long been the subject of scholarly interest, much of it in recent years being generated by scientific concerns. Some have concentrated on the astronomical features of the story, the fact that the Magi are guided to Bethlehem by a star. There have been a number of attempts to explain scientifically the Bethlehem star and its appearance in the eastern sky.[1] Many New Testament commentators follow the suggestion (first put forward by the astronomer Johannes Kepler in 1603)[2] that the 'star' was most probably a convergence of the planets Jupiter and Saturn in the zodiacal sign Pisces during the year 7 BCE.[3] Others, including astronomers and physicists, associate the 'star' with other astronomical phenomena, such as the appearance of Halley's comet in August–October of 12 BCE,[4] or a star going nova or even supernova, such as occurred in 5–4 BCE, observed by astronomers as far away as China.[5]

Yet even here the scientific experts disagree, with others asserting that the story in Matthew is mythological in nature and not subject to the kind of empirical verification proposed.[6] Thus, it has frequently been argued

1.   Hughes (1979) offers a comprehensive treatment along these lines. A recent less scientifically credible attempt is that of Gilbert (1996), which blends a neo-gnostic quest for knowledge of mysteries with pseudo-scientific concerns. For other specialized studies on the matter see Hughes 1976: 513-17; Yamauchi 1989: 15-39; Ferrari-D'Occhieppo 1978: 517-20; 1989: 41-53; Kokkinos 1989: 157-62; Finegan 1998: 306-320.

2.   For more on the importance of Kepler in this regard, see Screech 1978: 399-402.

3.   Stauffer 1970: 32-35; Rosenberg 1972: 105-109; Hill 1972: 82; R.E. Brown 1979: 172-73; Hagner 1993: 27.

4.   Burrows 1938: 97-100; R.E. Brown 1979: 171-72; Beare 1981: 75; Vardaman 1989: 66.

5.   Clark, Parkinson and Stephenson 1977: 443-49; Morehouse 1978: 65-68; Seymour and Seymour 1978: 194-97.

6.   Bourke 1960: 166-67; Cullen 1979: 153-59. Many biblical specialists, aware of the scientific evidence, also counsel caution in such matters. See Meier 1980: 11, for example.

that Matthew is pursuing a christological agenda here rather than an astronomical one, perhaps under the influence of the story of Balaam and Balak in Numbers 22–24, a passage that contains a reference to a 'star' coming forth out of Jacob and one which was known to have considerable messianic speculation attached to it.[7] Clearly the 'Bethlehem star' still has the power to attract the attentions of modern readers of Matthew's Gospel, even if we are driven by the scientific complications involved to nod politely in the direction of a naturalistic explanation while pursuing more fruitful avenues as to its significance. Perhaps the description of Mt. 2.1-12 as 'the First Star Trek' (Keener 1997: 64) illustrates an appropriate blending of science and mythology necessary to enable a twenty-first-century audience well-acquainted with the power of science fiction to create imaginative new worlds and illustrate that religious truth need not always be historical.

What remains certain is the abiding force of the story of the Magi, or the Three Kings as they quickly become known, and the fascination of succeeding generations with their story. Legends and traditions about them sprang up in an astonishingly diverse number of places. For example, the Venetian explorer Marco Polo, en route to China in 1272, found in the city of Sávah in modern Iran three beautiful tombs which were said to be the burial sites of the Magi. Local legends about the Magi were also narrated to him, no doubt building on the traditions describing Persia as a centre of Zoroastrianism.[8]

Several recent interpretations of the Gospel accounts have stressed the explicit references to the timing of the crucifixion of Jesus as narratives which are invested with tremendous theological weight. The provocative imagery which is included in the Gospel of Mark, for example, has often been remarked upon. For example, Kenneth Grayston identifies the darkness motif of Mk 15.33 as especially significant in this regard. He writes:

> At the heart of this narrative there is a mystery; a darkness which seems at first to distract attention from the central thing, to fill our minds with credulity or incredulity at the most inappropriate moment. A darkness beginning at midday, of all times, and lasting three hours—is this sheerly unnatural or an aberration of nature? Is St Mark prosaically recording the overshadowing clouds, and regarding them as a portent—and if so, what do they portend? Or is he treating with proper reserve three agonized hours of

---

7.   Senior (1998: 43–46) is a recent proponent of this as part of what Matthew's purposes are in the passage. Also see Davies and Allison 1988: 233-35.

8.   Olschki (1951: 375-95) and Duchesne-Guillemin (1973: 91-98) discuss this.

waiting, and yet fixing its character by the word 'darkness'? Whichever
way one decides, the word 'darkness clearly becomes a symbol, a focus of
associations, so that power is released into the imagination, and imagination
in its turn becomes a servant of the understanding (Grayston 1952: 123).

Similarly, Ched Myers argues that Mark plots the story of the life of Jesus
of Nazareth against a backdrop of apocalyptic mythology, a war of myths
in which the confrontation between the forces of good and evil is played
out. He suggests that the imagery of the three hours of darkness over the
land comes straight from the Old Testament: 'This is taken from Exodus
10.22, when Yahweh, in the war of myths with the pharaoh, blotted out the
sun in Egypt for three days—the repudiation of the imperial order
legitimized by the worship of the sun god Ra.'[9]

In Chapter 3, I consider two films, each of which in its own way offers a
vision of an apocalyptic confrontation between the forces of good and evil.
The films are from two well-defined genres: Fred Zinnemann's *High Noon*
is a Western made in the heyday of Hollywood's fascination with the
genre, and Peter Hyams's *Outland* (which is an adaptation of Zinnemann's
film) is a creative work of science fiction. It is the way that the confrontation is set within a chronological structure that occupies our interest,
particularly as this bears a remarkable similarity to a specialized feature of
the Gospel narratives. How significant is this?

High Noon is a good example of how Hollywood has tackled timeless
themes through its own well-defined genres of film. As *Life* magazine put
it: 'Although *High Noon* has some defects, few recent Westerns have
gotten so much tension and excitement from the classic struggle between
good and evil' (cited in Dickins 1970: 237). The film's original promotional trailer focuses on the terrible confrontation which is to take place at
an appointed hour. As the title of the film suggests, it is a confrontation set
for noon, and the audience watches helplessly as clocks tick away the
minutes and the hands move inexorably to mark twelve o'clock noon.
Over a montage of scenes taken from the film, and against a graphic which
reads 'Time was his deadly enemy!', we hear the rich tones of a narrator
summarize its essential plot:

> A terror-stricken town left him to face four killers, single handed, at high
> noon. With every swing of the pendulum, with every second, a man's life
> ticked away. Never have so few moments held such excitement.

9.   Myers 1990: 389. Also see Marcus 1995: 205-33 for a recent study of how Old
Testament texts were used by the Gospel writers.

Outland manages to convey a vision of an apocalyptic confrontation between good and evil which is remarkably relevant to our contemporary world. David Shipman's words remain as true for us today as when they were written over fifteen years ago: 'Hyams's view of the future is as chilling as any in cinema or literature, partly because of the importance that drugs and violence have achieved in our society' (Shipman 1985: 160).

The chapter on Conrad's *Heart of Darkness* (1899) focuses on the famous death-cry of the enigmatic Kurtz as he dies in the jungle wilderness. Kurtz's last words are 'The horror! The horror!', a cry as open-ended and as ambiguous as, perhaps, Jesus' own so-called 'cry of dereliction' in Mt. 27.46/Mk 15.34: 'My God, my God, why have you forsaken me?' However, even more significant as a biblical springboard for the exploration of Conrad's novel are the words of Jesus recorded in Mk 13.14 about the so-called 'abomination of desolation', or as it is perhaps better translated, 'the abominating horror'.

Joseph Conrad's novella, though firmly enrolled in the annals of literature as a classic piece of writing, was for many years considered unfilmable. The complexity of the prose makes it exceedingly difficult to adapt the work into a screenplay, at least as far as the original setting of the story is concerned. Yet the central idea of *Heart of Darkness* has been the subject of a number of interesting recent adaptations, including some from rather unexpected quarters. Conrad Ostwalt, for example, has suggested (1996) that Kevin Costner's multi-award winning *Dances with Wolves* (1990) shares many thematic similarities with Conrad's classic. He notes that both works concentrate on a journey of self-discovery and both set up a clash between an indigenous, native culture in the wilderness and an oppressive, colonialistic power which seeks to exploit the riches of the land and its people in the name of 'civilization'.

Even more intriguing is the way that the basic story-line of Conrad's novella has been picked up and reworked in J.D. Athens's *Cannibal Women in the Avocado Jungle of Death* (1988). This is a comedy-spoof which takes a sideways swipe at both feminism and male machismo, leaving no subject on the political-correctness agenda sacrosanct. It stars former Playmate of the Year (1982) Shannon Tweed[10] as Dr Margo Hunt, a feminist anthropologist, who goes in search of the militant Dr Kurtz. Kurtz (played by Adrienne Barbeau) has gone missing in the avocado

10. This is a connection here to Francis Ford Coppola's *Apocalypse Now* (1979) which uses Playboy bunnies in one of its most famous sequences. See below for fuller discussion.

jungles surrounding Bakersfield, where she has gathered to herself a group of beautiful, but deadly, Piranha Women. The Piranha Women are cannibals (the sexual pun of 'man-eater' is deliberately exploited), and Hunt hires a guide named Jim (played by Bill Maher) to take them safely through the avocado groves. Jim is a chauvinistic version of Indiana Jones from *Raiders of the Lost Ark* (1981), whose ineptitude and false bravado make for some interesting exchanges with the calmly proficient Dr Hunt and the seriously deranged Dr Kurtz. Even the death-bed cry of Kurtz in Conrad's novella becomes a vehicle for satire. In this case it comes as *Empress* Kurtz explains her antics in the Bakersfield 'jungle' to her would-be rescuer Dr Hunt, alluding to the debate surrounding late-night television in 1980s America in the process:

> All right, I was exploiting the Piranha women. You don't know what it was like. David Letterman, God, the horror...the horror of that show... the horror.

However, it is almost universally acknowledged that to find the premiere modern interpretation of the 'horror' of Conrad's character Kurtz we need to look elsewhere—namely to Francis Ford Coppola's *Apocalypse Now* (1979). Thus, the most important cinematic expression of 'horror' comes from an altogether different quarter, one that requires that the biblical basis for the imagery be enlarged beyond the cryptic declaration by Jesus about 'the abominating horror' to an image even more hypnotic and repulsive. Perhaps Jesus' words need the powerful imagery of the Seer of Revelation to help communicate their force. James Blevins captured something of the essence of this point when, commenting on the destruction of Babylon/Rome as portrayed in Rev. 18.1-24, he said:

> In modern times, it would be like a newsreel team showing us the ravished streets and disrupted lifestyle of a bombed-out city. John is at his very best in describing a major city—Rome—that has fallen. The scene is punctuated by funeral laments or dirges in the background. *One gets the feeling that a gigantic movie screen is needed to capture the force of what John is portraying* (Blevins 1984: 88, my emphasis).

Indeed, a good case could be made for suggesting that Francis Ford Coppola's *Apocalypse Now* (1979) attempts to do precisely that—to capture the force of what John the Seer was attempting to portray, and to do so by using the backdrop of Conrad's novella, as it is reset in the Vietnam war. In this respect, Jesus' words about the 'abominating horror' and the Seer's vision of the 'Great Whore of Babylon' are complementary, even mutually reinforcing images. The chapter on *Heart of Darkness* explores the relationship between these two apocalyptic anchor points in the Biblical witness and the literary and cinematic worlds of Conrad and Coppola respectively.

As in my earlier volumes on *The Old Testament in Fiction and Film* (1994) and *Pauline Images in Fiction and Film* (1999), I have included as a matter of deliberate strategy a chapter on a classic work of fiction which has been produced by a woman writer. In this case the choice is Margaret Atwood's *The Handmaid's Tale* (1985), one of the most interesting examples of dystopian fiction published in the past twenty years or so—a critically-acclaimed work in the tradition of such classics as Yevgeny Zamatkin's *We*, Aldous Huxley's *Brave New World* and George Orwell's *Nineteen Eighty-Four*.[11] My interest in Atwood's novel was sparked in part by a study I wrote on Nathaniel Hawthorne's *The Scarlet Letter* (1850) in which the themes of sin, secrecy and sexuality were explored (see Kreitzer 2000). Here, however, Atwood effectively turns the tables on the place of adultery within a religious society which is based on the repression of human freedom. What was regarded as the ultimate sin in Hawthorne's Bostonian community in the 1640s becomes the essential focal point in Atwood's neo-Bostonian community in the near future, the dystopian Republic of Gilead. Although the two works of fiction were composed nearly 130 years apart, there are many similarities between them, not least the preoccupation with the colour red as an identity-marker for the central female character concerned.[12]

To establish a connection between Atwood's dystopian fiction and the Gospel narratives within the New Testament we need look no further than

11. The *Oxford English Dictionary* (1994, 2nd ed.) defines a dystopia as: 'An imaginary place or condition in which everything is as bad as possible'. Ferns 1989: 373-82 contains an interesting discussion of how *The Handmaid's Tale* compares to these three works of dystopian fiction. Ehrenreich (1986: 33-35) also has some interesting remarks comparing Atwood and Orwell.

12. Walker (1988: 219-20) and Kauffman (1989: 235) note this. Also see Turner 1988: 85-86, Cowart 1989: 105-119 and Kaler 1989: 45 for further discussion comparing Atwood's novel with the Puritanism of New England. It is not without significance that Atwood dedicated the novel to Mary Webster, one of her ancestors who was hanged as a witch by the Puritans in Connecticut (or Massachusetts?) in 1683, and to Perry Miller, one of her Harvard professors who is an expert on seventeenth century American literature. See Bergmann 1989: 851-52; Carrington 1987: 130; D. Jones 1989: 31-32; M. Evans 1994: 177-88; Howells 1996: 130-31 and Atwood 1996: 51-52 for more on this intriguing point.

the accounts of the birth narratives of Matthew and Luke. The story of the annunciation and the miraculous impregnation of Mary provides an obvious point of comparison, particularly if, as has sometimes been suggested, the story contains a veiled account of the exploitation of the virginal Mary by a domineering and forceful male deity. Whether we would want to go so far as to describe the miraculous conception of Jesus by Mary as divine *rape*[13] is questionable, to say the least. Nevertheless, the parallels between Mary as a faithful and obedient handmaid of the Lord, and the character of the handmaid Offred in Atwood's novel are certainly well worth exploring.[14] Perhaps the best illustration of this comes in the form of a line frequently prayed in praise of Mary, the Handmaid of the Lord. In *The Handmaid's Tale* much is made of the first half of a well-known phrase taken from Elizabeth's declaration to Mary in Lk. 1.42: 'Blessed art thou among women and blessed is the fruit of thy womb'. The declaration is taken up in a Roman Catholic prayer to the Virgin Mary known in the English-speaking world as the 'Hail Mary' ('Hail Mary, full of grace, the Lord is with thee. Blessed art thou amongst women and *blessed is the fruit of thy womb*, Jesus'). In the novel, 'Blessed be the fruit!' is transformed into a standard greeting within the Republic of Gilead, evoking the response 'May the Lord open!'[15]

However, in keeping with our theme of taking up some of the sayings of Jesus and examining how these are expanded and adapted in literature and film, our focal text comes in the form of another familiar set of Beatitudes. To be more precise, our focal text involves the Beatitudes which Jesus utters at the beginning of the Sermon on the Mount as contained in Matthew's Gospel, and the way in which those sayings become adapted and refashioned. Most importantly, an extra Beatitude is attributed to the sayings of Jesus, one which is taken to embody a principle essential to the preservation of society within the futuristic Republic of Gilead: 'Blessed

13. A good example of this sort of argumentation is Ledbetter 1996: 129. He states: 'The narrative scar of the annunciation stories is that until Christianity defines its God in language other than the male body, there is no role for women in the Christian faith, except as victim and handmaid'.

14. The rape of women is certainly a theme that comes through elsewhere in Atwood's fiction, notably in her novel *Surfacing* (1972). See R. Wall 1988: 155-70 for a study of this.

15. Kaler (1989: 48) discusses this, even going so far as to suggest that the naming of the character Luke within the story is based upon the fact that it is Luke's Gospel which gives such prominence to Mary within the birth narratives. Kaler's article, although outrageously idiosyncratic at times, makes for fascinating reading.

be the silent'. Thus, my study of Atwood's novel explores how this supposed saying of Jesus is reworked and a religious justification for a repressively patriarchal society formed. Other biblical passages are called in to assist in this regard (as we shall see), but the (allegedly) dominical saying about silence stands as a key background text in Atwood's novel.

Finally, the short chapter on the *Star Trek* episode entitled 'Bread and Circuses' examines how the basic story of the rise of Christianity is handled within what is arguably the most influential television series ever. The *Star Trek* phenomenon is unparalleled in the annals of the entertainment business and much of the credit for it is due to its creator Gene R. Roddenberry. Roddenberry's humanistic beliefs are stamped all over the world of *Star Trek*, both in the various television series and in the full-length feature films. His antipathy to organized religion is well known and it certainly comes through within the *Star Trek* universe, particularly in the original television series first aired during 1966–69.

That is not to say, however, that religion was completely ruled out of court in the television episodes. The episode entitled 'Bread and Circuses' here discussed is the best example of the intersection of Christian history and the world of *Star Trek*. Specifically important in this regard is the way in which the christological declaration that 'Jesus of Nazareth is the Son of God' sets the tone for the episode. At the same time, several other parallels to ideas contained within the Gospel of Luke are also on view in 'Bread and Circuses', the title of which recalls a famous phrase taken from the Roman writer Juvenal's *Satires*. All of which is to suggest that *Star Trek* offers fruitful ground for an exploration of how biblical texts, great works of literature, and imaginative works of cinema or television can interrelate and enrich each other.

Chapter 1

'THE JOURNEY OF THE MAGI':
INTIMATIONS OF PASSION IN THE BIRTH NARRATIVES

Although modern critical scholarship has raised questions about the historicity of Mt. 2.1-12 as it now stands,[1] the story of the 'Three Wise Men' continues to attract the attention of scholars today on a variety of levels. Several key points are now generally agreed. For example, most commentators note the importance of the Magi offering gifts to the infant Christ and suggest that this is in some way symbolic of the Gentile world coming to worship him as Lord.[2] The fact that the Magi are described in v. 1 as coming 'from the east' (ἀπὸ ἀνατολῶν) emphasizes this fact.[3] The christological implications of the story have been another point of widespread scholarly interest, including the fact that Matthew places the birth in the Davidic town of Bethlehem. More often than not the focal point for the scholarly interpretation has been the way in which the story serves Matthew's presentation of Jesus Christ as the Jewish king, the royal Son of David, particularly with regard to the clash between King Herod and the infant Christ-child. Such a clash is set up as taking place in the heart of the Jewish nation, in the city of Jerusalem. Thus, according to Luz (1990: 134), 'The place of action is Jerusalem from the beginning. The

---

1.   Many of the concerns about the historicity of the Magi episode were first set out in David Strauss's *The Life of Jesus Critically Examined*, first made popular in English via the translation of George Eliot in 1840 (see Strauss 1973: 162-81 for details). R.E. Brown (1979: 188-90), Beare (1981: 72-85), Davies and Allison (1988: 224-84), Luz (1990: 127-41) and M. Davies (1993: 35-39) continue the movement to interpret the story as myth. Gaechter (1968) offers a comprehensive study which argues for the plausibility of the Magi episode. Other recent commentators who accept the historicity of the Magi episode include France (1985: 80-88) and Keener (1997: 64-73).

2.   On this point and its importance for Matthew's overall concern to present the mission to the Gentiles, see Gundry 1994: 26-32; Senior 1997: 45-52.

3.   France (1981: 239-40) discusses the importance of geography for Matthew's christological concerns.

journey of the magi is not of interest to Matthew; his interest lies with the confrontation with Herod.'

Most commentators acknowledge that there is another christological subtext within Matthew's story, namely the fact that the incident with Herod is made to serve the presentation of Christ as a new Moses figure within the Gospel as a whole.[4] Nowhere is this more clear than in Mt. 2.16-18, where the confrontation between Herod and Christ is set against a backdrop of Exod. 1.15-22 which relates the threat to Moses's life from a hostile Pharaoh.[5] The allusion to Exod. 4.19 ('those seeking your [Moses'] life') in Mt. 2.20 also supports such an understanding. But we should not assume that Mt. 2.1-12 has remained the exclusive province of recent biblical scholarship, or that such christological pre-occupations form the only focal point of the story.

The story of the visit of the Magi to Bethlehem, where homage is paid to the Christ-child, remains one of the most cherished in the Christian church. It features prominently in Christian art across the centuries, beginning with the simple drawings of the Capella Greca in the Catacomb of Priscilla on the Via Salaria in Rome which are dated to about 200 CE. Here the figures of the three Magi, painted in the colours of green, red and white and carrying before them boxes containing their gifts, advance toward the seated figure of Mary, who holds the Christ-child in her lap. Perhaps the most enduring contribution to Christian iconography in this regard was made in the 1220s by St Francis of Assisi, who created the nativity scene now so familiar to us, complete with manger, shepherds, Magi, donkeys, cows and sheep.[6]

4.   Allison (1993) offers an excellent study on the subject. Also see Hill 1972: 80-86 and Schweizer 1976: 39-40.

5.   France 1979: 105-106; 1980; Allison 1993: 140-65.

6.   For an excellent discussion of Christian art depicting the adoration of the Magi, see Macgregor (2000: 9-63). The book, published to accompany the splendid television series *Seeing Salvation* which was aired on BBC2 during Lent 2000, includes detailed studies and colour photographs of a number of important mosaics, paintings and reliquaries. These include the *Adoration of the Magi* painting in the Capella Greca, Rome, the mosaic of *The Empress Theodora and her Attendants* in San Vitale, Ravenna from c. 547 CE (which depicts the Adoration of the Magi within the folds of the Empress's dress), the mosaic in Sant'Apollinare Nuovo, Ravenna (dated 556–569), the Reliquary of the Three Kings in Cologne Cathedral (begun 1181), Jan Gossaert's painting of the *Adoration of the Magi* (c. 1510), Pieter Brueghel's painting *Adoration of the Magi* (1564), Benozzo Gozzoli's *The Journey of the Magi* (dated to 1459–1461), and Diego de la Puente's painting *Adoration of the Kings* (c. 1650). Also worth noting

The Magi have continued to captivate the imagination of countless artists over the centuries. Most have concentrated on the representation of them offering their gifts to the infant Christ and kneeling in worship, although occasionally it is their journey from the east to Jerusalem which is depicted. A good example is the painting entitled *The Journey of the Magi* by the French artist James Jacques Tissot (1836–1932), part of a series of paintings which took as their theme the stories of the birth and infancy of Jesus Christ.[7] Here something of the urgency of the Magi's journey is powerfully, and colourfully, presented (see the illustration on the cover of this book).

Legends surrounding the three wise men quickly developed in the early church. Names were soon attached to the three, beginning with the sixth-century *Armenian Infancy Gospel*.[8] The three were taken to be representatives of the different races of the human family, as well as representatives of the three regions of the inhabited world to the east. This is particularly evident in artistic representations of the three within the western half of Christendom, with many of the world's great painters following a fairly standard pattern of depiction in terms of the Magi's number, race, order and dress. Thus, Balthasar, the King of Chaldea, is commonly portrayed as a white man; Gaspar, the Ethiopian King of Tarshish, as a brown man, and Melchior, the King of Nubia, as a black man. Alternatively, Melchior is sometimes said to represent Europe, Gaspar to represent Asia, and Balthazar to represent Africa.

The story of the Magi has also served to fire the imaginations of musicians, writers and poets over the past two millennia. One of the most celebrated literary instances of the past century is T.S. Eliot's poem entitled 'Journey of the Magi' (1927), a short work which is only occasionally acknowledged by modern commentators on Matthew's Gospel.[9] The poem is readily available in various editions of Eliot's collected works. An

on the subject of art depicting the adoration of the Magi are R.E. Brown 1979: 197-200; Trexler 1997; Jensen 2000: 80-84, 91-92, 95, 179-81.

7.   Thomson (1984: 86-93) discusses Tissot's religious art.

8.   The sixth-century *Armenian Infancy Gospel* is the earliest document to give the names of the three Magi and their geographical homelands. It gives Melchon as the ruler of Persia, Balthasar as the ruler of India, and Gaspar as the ruler of Arabia. See Metzger 1970: 79-85 for more details on the traditions about their names.

9.   I.H. Jones 1994: 11; Davies and Allison 1988: 254; Jeffrey and Gussin 1998: 203-204. Goldberg 1992: 472-73 offers a good survey on how the Magi are represented in English literature.

audio-tape version of Eliot reading his 43-line poem is also commercially available, offering the rare treat of hearing how the author of a much-loved poem such as this intones the lines and lays stress on certain phrases.[10]

It first appeared in August 1927 as part of a series of greeting cards for Christmas published by Faber & Gwyer. The poem appeared together with drawings by E. McKnight Kauffer. Originally 5,000 copies of the card were produced, but they did not sell very well. Now, of course, they are collectors' items and extremely valuable. 'Journey of the Magi' marks an important shift in Eliot's poetry, for here the fertility myths so foundational to *The Waste Land* (1922) give way to mythological symbols of the Bible as a means of expressing the hopes of re-birth and new life.[11] Clearly Eliot's own spiritual journey is reflected in the transition to the biblical stories, and it is no coincidence that he had made a decision to be baptized and join the Church of England on 29 June 1927, two short months before the publication of 'Journey of the Magi'.[12] David Ward goes so far as to describe the poem as 'a mythical record or re-enactment' of Eliot's own conversion experience, a journey of his own soul, as it were.[13]

The poem begins in lines 1-5 with a reworking of some words from a nativity sermon by the Bishop of Winchester, Lancelot Andrewes (1555–1626), which was preached before King James I at Whitehall in London on Christmas Day 1622.[14] The sermon was based on the opening lines of Matthew's story of the visit of the wise men. Andrewes' sermon

10. See Eliot 1971. Interestingly, it was the hearing of another reading of the poem, that by the distinguished Shakespearean actor Sir John Gielgud, which first alerted Valerie Fletcher to the genius of Eliot (see Gordon 1998: 497-98 on this point). She was eventually (in January of 1957) to become Eliot's second wife and provide for him a measure of personal happiness and contentment that he had longed for all of his life.

11. Maxwell (1952: 149-55) discusses this. Also see Southgate 1999.

12. The baptism took place in the parish church in the village of Finstock in Oxfordshire and was performed by William Force Stead, the Chaplain of Worcester College. Interestingly, the renowned New Testament scholar B.H. Streeter, Fellow of Queen's College, Oxford, served as one of Eliot's god-parents for the baptismal ceremony; the other was Vere Somerset, a historian and Fellow of Worcester College. Eliot was confirmed in the Church of England the next day at Cuddesdon Theological College near Oxford by Thomas Banks Strong, the Bishop of Oxford. For more on Eliot's conversion, see Ackroyd 1984: 161-63; Gordon 1985: 77-94.

13. D. Ward 1973: 164. G. Martin (1970: 121-23) discusses the journey motif within Eliot's poetry in general.

14. For more on Bishop Andrewes' sermon see Gardner 1949: 124-25; Drew 1950: 150; G. Smith 1956: 122; Pinion 1986: 171-72. Matthiesson (1958: 197) cites the passage as an example of how prose is transformed into poetry within Eliot's work.

imaginatively describes the journey of the Magi as they pursue the star
toward Bethlehem:

> A cold coming they had of it at this time of the year, just the worst time of
> the year to take a journey in. The ways deep, the weather sharp, the days
> short, the sun farthest off, *in solstitio brumali*, the very dead of winter.

His point seems to have been to exhort his rather well-off, comfortable
congregation to follow in the footsteps of the Magi and share the arduous
journey of the Wise Men from the East.[15]

Much of the poem 'Journey of the Magi' is written from the perspective
of one of the Magi who reflects back over the events surrounding the birth
of Christ,[16] reflections which take us outside the bounds of Gospel
narrative as it stands.[17] Indeed, at least one interpreter of the poem
speculates that lines 33-35 of the poem ('…set down/This set down/This')
hint at the Gospel writer Matthew as the invisible recorder of the Magus's
thoughts (Barbour 1988). However, the open-endedness of these lines has
prompted other interpretations. For example, there are good grounds for
suggesting that Eliot had the traditional legends about the racial identity of
the Magi in mind here, and that he was intimating that the Magi whose
recollections form the basis of the poem was a black man. The fact that the
line appears to allude to the final speech in Shakespeare's *Othello*
(V.ii.410-18) points unmistakably in this direction.[18] Not only is the
critical phrase 'Set…down this' used, but so too is the imagery of the

15. It is worth noting that in T.S. Eliot's *Murder in the Cathedral* (1935) Thomas à
Becket also preaches a nativity sermon which blends notions of Christ's birth and
death, mixing imagery of Christmas and Calvary (see the Interlude between Parts I and
II of the play). I am grateful to my colleague Julian Thompson for calling my attention
to this point.

16. Braybrooke (1967: 23) says that the Magus 'assumes something of the air of a
correspondent in *The Times*'.

17. Shea (1983: 176) notes: 'The religious dynamics which Eliot expresses in
Journey of the Magi are far from the Matthean use of story and barely suggested by
anything within the text itself'.

18. The relevant portion of Othello's speech, uttered just before he kills himself,
runs: 'Nor set down aught in malice: then must you speak/Of one that loved not wisely
but too well;/Of one not easily jealous, but being wrought/Perplex'd in the extreme;
of one whose hand,/Like the base Indian, threw a pearl away/Richer than all his tribe;
of one whose subdued eyes,/Albeit unused to the melting mood,/Drop tears as fast
as the Arabian trees/Their medicinal gum. Set you down this'. See Wills 1954: 32; G.
Smith 1956: 331; Rajan 1976: 49; Pinion 1986: 172; Fleissner 1994: 65-71 for more on
Eliot's use of Shakespeare here.

Arabian trees and their medicinal gum,[19] a clear reference to the frankincense and myrrh which form part of the Magi's gifts to the infant Christ.

At one level, the poem comes as something of a surprise, for nowhere is there any mention of the gifts of gold, frankincense and myrrh offered to the infant Christ,[20] gifts which are traditionally associated with the three wise men from the est and are a universal feature of their depiction in Christian art.[21] The Magus narrates his recollections of the journey to Jerusalem, the impressions that remain with him, and the difficulties that he has had returning to his former kingdom, his 'old dispensation',[22] where he feels out of place, an alien among his own people. As Tony Sharpe puts it: 'It is a story of an uncompleted transition, told by an old man who knows what he has lost, but not what he has found'.[23] The poem closes with a mournful longing for the death which will bring spiritual life, although this is ambiguously phrased in such a way that the reader is not quite sure whose death is in mind here. Is it Christ's death, or the Magus's, and by extension, ours?[24]

The poem contains a number of obvious allusions to the Gospel stories of the passion of Christ; several of these are generally agreed by critics. Thus, the mention of 'three trees on the low sky' in line 24 is taken to be an allusion to the crosses upon which Jesus and the two thieves were crucified outside the city walls of Jerusalem (Mt. 27.38/Mk 15.27/Lk. 23.33/Jn 19.18); the mention in line 27 of the 'dicing for pieces of silver' a double reference to Judas's betrayal of Christ for thirty pieces of silver (Mt. 26.15; 27.3-10) and a reference to the Roman soldiers gambling at the foot of the cross for the seamless robe which Jesus wore (Jn 19.23-25a). Less immediately obvious is the reference in line 26 to 'a tavern with vine-

19. See Abercrombie 1985 for a fascinating study of Arabia's spice trail. J.I. Miller (1969: 98-109) offers a discussion of the trade of Arabian spices within the Roman world.

20. Andrewes' sermon does not mention the gifts offered by the Magi either.

21. On this point, Crawford (1987: 185) notes that 'the poem is deliberately unconventional'.

22. G. Smith (1956: 317) notes that the reference to 'the old dispensation' may refer to Eph. 3.2 which speaks of 'the dispensation of the grace of God'. The passage was one of the lectionary readings for the Feast of Epiphany in *The Book of Common Prayer* and as such would have been familiar to Eliot in the context of the Magi.

23. Sharpe 1991: 117. Scofield (1988: 146) similarly remarks that the Magus has 'the experience of conversion without the full benefit of assured faith'.

24. G. Williamson (1967: 165) states: 'This poem centers in the ambiguity of "Birth or Death"'.

leaves over the lintel', almost certainly an allusion to the Old Testament story of the preparations for the first Passover in which the blood of a sacrificial lamb was daubed on the door-posts and lintel of Jewish houses (Exod. 12.7). The mention of 'empty wineskins' in line 28 builds upon Jesus' words about 'new wine and old wineskins' (Mt. 9.17/Mk 2.22/Lk. 5.37-38). The line hints suggestively that those who kick the empty wineskins anxiously await the time when they will be filled with new wine in the kingdom of God.[25]

The reference in line 31 to the Magi finding the place of the birth of the Christ-child 'satisfactory' has engendered considerable discussion, particularly as it relates to 'satisfaction' theories of the atonement.[26] Although there is much to commend such a theological interpretation of the line, it seems much more likely that Eliot here is alluding to W.B. Yeats' poem 'The Magi' (1913), which speaks of the Magi as 'the pale *unsatisfied* ones' who remain 'by Calvary's turbulence unsatisfied', and who long to experience the wonder and intensity of emotion of 'the uncontrollable mystery on the bestial floor'. In other words, Eliot is offering an understated assessment of the birth of Christ as 'satisfactory' when it is seen from the standpoint of faith. The humble circumstances surrounding Christ's birth may be unspectacular and, indeed, unremarkable from a human (Magi's) point of view, but the birth is none the less satisfactory as a basis for Christian faith.

The reference in line 25 to 'an old white horse [which] galloped away in the meadow' presents something of a mystery. Commonly it is taken to be an allusion to the 'white horse' which the risen Christ rides in eschatological judgment in Rev. 19.11-16.[27] The passage speaks in v. 13 of the Lord

25. Tamplin 1988: 144. G. Smith (1956: 124) takes it to refer to the pilgrims at the open tomb in the garden who discover the empty graveclothes of the risen Lord on the first Easter morning. Broes (1966: 130) associates the 'empty wine-skins' with the story of Jesus at the wedding in Cana found in Jn 2.1-11.

26. See Franklin 1968; R.D. Brown 1972: 136-40; Wohlpart 1992.

27. Williamson (1967: 164); Southam (1994: 119); Moody (1979: 133); Pinion (1986: 173) and Tamplin (1988: 144) all take the line to refer to the descriptions of the 'white horse' in Rev. 19 (or perhaps the related image of the so-called 'four horsemen of the Apocalypse' in Rev. 6.2). Kaplan and Wall (1960: 8) take the line to be a reference to the death of paganism under the onslaught of Christianity, building upon the imagery contained in G.K. Chesterton's poem 'The Ballad of the White Horse' (1911). Similarly, Jones (1964: 191) takes it to be a symbol of the triumph of Christianity in England, as exemplified by the White Horse cut into the hillside near the town of Westbury in Wiltshire. However, S. Ellis (1991: 178) describes such an interpretation as

wearing 'a robe dipped in blood'—a feature that fits well within the overall passion theme at the heart of Eliot's poem.[28]

We turn now to consider some of the film versions of the life of Jesus Christ, particularly paying attention to those which follow up in some way the suggestion contained within Eliot's poem that the birth of Christ and the death of Christ are intimately connected.

Film Interpretations of the Magi

Some cinematic interpretations of the life of Christ present the story of the visitation of the Magi in a minimalist fashion. A good example is Nicholas Ray's *King of Kings* (1961), which manages to convey the story in less than two minutes (the death throes of Herod the Great last longer!). In this version the Magi do not even manage to utter a single word, nor is anything ever said to them by Joseph, Mary or, somewhat remarkably (given the narrative in Mt. 2.1-9), King Herod. They simply appear on the scene, sumptuously dressed and riding their camels; they bring their gifts of gold, frankincense and myrrh, lay them on the stable floor, and prostrate themselves in worship. The most interesting feature of the film occurs as the narrator introduces the sequence, stating their traditional names and assigning to each a geographical homeland:

> Now when this holy child was born in Bethlehem of Judaea, three wise men came from the East. And these were Gaspar, Melchior and Balthasar, of Mesopotamia, Persia and Ethiopia.

However, there are several other films in which the story of the visitation of the Magi is given a much more elaborate treatment. We have space to consider four films in some detail: Pier Paulo Pasolini's *The Gospel According to St Matthew* (1964); Franco Zeffirelli's *Jesus of Nazareth* (1977); William Wyler's *Ben-Hur* (1959); and George Stevens' *The Greatest Story Ever Told* (1965). Each of the films puts a distinctive spin on the narrative contained in Mt. 2.1-23. Most importantly for our considerations is the way in which these films incorporate in some way

'misplaced critical ingenuity'; Canary (1982: 202) offers a similar assessment. Also see Smailes 1970 and Dean 1979 for additional interpretations of the line.

28. Several other features of the imagery underlying the poem have engendered considerable debate, including Eliot's ideas about the identification of the Magi. Some have taken them to be a sign of Eliot's interest in Eastern mysticism, identifying the three Magi as Zoroastrian priests who were following the astronomical signs of the heavens. On this point, see Burgess 1984.

suggestive hints of Christ's ultimate passion within the story. In this respect the birth of Christ contains within it intimations of his death, just as we noted above in relation to T.S. Eliot's 'Journey of the Magi'.

Pier Paulo Pasolini's The Gospel According to St Matthew *(1964): The Motherless Child and the Long Journey from Home*
Pasolini's film gives considerable attention to the birth narratives, including the stories associated with the three Magi. We first catch sight of them as they ride into Jerusalem on horses (*not* the traditional camels!) at the head of a long train of donkeys, supplies and servants. The three Magi are all clean-shaven Caucasians; two are dressed in white robes and headgear and one is similarly attired in black. They are shown approaching King Herod and asking him where it is that the king of the Jews is to be born. Herod consults his advisors, all of whom are dressed in ecclesiastical robes and papal-like tiaras, and then reports to the Magi that Bethlehem is the place. We next see the three Magi and their entourage making their way down a rocky landscape to a cave cut into the side of the hill. Mary sits outside the entrance holding the Christ-child with Joseph standing nearby. The three Magi approach cautiously and reverently, surrounded by a number of village children, and kneel before mother and child. Mary stands up and stretches out her arms, offering the child to the middle Magus, who receives him carefully and lifts him upwards as if to offer him to God. One of the other Magi kisses the exposed feet of the infant. The camera then focuses in on close-ups of the faces of the Magi, Mary and Joseph, and the surrounding onlooking children. The sequence closes with some of the servants of the three Magi bringing forward their gifts in the form of gold and silver vases.

Somewhat surprisingly, no words are exchanged in the scenes depicting the Magi's visitation. In the place of dialogue there is a voice-over soundtrack of the old African-American spiritual 'Sometimes I Feel Like a Motherless Child', performed with mournful solemnity by an uncredited Billie Holliday. It is in the words of the song that we have the closest thing to an intimation of Christ's passion, or at least the sense of isolation and loneliness which forms part of it.[29] The words sung are:

29.   Garland (1993: 30) remarks upon King Herod's attempt to annihilate the infant Christ just as the Egyptian Pharaoh tried to destroy the Hebrews and contrasts this with the birth narrative contained in Lk. 1–2. He perceptively comments: '[N]o one sings in Matthew's infancy narrative as they do in Luke's; instead they weep'.

> Sometimes I feel like a motherless child,
> Sometimes I feel like a motherless child,
> Sometimes I feel like a motherless child,
> A long way from home.
> A long way from home.
>
> Sometimes I feel like I'm almost done,
> Sometimes I feel like I'm almost done,
> Sometimes I feel like I'm almost done,
> A long way from home.
> A long way from home.
>
> True believer.
> True believer.
> A long, long way from home.
> A long, long way from home.

It is not entirely clear to whom the words of the song refer, nor whose perspective they are intended to represent. Is it the infant Christ, who, even though he now is in the arms of his mother, will one day be rejected and feel the humiliation and isolation of an orphan? In this sense, the 'long, long way from home' could be seen as a symbolic statement of the incarnation, the fact that Christ's true home is in heaven and that his birth means that a long and difficult journey has been undertaken. Alternatively, does the song mean to imply that the Magi are the ones who have come 'a long, long way from home' in that they have travelled from the east to witness the birth of the child? If this is the case, then the sentiment of feeling 'like a motherless child' is a fair reflection of the weariness and disillusionment of the Magi as contained in Eliot's poem. In point of fact, we need not decide between the two interpretations of the song, as if they were mutually exclusive. It is entirely possible to take the song to be delightfully ambiguous, just as Eliot's poem plays on the ambiguity of what the Magi had witnessed: was it a birth or a death, and whose precisely?

Franco Zeffirelli's Jesus of Nazareth (1977): Bitter Herbs and Crushing Scorpions

Zeffirelli's *Jesus of Nazareth* is perhaps the most reverential of films about the life and ministry of Jesus Christ. One of the ways in which it achieves this is by careful attention to the New Testament texts, even to the point of interweaving stories from the various Gospel accounts and effectively creating a harmony of the life of Jesus. This is certainly the case with regard to the birth and infancy narratives, for example, where the very first glimpse we get of Matthew's story of the visitation of the Magi is interwoven with Luke's story of the Roman census and the journey of Mary and Joseph to Bethlehem. Here Mary's arduous travel over very rough terrain on the back of a donkey is juxtaposed with scenes of the three wise men following the heavenly star. Interestingly, the three Magi are not shown as travelling together as a single group, but come from different geographical areas, wear different styles of dress, and arrive by different means (horses and camels are both used). The three simultaneously arrive at a wooded clearing and greet each other warmly, recognizing each other as brothers in a common pursuit. They set up camp together and, under the canopy of a shared tent and seated around a campfire, relate to one another how they have come to follow the guiding star.

The film takes an interesting angle on presenting the relationship between the Magi (Balthazar is played by James Earl Jones, Melchior by Donald Pleasance, and Gaspar by Fernando Rey) and King Herod (who is played by Peter Ustinov). The Magi are not depicted as first visiting Herod at his palace in Jerusalem and discovering information from Herod's advisors about Bethlehem as the actual place of the Messiah's birth. Instead, Herod's advisors simply inform him that the Magi have crossed his territorial borders and that they are heading towards Bethlehem, while Gaspar and Melchior are shown to have determined the place of the birth by their astronomical charts and calculations and their knowledge of Jewish scriptures (namely Mic. 5.2). Thus, the film avoids one of the historical difficulties of the Gospel story-line, namely the improbability of Herod sending the Magi on to Bethlehem without following them and inviting them to send back news of what they find there.

The actual encounter between the Magi and the infant Christ takes place as Joseph and Mary return to their stable following the circumcision of the child at the Jerusalem temple. In other words, the Messiah that the Magi come to worship in Bethlehem is a newly-born infant, not a two-year-old child as he is sometimes portrayed in films which focus on Mt. 2.16 (where Herod is said to order the slaughter of all male children in Bethlehem two years old and younger). Once again this is an illustration of the tendency in *Jesus of Nazareth* to offer a harmonized account of the Gospel narratives, ironing out the differences between them and creating a seamless story-line.

The three Magi wait eagerly for the holy family and offer their words of worship and the traditional gifts of gold, frankincense and myrrh.[30] The

30. The symbolism of the gifts as representing Christ's kingship (gold), his priesthood and divinity (frankincense) and his passion and death (myrrh) arises early

order of the presentation of the gifts is altered slightly, and the significance of myrrh as a symbol of the passion is emphasized. This builds upon the traditional association of myrrh with the death of Christ (the only other New Testament references to the spice are found in Jn 19.39, where Nicodemus brings spices for the burial of the body of the crucified Christ, and Mk 15.23, where the wine offered by a Roman soldier to Jesus as he hangs dying on the cross is said to have been 'mixed with myrrh' [ἐσμυρ-νισμένον]).[31] Note in this scene how the 'bitterness' of this valuable spice/herb is made the culminating focal point of the Magi's gifts, and then immediately followed up by a warning to Joseph about the safety of the child:

> Melchior: This is the king of Israel, who will take away the sins of the world.
> Balthazar: I did not know what we were to find in coming here—a stable. I thought my brothers were mistaken, but now I see the justice of it. There could be no other place.
> Gaspar: *[Nodding approvingly.]* Not in glory…but in humility.
> Balthazar: Accept these poor tokens of our homage. Incense…to perfume the halls of the mighty.

within the Christian church, as can be seen in Irenaeus, *Adv. Her.* 3.9.2 (c. 185 CE). The tradition is maintained in a number of popular nineteenth-century Christmas carols, including 'We Three Kings of Orient Are'. The carol has verses sung by each of the three Magi:

> *Melchior:* Born a king on Bethlehem plain,/Gold I bring, to crown him again,/King for ever, ceasing never,/Over us all to reign
> *Caspar:* Frankincense to offer have I,/Incense owns a deity nigh;/Prayer and praising, all men raising,/Worship him, God most high.
> *Balthazar:* Myrrh is mine; its bitter perfume/Breathes a life of gathering gloom;/Sorrowing, sighing, bleeding, dying,/Sealed in the stone-cold tomb.

See Dearmer, Williams and Shaw (1964: 432-34); Bardley (1999: 377-79) for more on this beloved hymn, written by an American Episcopalian priest named John Henry Hopkins (1820–71) and first published in 1865.

31. If the reference to myrrh in Mt. 2.11 is intended to be an intimation of the passion of Christ, then Matthew has failed to follow it up in the passion narrative itself. In 27.34 he alters Mark's allusion to Ps. 68.22 (LXX) by dropping the suggestive 'mixed with myrrh' (ἐσμυρνισμένον) and substituting in its place 'mixed with gall' (μετὰ χολῆς μεμιγμένον). This may indicate that Matthew does not see the gifts of the Magi as an intimation of Christ's future passion, although such an association is taken up early in the Christian church, as I noted. See Davies and Allison 1988: 249-50 for details.

Gaspar: Gold…for kingly rule.
Melchior: Myrrh. The most precious herb of the east…and the most bitter.
            *[The camera focuses in on the faces of Joseph and Mary, before
            returning to shots of the Magi.]*
Gaspar: And now…a word of warning. Leave here as soon as you can.
Balthazar: Herod's soldiers have followed us, hoping we will lead them to
            you. He knows of this birth. He will seek out the child to kill
            him.
Melchior: Go into Egypt. It may not be for long. Herod's days are num-
            bered.

Indeed, the graphic depiction of Herod's slaughter of the innocents
follows immediately after this exchange and it is here that we have the
clearest suggestion of the passion of Christ which is to come. The struggle
between the earthly rule of King Herod (and his sons) and the spiritual
kingdom of the new-born Messiah is the focus of two very interesting
scenes involving Herod, two scenes which form something of a dramatic
inclusio to the larger story of the birth of Jesus itself. Both of these are set
within Herod's palace, the first as Herod entertains his Roman friends,
including an official named Proculus:

Proculus: Majesty, I have heard the word 'Messiah'. What exactly is a
          'Messiah'?
Herod: Oh, even you have heard that awful word, Proculus.
Proculus: Is he a prophet, or is he something even…?
Herod: Well, Rome, even Rome, cannot influence men's dreams. And the
          Messiah is a bad dream, disguised as a solution to every problem. It is
          a leveller of scores, a rewarder of righteousness, a scourge for the
          wrong-doer. It is the bringer of everlasting peace.
Proculus: Then as I understand it, from what you have said, a Messiah is worse
          than a prophet…from the Roman point of view.
Herod: Oh, from the Jewish viewpoint too! Only you try telling that to the
          Jews! No, don't, don't… It's much wiser not to consult them. Just
          when a Messiah appears crush it underfoot, like a young scorpion. No,
          you can tell great Augustus, that he can rest in peace in Rome. There
          will be no Messiahs, true or false, in Palestine while I am alive.

Note the way in which the gift of myrrh is immediately associated with the
threat of Herod the Great for the child's safety, a threat which ominously
portends evil for the future. Thus, the image of King Herod crushing the
upstart Messiah, as one would crush a scorpion underfoot, is continued in
our third scene. It is this sequence which sets up the depiction of Herod's
soldiers descending upon the town of Bethlehem and killing the young
male children. Once again, Herod is in his palace in Jerusalem, surrounded

by his soothsayers and advisors. He has sought their advice about the progress of the Magi out of his territory, and then reaches the fateful moment when murder of the innocents is decided:

Herod:	Kill every male child up to one year old. *[He pauses a moment to recalculate]*… No, *two* years old. Better the innocent should die, than that the guilty should escape.
Blind Advisor:	Guilty? Your majesty, a child?
Herod:	*[Ranting and raving as he wanders around his palace.]* Guilty in the womb! Guilty in the stars! I'll bring down their stars! I'll snuff them out in blood! This is *my* world. I will not share it with an infant! There's no room for two kings here! Like a new-born scorpion *[stamping his foot down on marble floor and grinding an imaginary scorpion into the dust]* Underfoot! You know the mark of a real king? Courage! Even in the face of Jewish prophecy, bits of old parchment. *[Gesticulating wildly at the blind advisor.]* Old blind men! Hah! Now go to Bethlehem…and make history! Kill!
One of the Advisors:	*[Pleading.]* But your majesty!
Herod:	Kill! Kill them all! Kill! Kill them all!

William Wyler's Ben-Hur *(1959): The Bewilderment of Balthasar*
William Wyler's *Ben-Hur* begins with a five-minute pre-title sequence which depicts several scenes from the birth and infancy narratives of Matthew and Luke. Included within this montage is a sequence in which the guiding star in the heavens is shown moving across the skyline towards the hillside village of Bethlehem before it stops over the nativity stable and emits a searchlight beam of light downwards. Images of both shepherds and Magi are presented gazing up at the mysterious star, effectively blending together the nativity accounts of Matthew and Luke in the process.[32] The three Magi are initially shown seated on their camels, watching the star in the sky. When the action shifts to Joseph and Mary and the child inside the manger we are again presented with an image of the three Magi entering, to the amazement of the assembled shepherds and assorted onlookers. The three are dressed in different styles of clothing and, predictably, they are

32. Such blending is seen in many cinematic treatments of the birth and infancy of Jesus, some purporting to be based on the Gospel of Luke. A case in point is the short film entitled *The Nativity*, produced by the Church of Jesus Christ of Latter-Day Saints. The film purports to depict the birth of Jesus Christ as recorded in Lk. 2, but it also shows the three Magi following the heavenly star to the stable of Bethlehem.

representative of different races and geographical regions: the first wears costuming which is Egyptian in appearance, the second wears a head-dress which suggests the deserts of Arabia, and the third, a black man, suggesting he is a Nubian, wears a red turban. None of them says anything, but they present their gifts of gold, frankincense and myrrh in turn. There is nothing intimating the passion which will come to the Christ-child within this opening sequence, and at this level, at least, the close correspondence of death and birth suggested by Eliot's poem is not in evidence. However, this is not the only time that we encounter the Magi within the film. There are two other occasions on which one of the Magi appears. The first occurs as Ben-Hur returns to Judaea following his adventures as a galley slave and his adoption as the son of the Roman consul Quintus Arrius. He arrives riding a camel at a small settlement and, exhausted from his journey, helps himself to a cup of water from the village well before lying on the ground under the shadow of a palm tree to rest. As he lies there Balthasar comes to stand over him; his arrival startles Ben-Hur, who leaps to his feet. They speak together:

> Balthasar: Forgive me! You're a stranger here. Would you be from Nazareth?
> Ben-Hur: Why do you ask?
> Balthasar: I thought you might be the one…the one I have come back from my country to find. He would be about your age.
> Ben-Hur: Who?
> Balthasar: When I find him, I shall know him. But forgive me, I am Balthasar from Alexandria. I am the guest of Sheik Ilderim.

The conversation between Ben-Hur and Balthasar continues as the two share a meal with Sheik Ilderim in his tent. Ben-Hur learns of the success of his arch-enemy Messala and begins to contemplate how he might wreak revenge on the Roman:

> Sheik Ilderim: Judah Ben-Hur, my people are praying for a man who could drive their team to victory over Messala. You could be that man. You could be the one to stamp this Roman's arrogance into the sand of that arena. You have seen my horses—they need only a driver who is worthy of them, one who would rule them with love and not the whip. For such a man they would outrace the wind.
> Ben-Hur: It is not possible!
> Sheik Ilderim: Oh, that is a pity. Think of it! To break his pride. To humble this tribune before the very people he has degraded. Just think! His defeat and humiliation at the hands of a Jew!

Ben-Hur: I must not!
Sheik Ilderim: I know it is not possible. But is it not a delight to your
                imagination? Does it not answer your purpose?
Ben-Hur: I must deal with Messala in my own way.
Balthasar: And your way is to kill him. I see this terrible thing in your
                eyes, Judah Ben-Hur. But no matter what this man has
                done to you, you have no right to take his life. He will be
                punished inevitably.
Ben-Hur: I don't believe in miracles.
Balthasar: But all life is a miracle. Why will you not accept God's
                judgement? You do not believe in miracles, yet God once
                spoke to me out of the darkness and a star led me to a
                village called Bethlehem where I found a new-born child in
                a manger, and God lived in this child. By now he is a
                grown man and must be ready to begin his work. And that
                is why I have returned here so that I may be at hand when
                he comes among us. He is near. He saw the sun set this
                evening as we did. Perhaps he is standing in a doorway
                somewhere, or on a hilltop. Perhaps he is a shepherd, a
                merchant, a fisherman. But he lives, and all our lives from
                now on will carry his mark.

The next exchange between Ben-Hur and Balthasar takes place after the
cinematic showpiece of the film, the climactic chariot-race between Ben-
Hur and Messala. Ben-Hur is victorious and defeats Messala in spectacular
fashion, but with his dying breath the Roman tribune reveals that Ben-
Hur's mother and sister are not dead (as Ben-Hur had been led to believe).
Rather, they are banished to the valley of the lepers where they eke out a
miserable existence and live off the generosity of others. Judah Ben-Hur is
despondent and sets off across the countryside where he stumbles upon a
large crowd of people flocking to hear Jesus speak to them (this is the
film's version of the Sermon on the Mount). Ben-Hur is hailed by Balthasar, who is among the crowds going to hear the Lord speak. Balthasar
and Ben-Hur exchange these words:

Balthasar: Judah! Judah! He is here! I have found him! The child has
            become a man and the man… Oh, I know it now! He is the Son
            of God. The promise is true.
Ben-Hur: Happy Balthasar. Life has answered your questions.
Balthasar: Life has been answered. God has answered it.
            [Ben-Hur sits down and scoops up a handful of water from a
            stream running nearby.]
Balthasar: Come, come with me.

> Ben-Hur: *[Looking at his hand and the water contained within it.]* When the Romans were marching me to the galleys, thirst had nearly killed me—until a man gave me water to drink. I went on living. I should have done better if I had poured it into the sand.
> Balthasar: No!
> Ben-Hur: I am thirsty still.
> Balthasar: *[Pointing to the hillside and the gathering crowd.]* Come and listen.
> Ben-Hur: I have business with Rome.
> Balthasar: *[Shaking his head.]* You insist on death.

Balthasar also appears at the side of Ben-Hur towards the end of the film, as Jesus of Nazareth is crucified by the Romans. The two men both stand looking up at the tragic figure of the dying Christ, their faces showing shock and bewilderment at what is taking place before their very eyes. The following exchange takes place, building on the evocative imagery of Christ offering the water of life through his death.[33]

> Ben-Hur: This is where your search has brought you, Balthasar.
> Balthasar: *[Shakes his head slowly and looks down at his feet despondently.]*
> Ben-Hur: He gave me water. And a heart to live. What has he done to merit this?
> Balthasar. He has taken the world of our sins onto himself. To this end he said he was born...in that stable where I first saw him. For this cause he came into the world.
> Ben-Hur: For this death?
> Balthasar: For this beginning.
> *[The camera shifts from the two men to show the Roman soldiers working with one of the crosses bearing one of the two thieves. The cross drops into place with a resounding thud. The camera then moves back to Balthasar and Ben-Hur.]*
> Balthasar: *[Shaking his head sadly.]* I have lived too long.

Of all the cinematic portrayals of the Magi, it is here that we have the closest equivalent to the character portrayed in T.S. Eliot's 'Journey of the Magi'. For here we see an elderly and somewhat disillusioned Magus, confronting the mystery of Christ's passion and struggling to comprehend how birth and death fit together in the divine plan.

---

33. See Kreitzer 1993: 44-66 for a study of this motif within both Lew Wallace's novel *Ben-Hur* and the film adaptations of it.

George Stevens' The Greatest Story Ever Told *(1965):*
The Infant Glimpses the Cross

George Stevens' underrated version of the life of Christ opens with an extended twenty-minute sequence depicting events surrounding the birth and infancy of Jesus Christ, including a section depicting the three wise men journeying to Jerusalem on their camels and approaching the court of Herod the Great. The film contains a star-studded cast: Herod is played by Claude Rains, with the three Magi played by Mark Lenard, Frank Silvera and Cyril Deleranti; Mary by Dorothy McGuire, Joseph by Robert Loggia, Herod Antipas by José Ferrar and Herod Archelaus by Joseph Perry.

Here it is not the Lukan stories of the Annunciation which set up the story of the birth of Christ (as is so often the case in cinematic versions of the life of Jesus), but the story of the conflict with the jealous Idumean, King Herod. In this respect it is Matthew's version of the birth stories which dominates, although not inconsiderable attention to Josephus' account in *Antiquities of the Jews* 17 concerning the life of Herod and his sons is also to be seen. Also worth noting is the fact that this is one of the few films about the life of Jesus which gives an explicit explanation of the meaning of the gifts of the Magi.[34] However, it is the clash between the Herodian kings and the infant Messiah which provides the most interesting food for thought within the film.

There is an interesting exchange between the Magi and Herod and his advisors over the prophecies proclaiming the birth of the Messiah. The prophecy of Mic. 5.2 is invoked by one of Herod's advisors, thereby giving the Magi confirmation about the direction they are to take; they politely bid farewell to Herod and make their departure. However, Herod calls over one of his soldiers and orders that the Magi be followed and that he be kept informed as to their movements. The ominous threat of the soldiers is the primary means by which the passion of Christ's later life is intimated in the film's relation of the story of the Magi. We see this

---

34. Many New Testament commentators point to a number of Old Testament texts as providing the basic imagery of the Gentile nations bearing gifts as an act of worship, including Isa. 18.1-3; 45.14-15; 60.6; Zeph. 3.10; Pss. 68.29-31; 72.10-11, 15; 2 Chron. 9.1-2. For more along these lines, see Bruns 1961: 53-54 and Derrett 1975: 103-105. The visit of the Armenian king Tiridates to the Emperor Nero at Naples in 66 CE is also frequently cited as a possible parallel (the visit is mentioned in Pliny, *Natural History* 30.1.16-17; Dio Cassius, *Roman History* 63.1-7; Suetonius, *Nero* 13). See Dietrich 1902; Beare 1981: 73-75; Davies and Allison 1988: 232-34; and Trexler 1997: 15-18 for further details.

especially when the three Magi first appear before Mary and the child, entering the doorway of the house in which they are staying in Bethlehem, a group of eager shepherds looking on. The three, who are never named, approach Mary and the Christ-child and we hear the following exchange:

Mary: Who are you?
Magi no. 1: We have come from a far land to see your child.
Magi no. 3: What will you name him?
Mary: Jesus. Jesus will be his name.
                 [The camera cuts to one of the shepherds looking out of the doorway to the surrounding hilltops. We then catch sight of a group of six of Herod's soldiers mounted on horseback.]
Magi no. 3: *[Moving forward and placing his gift before Mary.]* I bring gold…for the sovereignty of our king.
Magi no. 1: *[Unwrapping and offering his gift.]* And frankincense…for the worship of God.
Magi no. 2: *[Unwrapping his gift and laying it before Mary.]* And myrrh for preservation…until time everlasting.
                 [A dog barks and the camera moves to show one of the shepherds again looking towards the open doorway. The six mounted soldiers begin to depart. The Magi also look towards the open doorway.]
Magi no. 3: *[Seeing the soldiers beginning to leave the hilltop.]* The old king! We leave at once.

The threat to the Christ-child posed by an insecure and fearful Herod is given an interesting twist as the scene shifts to the Herodian palace in Jerusalem and King Herod discusses the recent events with his three sons. The three sons are seated around a burning brazier as the old king paces nervously and addresses them:

King Herod: The stars foretold that one day I would be king. And I am king.
Herod Antipas: *[Nodding approvingly.]* Truly
Herod Archelaus: If there is anything in prophecy, surely it is not the stars but God who has sent this child…
King Herod: Hah! God! Where is God? Or the child of God, except in man's most dangerous imagination? *[He sits near the brazier and moves to come face to face with his son Antipas, grasping him about the neck and whispering in an ominous tone.]* The child of imagination is the child I fear. And my son, when you reign—if you do—remember that!

We are then presented with a graphic portrayal of the slaughter of the innocents, which builds much upon the prophecy of Jer. 31.15 about Rachel weeping for her lost children in Ramah (see Mt. 2.18).[35] At one point Herod the Great is even made to cite the words of Jeremiah in ominous anticipation of the killing spree. The depiction of the slaughter of the innocents is juxtaposed with an extended sequence showing Joseph and Mary's flight into Egypt with the Christ-child. This includes a scene in which Joseph stands reading from Isa. 9.1 to Mary and the child; they are camped alongside the Nile, the pyramids visible in the background. A young boy comes splashing his way across the water, announcing that a caravan (which we see slowly moving across the landscape) has brought news that King Herod is dead. This sets up a sequence which gives one of the most explicit intimations within the film of Christ's passion. This intimation comes in the form of images of crucified bodies, which illustrate the turbulent nature of Jewish–Roman politics in first-century Palestine.

Soon after the news of King Herod's death there is a complex sequence in the film in which we see Herod Antipas being confronted by rioting following his father's death. Antipas sends for the Roman legion in Syria for help in suppressing the rioters. The Roman legionary commander arrives, announces that henceforth the troublesome province is to be governed by a Roman governor based in Jerusalem, and takes possession of the vestments of the Jewish high priest as a symbol of the nation's subjugation. A number of the rebels are crucified along the roads leading to Jerusalem and we are given a poignant shot of Joseph and Mary with their son returning from Egypt and travelling down one of these cross-lined roads. We see Mary holding the infant and riding a donkey, which is led by Joseph along the dusty road. Crucified corpses trail off into the distance as far as the eye can see, while a voice-over, sounding like disembodied spirits, recites from Psalms, including the words of Ps. 22.1 uttered by Jesus on the cross (Mt. 27.46/Mk 15.34): 'My God, my God! Why have you forsaken me?' The camera even lingers momentarily on a close-up of the infant Jesus (who appears to be about a year old) as he looks upon the spectacle.

There is no doubt about the associations with Calvary here. The infant Christ is indeed destined to die on a Roman cross. That is why he returns from exile in Egypt; indeed that is the very reason he was born at all.

---

35. The Nobel Prize-winning author José Saramago builds much of his imaginative tale of the earthly life of Jesus around the story of the slaughter of the innocents and its subsequent impact upon Joseph, Mary and their family. See his *The Gospel According to Jesus Christ* (1991).

Conclusion

T.S. Eliot's 'Journey of the Magi' remains one of the poet's best-known and beloved works, perhaps more for its vividness of detail and its ability to invoke the imagination of its readers than for its ability to explore new theological depths of the Christian story. Yet the poem does touch upon, if not rest firmly upon, one of the most profound mysteries arising out of the tale of the birth of Jesus Christ: how are we to understand the relationship between the Christ-child's birth and his eventual death on a Roman cross? In what sense is he a child 'destined to die'? And perhaps even more importantly for the reader, what difference does his death mean for me? In what sense am *I* implicated in his birth and death; in what sense does it draw *me* in?

These are all questions gloriously provoked by the poem, and they invite us to contemplate how the complex of stories contained in Matthew 2, several of them revolving around the visit of the Magi to Bethlehem, are all intimations of the passion of Christ. Eliot certainly fastened on a rich treasury of theological truth here, and it is one that has been followed up quite extensively by a number of film-makers all concerned to give their versions of the life of Jesus Christ. We have looked briefly at four such film interpretations of the Lord's birth (and death), and have noted how each director presents his own version of a cinematic Christ. One thing unites all four films: the dramatic power of portraying the birth of an infant as intimately, and inextricably, bound up with his death, a death for us.

The words of some verses from Timothy Dudley-Smith's 'Where do Christmas Songs Begin?' capture something of the mystery:

> Where do Christmas songs begin?
> By the stable of an inn
> Where the song of hosts on high
> Mingled with a baby's cry.
> There for joy and wonder smiled
> Man and maid and holy child.
> Christmas songs begin with them,
> Sing the songs of Bethlehem.
>
> Only love can answer why
> He should come to grieve and die,
> Share on earth our pain and loss,
> Bear for us the bitter cross.
> Love is come to seek and save,
> Life to master death and grave,
> So in Christ is all restored,
> Risen and redeeming Lord!

Chapter 2

HEART OF DARKNESS:
THE ABOMINATING HORROR/WHORE

In John Sutherland's latest collection of short investigations into the puzzles, problems and unsolved mysteries in the world of fiction, Conrad's *Heart of Darkness* (1899) features in one chapter entitled *'L'horreur! l'horreur!'*. Sutherland playfully picks up on the fact that the character Kurtz within the novella is supposed to be a French-speaking employee of a Belgian company, the thinly-disguised *Société Anonyme-Belge pour le Commerce du Haut-Congo*. Commenting on the cryptic words which Kurtz utters as he dies, words which have both perplexed and fascinated interpreters of the novel ever since it was published, Sutherland asks:

> When, therefore, Kurtz croaks his famous last words, 'The horror! The horror!', has he reverted to his mother (or half-mother) tongue, English? or is Marlow translating from the French, for the benefit of his English listeners on the *Nellie*? (Sutherland 1998: 9).

The question posed by Sutherland is rather tongue-in-cheek because he is perfectly aware of how careful Conrad was to avoid giving any explicit geographical clues as to the central-African, French-speaking setting of his story so as to make it universal in scope. However, Sutherland's point about the enigmatic nature of 'The horror! The horror!' is well taken, and it is an illustration of one of the many interpretative difficulties which the reader of this complex novella faces. Indeed, the story is one of the most critically discussed works of fiction ever published. Given that Conrad's *Heart of Darkness* has such an enviable place within world literature, it is somewhat ironic that for many people the work is known not so much because they have actually *read* it, but because they know that Francis Ford Coppola's film *Apocalypse Now* (1979) is based on it and they know the film. Yet, as I hope to demonstrate, there is much that is to be gained from a study of both the novel and the film, particularly as concerns the crucial words attributed to Kurtz as he dies in the darkness which lies at the heart of the jungle.

One of the more interesting recent interpretations of *Heart of Darkness* suggests that the novel could be profitably read against the biblical genres of parable and apocalypse. This is the fascinating study by J. Hillis Miller (1985) in which parallels in *Heart of Darkness* to both of these well-established biblical categories of literature are identified and discussed. For example, Miller argues that *Heart of Darkness* has a well-maintained distinction between 'insiders' (who hear the voice of the wilderness) and 'outsiders' (who do not). In this sense it is strikingly reminiscent of the puzzling words of Jesus recorded in Mk 4.10-12 about the mystery of the kingdom of God being given to the disciples who are on the 'inside'.[1] More important for our consideration within this study are the features of *Heart of Darkness* which demonstrate its character as a revelatory text, one in which the narrative unveils image after image, idea after idea, to the reader by means of the narrative complexities of the work. Miller explains:

> The reader of *Heart of Darkness* learns through the relation of the primary narrator, who learned through Marlow, who learned through Kurtz. This proliferating relay of witnesses, one behind another, each revealing another truth further in which turns out to be only another witness corresponds to the narrative form of *Heart of Darkness*. The novel is a sequence of episodes, each structured according to the model of appearances, signs, which are obstacles or veils. Each veil must be lifted to reveal a truth behind which always turns out to be another witness, another veil to be lifted in its turn (Miller 1985: 42).

On this basis, Miller suggests, *Heart of Darkness* is an apocalypse in the true sense of the term, insofar as it is continually engaged in the process of unveiling, of revealing the truth. This point can be extended to include some of the cinematic interpretations of Conrad's novel, notably Francis Ford Coppola's *Apocalypse Now* (1979). Thus, Christopher Sharrett goes so far as to suggest that Captain Willard (the film's Marlow character) is comparable to John of Patmos:

> Like a modern St. John, Willard sees that his Book of Revelations [*sic*] involves a decoding of complex metaphor before a set of truths can be perceived. The journey up the Nung river becomes a process of discovering reality in disinformation, of distancing oneself from a general hallucination which is, in fact, the substance of the war strategy.[2]

---

1.   Miller is here building upon the creative ideas of Kermode (1979: 23-47).
2.   Sharrett 1980: 35. Tomasulo (1990: 156) similarly describes Revelation as 'one of the film's mythic substrata', and Coupe (1997: 75) notes that 'Coppola's film itself draws its power, however indirectly, from Revelation'. Indeed, several images and

There is much to be said about this as a way of approaching the novel and its cinematic adaptations, even if we would not wish to go as far as Miller does and attempt to identify the *content* of that unveiled truth. For Miller the ultimate source of the truth to which *Heart of Darkness* points, the final witness, as it were, is Kurtz himself and his encounter with 'the horror', which is death itself. Miller continues:

> The truth behind the last witness, behind Kurtz for example in *Heart of Darkness*, is, no one can doubt it, death, 'the horror'; or, to put this another way, 'death' is another name for what Kurtz names 'the horror' (1985: 43).

For Miller the fact that the narrative of *Heart of Darkness* is so multi-layered, and ultimately derivative in nature and never capable of being absolutely pinned down with any degree of certainty, confirms its nature as an apocalyptic text. As he says:

> The absence of a visible speaker of Marlow's words and the emphasis on the way Kurtz is a disembodied voice function as indirect expressions of the fact that *Heart of Darkness* itself is words without person, words which cannot be traced back to any single personality. This is once more confirmation of my claim that *Heart of Darkness* belongs to the genre of an apocalypse. This novel is an apocalyptic parable or a parabolic apocalypse. The apocalypse is after all a written not an oral genre, and it turns on the 'Come' spoken or written always by someone other than the one who seems to utter or write it (1985: 46).

In the novel Conrad piled adjective upon adjective in an attempt to communicate something of 'the horror' that was Kurtz's camp up-river, his Inner Station, but the precise nature of this horror remains mysterious and undefined.[3] At one level, we could say that the technique is similar to

features of Revelation have been identified in *Apocalypse Now*. One of the most intriguing is that of the Archangel Michael who fights a holy war against the dragon-like foes of God in Rev. 12.7-9. This is echoed in Kurtz's first campaign against the forces of Communism, a campaign which was given the codename 'Operation Archangel', as Bogue (1981: 619) points out. Also worth noting are the comments of D.M. Martin (1975), who argues that Conrad himself associates the imagery of Rev. 12.7-9 (where Satan is portrayed as the Prince of the Earth) with the characterization of Kurtz.

3.   Leavis (1993: 204-208) laments this feature of *Heart of Darkness*. Other critics dispute Leavis' interpretation, suggesting that it misunderstands Conrad's intention and his struggle with Romanticism. See Guetti 1965; Karl 1968: 154; Garrett 1969: 160-80; Cox 1974: 49-50; 1981: 15-16; Thorburn 1974: 117-18; McLauchlan 1983: 12-13; Elliott 1985: 168-69; Murfin 1996b: 101-102. Maud (1971: 209) even adopts Conrad's

that of the writer of Mk 13.14 who relies upon the equally cryptic phrase 'the abominating horror' to communicate something of the horror of the impending judgment on Jerusalem.

The stage is thus set for a fresh investigation into Conrad's *Heart of Darkness* from the standpoint of it as an apocalyptically conditioned text which addresses the unspeakable 'horror'. Within this study I propose to examine Conrad's novella in considerable depth, paying particular attention to any similarities it displays to two apocalyptic images contained in the New Testament—the idea of the 'abominating horror' in Mk 13.14, and the image of the 'whore of Babylon' in Revelation 17–18. My contention is simply this: that Conrad's *Heart of Darkness* contains a number of linguistic and conceptual correspondences to these apocalyptic motifs and that when the novel and the motifs are taken together the two biblical passages open up a new way of understanding the meaning of the cryptic expression 'The horror! The horror!' which stands at the centre of much of the interpretative debate of the novel. These same correspondences also extend to the cinematic adaptations of Conrad's novel, namely Nicolas Roeg's *Heart of Darkness* (1992) and Francis Ford Coppola's *Apocalypse Now* (1979). In short, the study sets up a multi-layered dialogue between three different worlds: the world of the biblical texts (in the form of Mk 13.14 and Rev. 17–18); the world of literature (in the form of Conrad's *Heart of Darkness*); and the world of cinema (in the form of the films by Roeg and Coppola). At the centre of it all is the suggestion that it is the evils of colonial imperialism which are being addressed in all three worlds, that it is at this point that the three unite (see Table 1 for a chart outlining the key thematic correspondences). This is not to say that the forms that an oppressive imperialism takes in the three worlds are exactly the same; there is diversity of expression and detail appropriate to the changing contexts. But it is to say that there is common ground, a shared perspective, between them. In this sense what we are presented with is not so much a *collision* of three worlds, but a *collusion* of three worlds.

style in registering a rebuke to Leavis' claim of 'adjectival insistence' when he makes the following remark: 'If Marlow had told the story without his editorial 'incomprehensibles' it would have been too plain, too plain altogether. But Conrad means us to read the plain tale behind the other. Otherwise what is the point of 'The horror! the horror!'? A man goes into the center of Africa and does extraordinarily horrible things, and then in a final moment admits they are horrible. That is no story of consequence'.

Heart of Darkness: *Assessing Conrad's 'Loot' from Central Africa*

Joseph Conrad was born Józef Teodor Konrad Korzeniowski on 3 December 1857 near the town of Berdyczów in what is now the Ukraine, although at the time the town was part of a Russian-dominated Poland. His parents, Apollo and Eva, were deeply involved in the cause of Polish nationalism. Such patriotism left its mark on young Józef, who was orphaned at the age of eleven (his mother died in 1865, his father in 1869, both from tuberculosis contracted in political exile). Thus, Joseph Conrad (as he came to be known) was a Polish émigré, having taken British nationality in 1886. Given that Conrad did not learn to speak English until he was twenty years old, it is remarkable that he managed to write so beautifully and powerfully in the language.

Conrad was one of those people who seem to have crammed the equivalent of several lifetimes into a single lifespan, prompting one of his biographers to entitle his study of the man *Joseph Conrad: The Three Lives*.[4] Conrad lived a full and adventurous life, and endless attempts have been made to relate his literary output to his own life experiences. Nowhere are these experiences more clearly seen than when one considers *Heart of Darkness* (1899), which is probably his most influential work.

Conrad made a visit to the Congo Free State (as it was then known in English)[5] in June–December of 1890; he had been hired by the Belgian *Société Anonyme pour le Commerce du Haut-Congo* to pilot one of their steamers along the Congo river. There is little doubt that his experiences in the Congo had a profound impact upon him. It is universally acknowledged that the experience provided the raw material out of which *Heart of Darkness* was later fashioned.[6] Conrad once described the novella as the

---

4. Karl 1979: xiii. He refers to Conrad's 'lives' as a seaman, a writer, and a Pole. Conrad has been well served by a number of biographers over the years. Among the most influential have been Jean-Aubry (1927), Baines (1960) and Najder (1983).

5. There is some question about how the official French title of the country ('L'Etat Indépendant du Congo') came to be rendered as 'Congo Free State'. See H. Johnston 1971: 91 for details.

6. Sherry (1971) offers an excellent study along these lines. Also see Baines 1960: 105-19; Sherry 1972: 53-62; Karl 1979: 283-301; Watt 1980: 135-46; Najder 1983: 123-42; Meyers 1991: 91-108. There is some evidence that Conrad may have based his character Kurtz on General Gordon of Khartoum, whose death in 1884 generated a political scandal which endured right up to the time that Conrad was working on the novel. See Willy 1978 for details.

THE APOCALYPTIC IMAGES	THE BIBLICAL WORLD	THE LITERARY WORLD	THE CINEMATIC WORLD	
	The New Testament	Joseph Conrad's *Heart of Darkness* (1899)	Nicolas Roeg's *Heart of Darkness* (1992)	Francis Ford Coppola's *Apocalypse Now* (1979)
Mark 13:14: 'The Abominating Horror'	The 'horror' of Roman oppression culminating in a threat to the Jewish temple (reminiscent of the threat posed by Antiochus IV Epiphanes in 167 BCE)	The 'horror' of the ivory trade culminating in the moral disintegration and death of Kurtz and Marlow's lie to the Intended	The 'horror' of the ivory trade culminating in the moral disintegration and death of Kurtz and Marlow's lie to the Intended	The 'horror' of war culminating in the ritual killing of Kurtz in the Cambodian temple (reminiscent of the place of ritual sacrifice found in Frazer's *The Golden Bough*)
The Abominating Horror/Whore of Colonial Imperialism	Roman Imperialism	Non-Specific Imperialism	Belgian Imperialism	American Imperialism
Revelation 17–18: 'The Whore of Babylon'	The city of Rome and its Empire; symbolizing the exploitation of subjugated peoples and the dangers of the imperial cult to Christians	Kurtz's Intended back in the 'Sepulchral City'; symbolizing the exploitative ivory trade in the 'heart of darkness'	Kurtz's Intended back in the 'Sepulchral City'; symbolizing the exploitative ivory trade in the Congo (Brussels and London are the cities implicated)	The estranged wives back in the USA; symbolizing an ungrateful nation and the folly of intervention in Vietnam by the military/industrial complex

Table 1. *Heart of Darkness: Thematic correspondences between the biblical, literary and cinematic worlds*

main portion of 'the loot I carried off from Central Africa' (1921: x). G. Jean-Aubry, one of Conrad's early biographers, went so far as to suggest that the experience of going up the Congo river was a turning point in Conrad's life, transforming him from a seaman into a writer.[7] Such a suggestion seems justified when one considers some of Conrad's own reflections on the matter, not only in his diaries of the trip, but also within his surviving private letters and his published reflections on the journey. For example, in a letter to his friend Arthur Symonds he says:

> I know that a novelist lives in his work. He stands there, the only reality in an invented world, amongst imaginary things, happenings and people. Writing about them, he is only writing about himself. Every novel contains an element of autobiography—and this can hardly be denied, since the creator can only explain himself in his creations (Symonds 1971: 158).

Conrad's fatalism certainly comes through in *Heart of Darkness*, particularly in the central character Marlow, who is at times thoroughly pessimistic about life and its purposes.[8] Not surprisingly, many have attempted to associate Marlow's pessimism with Conrad's own attempted suicide, an obscure event in his life as a younger man in Marseilles. We can only guess as to the mental state Conrad was in and what it was that drove him to take such drastic action.[9] The subject has long fascinated biographers, and several psychological assessments of Conrad which have been undertaken fasten on the attempted suicide as a key to understanding the man.[10] Indeed, *Heart of Darkness* itself has often been viewed in psychological terms, with the journey into the heart of darkness symbolic of an interior night journey of self-discovery.[11] Much attention has been focused on the character Kurtz in this regard. How much of Conrad's own inner struggles are projected onto Kurtz? Are there circumstances of Conrad's

---

7.   Jean-Aubry (1927: 141) says: 'Africa killed Conrad the sailor and strengthened Conrad the novelist'.

8.   Many critics closely identify Conrad with his character Marlow in this regard; see Guerard 1958: 33-48. It is often suggested that Conrad's own sense of loneliness and isolation was due to his childhood experiences as an orphan. For further discussion, see Whitehead 1969–70; Cox 1977: 5-7.

9.   Karl (1985: 22-26), discusses this, suggesting that the suicide attempt was ultimately an act by Conrad to free himself from his uncle's dominance. For more on the matter, see Cox 1974: 1-18; 1977: 7-8.

10.   Moser 1957; Meyer 1967; Cox 1981: 12-13.

11.   Guerard 1958: 33-48. Watts (1977: 141-45) offers a convenient summary and critique of Guerard's 'night journey' theory.

own life which served as the inspiration for the creation of Kurtz, or should we look elsewhere for background people and situations? Fascinating though such questions may be, they are generally regarded now as dead ends. To put the matter simply, it is virtually impossible to determine how much of Conrad's writing is, in any sense, autobiographical, so cleverly is the line between fact and fiction blurred within his work. Yet his genius and artistry are undeniable.[12]

We are perhaps on the surest ground for establishing a relationship between the man and his work when it comes to Conrad's life as a sea captain, for his experiences at sea do inform his fictional writing at several points. Within *Heart of Darkness* itself there are many little touches which demonstrate Conrad's nautical expertise. Even something as seemingly insignificant as the mention of 'the turning of the tide' in the opening and closing words of the novel, voiced by the anonymous frame narrator, points to a deliberate structuring within the novel based upon a sea captain's knowledge.[13]

Heart of Darkness was written by Conrad between December of 1898 and February of 1899 when he was living at Pent Farm, Stanford, near Hythe in Kent. It was a period of enormous productivity (some of his most memorable work was produced between 1896 and 1902). The story originally appeared in three parts in *Blackwood's Magazine* in February, March and April of 1899[14] and then in book form in 1902 as part of Conrad's *Youth* (the original manuscript of *Heart of Darkness* is now in the Beinecke Library at Yale University). It is a short story of some 38,000 words, but it contains many images and scenes which are written in such a way that they are unforgettable. Included are the preposterous image of a French ship shelling the jungle,[15] the description of an overturned railway carriage with its wheels pointed skyward as looking every bit like a great

12.   Leavis (1993: 219) lists Conrad as one of the four masters of English fiction (he identifies the others as Jane Austen, George Eliot and Henry James).

13.   Williams (1963) demonstrates this.

14.   There is good evidence to suggest that the basic story-line as Conrad conceived it evolved in the course of the writing. In the beginning the novella concentrated on general socio-political concerns but later became focused on the character of Kurtz himself. See Levenson 1985–86.

15.   Cox 1977: 17-18; Berthoud 1978: 45-46. Meyers (1991: 97) suggests that this is a veiled reference to the French campaign against the African kingdom of Dahomey in 1893; Najder (1983: 126) argues that the image arises from Conrad's witnessing of the French man-of-war *Le Seignelay* shelling a Negro village near the town of Grand Popo on his way to Boma in 1890.

beast of the wild lying on its back with its legs in the air, and the frenzied attack by the natives on Marlow's steamer as it travels up-river.[16]

Moreover, it is not just the isolated images which have captured the attention of critics, but the impact of the novella as a whole. The economic exploitation which generates a slow-burning sense of outrage throughout the novel focuses on the trade in ivory. Ivory, or the obsessive pursuit of it, stands as a governing metaphor in the novel. The ivory also conveys the notion of death, remembering that every pair of tusks gathered represents the death of the animal concerned. An ivory-generated spectre of death hangs over the story from beginning to end, from the mention of the dominoes (described as 'bones') in the opening paragraphs, right through to the grand piano of Kurtz's fiancée (his Intended) with its ivory keys (described as 'a sombre and polished sarcophagus') in the closing paragraphs. Nor should we forget that the central character Kurtz is himself described at one point in terms of ivory, as his head is likened to 'an ivory ball' (Rogers 1975). So what are we to make of this story, which tantalizes our imaginations as to 'the horror' which lies behind the pursuit of ivory? Perhaps the most obvious place to begin is to note the place that *Heart of Darkness* has as a tale about the African jungle wilderness.

Heart of Darkness certainly contains elements of the 'jungle adventure story' so beloved by a Victorian readership,[17] but it fits uncomfortably into such a literary tradition (see White 1993: 167-92). For one thing, Conrad, although politically conservative and appreciative of the benefits of Empire, was not above levelling criticism against what he saw as the excesses of the imperialist system, particularly those pursued in the Congo by King Leopold II of Belgium.[18] In this way, he was effectively deconstructing the myth of colonial imperialism.[19] As Czeslaw Milosz put it, Conrad's *Heart*

---

16. The passage is discussed in Daleski 1977: 68-71; Seidel 1985: 85-86; Watts 1993: 115-16; B. Johnson 1985.

17. See White 1993 for a full-length study of the fascination that adventure stories held for Victorian readers. Thorburn (1974: 141-43) compares *Heart of Darkness* to some of R.L. Stevenson's South Sea adventures; Hunter (1983: 27-29) to H. Rider Haggard's *She* (1887).

18. By international agreement, the Congo was the private domain of King Leopold II from 1875. See Murfin 1996a: 5-7 for a convenient summary of this. For more on the sheer carnage unleashed on the Congo under Leopold's rule, see Hochschild 1999. The importance of the intrepid explorer Sir Henry Morton Stanley on the exploration of Africa cannot be overestimated. For more on how Stanley's life and work influenced Conrad's novel see Dean 1960 and Stanley 1960.

19. For more on Conrad's critique of imperialism, see Hay 1963: 108-157;

of Darkness 'was a Cassandra cry announcing the end of Victorial [*sic*] Europe, on the verge of transforming itself into the Europe of violence. The First World War, which ushered in the new epoch, destroyed many illusions' (Milosz 1960: 43). Conrad is frequently cited in discussions about Victorian presumptions regarding racial superiority, the benefits of colonialism, and the inexorable advance of science.[20] Indeed, in 1975 Conrad was the subject of a celebrated attack by the Nigerian novelist Chinua Achebe who asserted that *Heart of Darkness* stood as irrefutable evidence that Conrad was a racist.[21] But there are many other viable ways of approaching the novel.

In point of fact, the range of interpretative strategies applied to Conrad's *Heart of Darkness* is simply staggering. As Cedric Watts once remarked, 'interpreting the tale is in some ways like wrestling with an octopus; we extricate ourselves from one entanglement only to be re-entangled in our new position' (Watts 1977: 2). For example, many commentators on Conrad note his presentation of women in the novella, notably the deliberate contrast between Kurtz's Intended and his jungle mistress, the wild native woman with her splendid headdress and ivory-laden costume.[22] Not surprisingly, *Heart of Darkness* has been the subject of a considerable interest among feminist literary critics, not least because it depicts a predominantly androcentric universe and presents women as weaklings who must be protected from the harsh realities of life.[23] The novel has also enjoyed a number of Freudian or Jungian analyses which see the journey into the heart of darkness as symbolic of psychological struggle and/or as a journey of sexual discovery.[24] Marxist interpretations of the story are also

Fleishman 1967; Baum 1975; Hawkins 1979; 1981; Parry 1983: 20-39; Singh 1988: 268-80; Shetty 1989; Meyers 1991: 191-96.

20. Saveson 1970; Sarvan 1980; Harris 1981; Hawkins 1982; Brantlinger 1985a; 1985b; Watt 1996.

21. For an assessment of Achebe's charges, see Watts 1983; 1993: 126-27; Shetty 1989; Hampson 1990: 22-28.

22. Karl (1968: 155) says: 'Kurtz's two fiancées are contrasted, each one standing for certain values, indeed for entire cultures in conflict'. Also see Ridley 1963: 49-53; Bross 1969–70: 42-43; Lincoln 1972: 189-91; Cox 1974: 45-46; G. Thompson 1978; Land 1984: 74-77; Hawthorne 1990: 183-92.

23. Brodie 1984; London 1989; J.H. Smith 1989; Mongia 1993; Straus 1996.

24. On this point, see Hollingworth 1955; Guerard 1958; Karl 1968; Crews 1975: 41-62; Ong 1977: 155-60; Sullivan 1981; Staten 1986; Hyland 1988; Young 1989; Rising 1990: 40-50; Batchelor 1994: 91; Goodheart 1991: 23-43; Knapp 1991: 49-74; Stampfl 1991; S. Jones 1999: 171-72.

on offer, focusing on the character of Kurtz and seeing him as the embodiment of an unrestricted capitalism.[25] In recent years *Heart of Darkness* has also become an important focus for reader-response critics who find the work a convenient means of demonstrating many of the interpretative dynamics involved in reading, and re-reading, texts which lend themselves to multiple layers of meaning and engagement by the readership.[26]

Finally, we note in this regard that much has been made of the veiled language surrounding the 'unspeakable rites' which Kurtz participates in at his jungle compound. Marvin Mudrick, citing in part Kurtz's own seventeen-page report on the 'Suppression of Savage Customs', identifies the key issue thus:

> The problem, as Conrad sets it up, is to persuade the reader—by epithets, exclamations, ironies, by every technical obliquity—into an hallucinated awareness of the unplumbable depravity, the primal unanalyzable evil, implicit in Kurtz's reversion to the jungle from the high moral sentiments of his report: 'The peroration was magnificent, though difficult to remember, you know. It gave me the notion of an exotic Immensity ruled by an august Benevolence' (Mudrick 1966: 43).

It remains an open question precisely what these rites and practices are, and whether Conrad deliberately intended that they should remain shrouded in mystery within the novella. Nevertheless, many critics have attempted to penetrate the mystery. One of the most influential interpretations is that of Stephen A. Reid (1966: 45-54), who suggested that they involved human sacrifice and Kurtz's consuming a portion of the sacrificial victim as part of the ritual. Reid bases his case on Sir James George Frazer's *The Golden Bough* and the analysis of how primitive cultures practised ritual sacrifice and cannibalism as a means of ensuring stability in society and ensuring that the powers of a weakening man-god were transferred to a suitable successor. Reid suggests that this is precisely the case with Kurtz, who, as he grows older and weakened by illness, is forced to participate in the barbaric rituals again and again in order to maintain his position among the natives with whom he lives.[27] This interpretation may, in fact, help explain another memorable scene within

25. Eagleton 1976: 130-40; S. Smith 1987.
26. Rosmarin 1989; Rabinowitz 1996: 131-47.
27. For more on the presentation of cannibalism in the story, see H.R. Collins 1960; Meyer 1967: 168-84; Yoder 1969–70; Tanner 1976: 30-32; Watts 1977: 104-107; Berthoud 1978: 47-48; McLauchlan 1983: 13-14; Seidel 1985: 82-83; Singh 1988: 273-74; Knapp 1991: 62-64; Parrinder 1992: 88-92.

the story, namely the discovery by Marlow that Kurtz's hut at the Inner Station is surrounded by half a dozen or so heads, which are mounted on stakes and almost all face inwards as if in an attitude of reverence and worship.[28] Such a suggestion has many convincing aspects to it, and it provides a credible answer to many of the perplexing features of the story-line in *Heart of Darkness*. As we shall see below, it also provides a fascinating connection to Francis Ford Coppola's cinematic adaptation of *Heart of Darkness*.

However, in order for us to appreciate Coppola's reworking of Conrad's *Heart of Darkness* we move first to consider two apocalyptic motifs from the New Testament which together invite a reassessment of the novella.

Twin Apocalyptic Motifs: The 'Abominating Horror' (Mark 13.14) and The 'Whore of Babylon' (Revelation 17.1-18)

The place that religion had within the life and thought of Joseph Conrad has been a subject of considerable discussion.[29] In particular, his use of biblical imagery within *Heart of Darkness* has been a topic of special focus, with his reliance upon the Authorized Version of 1611 especially in evidence (see Purdy 1984). Joan E. Steiner, for example, has meticulously combed through the novella, pointing out the New Testament parallels, most of which, she suggests, derive from Matthew and Luke, notably Jesus' likening in Mt. 23.27 of the hypocritical Pharisees to whitewashed tombs.[30] Similarly, in *Heart of Darkness* the representatives of the Company are described as 'pilgrims', suggesting that they are like the Pharisees, unworthy disciples who bow before the ivory-coloured god of greed. Following through the logic of this line of interpretation, some interpreters have gone so far as to suggest that Kurtz is being deliberately presented as something of a Christ-figure within the work.[31]

---

28. Church (1987: 35-36) argues that the one head facing outwards towards Marlow symbolizes Kurtz himself.

29. Watts 1984: 54-59; 1993: 47-51. Several writers have pointed out the Buddhist themes within *Heart of Darkness*; see Stein 1956–57: 236; Lombard 1975, for example.

30. Steiner 1982–83. Also see S.C. Wilcox 1960: 4; Watts 1977: 10; Meyers 1991: 194.

31. Moseley 1962: 16-19; Godshalk 1969; Renner 1976. Also worth noting in this regard is the curious phrase 'It was as though a veil had been rent', which Marlow utters as part of his recollection of Kurtz's dying words. What precisely is meant here? Some interpreters, such as Stein (1965) and Pecora (1985: 1002), have taken it to be a

However, there are two additional biblical motifs which merit further investigation, both of which are expressions of the apocalypticism which was so much a part of the thought-world of the first-century Jews and Christians. Together these may help us understand better something of the significance of Kurtz's cryptic last words, the mysterious phrase 'The Horror! the horror!' which could be regarded as a summary expression for Conrad's *Heart of Darkness*.

The 'Abominating Horror' (Mark 13.14)

One of the most provocative images of the so-called Eschatological Discourse within the Synoptic Gospels is that of the 'abomination of desolation' (βδέλυγμα τῆς ἐρημώσεως), perhaps better translated as the 'abominating horror' (Mk 13.14).[32] In the midst of his extended discourse about last things, Jesus is recorded as saying:

> But when you see the abominating horror set up where it ought not to be (let the reader understand), then let those who are in Judaea flee to the mountains; and let the one who is on the rooftop not go down, nor enter his house to take anything away, and let him who is in the field not turn back to take his mantle. And alas for those who are with child and for those who give suck in those days! Pray that it may not happen in winter (Mark 13.14-18).

There have been many scholars who have argued that Jesus' Apocalyptic Discourse was based, in part, on an earlier Jewish apocalyptic tract which included these verses. This so-called 'Little Apocalypse' theory has received considerable attention, much of it directed towards an

reference to Schopenhauer's 'veil of Maya', which, once lifted, enables a person to see himself or herself as he or she really is. This may be what Conrad has in mind (he certainly was familiar with the work of Schopenhauer); but it may be that another explanation lies closer at hand. I refer to the description of Jesus Christ's death and the fact that his last words from the cross are accompanied by a reference to the 'veil of the temple being torn' (Mt. 27.51/Mk 15.38/Lk. 23.45). However, Lester (1988: xviii-xix, xxiii) advises caution in using such archetype criticism, which 'seems to have fallen into the dangers of overspecification…[and] …failing to treat the characters of a novel as characters'.

32. The phrase is also found in Mt. 24.15, which is probably dependent upon the Markan passage. Lk. 21.20 does not retain the phrase in its entirety, but speaks of the 'desolation' (ἐρήμωσις) of the city of Jerusalem. Dodd (1947) argues that Luke is not here reliant upon Mark but is following an independent tradition which builds upon Old Testament imagery associated with the capture of Jerusalem by Nebuchadnezzar in 586 BCE. See Wenham (1984: 175-218) for a full-bodied assessment of the pre-synoptic nature of Mt. 24.15-22; Mk 13.14-20/Lk. 21.20-24.

investigation into the literary and theological tensions perceived to be contained within Mark 13 as a whole, particularly since 13.14-18 seems to be based upon a different source from other sections of the chapter (such as 13.7-8, 13.9-13 and 13.24-27). Such an approach to the chapter has a long history within scholarship, starting with the provocative work of Timothy Colani in 1864.[33] Nevertheless, in modified form it continues to command the attention of many recent interpreters of the chapter. Thus, Vicky Balabanski recently suggested that 13.14-18 was part of an earlier Judaean oracle which becomes incorporated within Mark's eschatological discourse, an oracle which is the result of a specific, historical situation in Judaea. In particular, Balabanski associates the oracle with the traditions of the flight of Christians to Pella just prior to the outbreak of the Jewish Revolt in 70 CE.[34]

But what exactly is this 'abominating horror'? The phrase has been the subject of considerable scholarly interest, among Old Testament and New Testament commentators alike.[35] The cryptic Greek phrase is one which is firmly anchored in the apocalyptic traditions of Judaism, notably the book of Daniel (see 9.27; 11.31; 12.11; cf. 8.13) and 1 Macc. 1.54 (perhaps the earliest interpretation of the crucial phrase in Daniel).[36] Thus, most scholars agree that the phrase originally refers to the desecration of the Jewish temple in December of 167 BCE by Antiochus IV Epiphanes (Zmijewski 1990: 210). It is not entirely clear what the nature of this desecration was, whether it consisted of the Seleucid monarch dedicating the temple to the Olympian Zeus, or placing an image of himself, in the guise of the god Zeus, upon the great altar of sacrifice.[37] One ancient source is more specific about the desolating action: Josephus (*Ant.* 12.5.4) says that Antiochus

33. Beasley-Murray (1956: 14-18) discusses Colani's under-rated contributions. Also see D. Ford (1979: 17-21).

34. Eusebius, *Eccl. Hist.* 3.7.1 and Epiphanius, *Refutation of all Heresies* 29.7.7-8; 30.2.7 and Epiphanius, *Weights and Measures* 15 are the major sources for this tradition. See Balabanski 1997: 101-34. Luedemann (1989: 200-213) offers an alternative interpretation of the Pella tradition.

35. Some of the most significant discussions include Beasley-Murray 1957: 59-72; Ford 1979: 148-75; Wenham 1992: 28-32; Collins 1993: 357-58; Balabanski 1997: 88-92; Such 1999.

36. See Dyer 1998: 107-108 for a discussion of the Greek text of Daniel in connection with Mk 13.14.

37. Jerome is the first person to suggest this (in his *Commentary* on Dan. 11.31). See Collins 1993: 357-58 for details. Schürer (1973: 146-55) discusses the chronology concerned with the incident.

built a pagan altar upon the temple-altar and butchered a pig on it: 'The king built a pagan altar upon the temple-altar, and slaughtered swine thereon, practising a form of sacrifice neither lawful nor native to the religion of the Jews'.[38]

Among succeeding generations the threat of similar conflict with Roman forces (the oppressive successors of the Seleucids) helped to create an atmosphere of renewed apocalyptic fervour. Interestingly, the Roman military leader Pompey the Great committed a similarly sacrilegious act by entering the Holy of Holies of the Jerusalem temple in 64 BCE; and this may help provide the backdrop for the enigmatic 'desolating sacrilege' of Mk 13.14.[39] Similarly, some interpreters see the desecration fulfilled in the experiences of a later generation in 41 CE when the Emperor Caligula attempted to desecrate the Jewish temple in Jerusalem by erecting his statue inside it.[40] Others postulate a comparable desecration by the Roman general Titus in connection with the destruction of Jerusalem by his legions in August/September of 70 CE. Titus' declaration about the conquest of the city which was made in the temple courtyard is commonly identified as the desecrating act in this regard, although the appearance on Mount Skopos of Titus' army under the command of Cestius Gallus on 17 November 66 CE is sometimes identified as the specific desecrating act (Günther 1973). For others it is simply the desecrating presence of the Roman army, complete with the emblems of the Roman emperor affixed to its shields and legionary standards, that provides the historical key to the mystery.[41] Still others associate the desecration with the installation of Phanias as a puppet high priest in late 67 CE (Sowers 1970; Balabanski 1997: 122-34). This was a

38. *Ass. Mos.* 8.5 also appears to allude to the slaughter of a pig as the sacrilege.

39. Asimov (1974: 199-213) offers a fascinating study of this little-noted event. He suggests that Pompey's rash act was a watershed in his career, and that thereafter his political fortunes waned dramatically. Asimov playfully speculates that the collapse of Pompey's public career might be attributed to divine judgment for his 'abomination of desolation'. Interestingly, Nicholas Ray's film of the life of Jesus entitled *King of Kings* (1961) begins with a five-minute sequence depicting Pompey's sacrilege of the Jerusalem temple; the film also depicts the so-called 'Golden Shields' incident in the temple which took place during Pilate's governorship (see Josephus, *War* 2.9.2-3). These are some of the many ways in which this underrated film sets up a contrast between Rome's worldly power and Jesus Christ's heavenly authority.

40. Manson 1957: 329-30; Gaston 1970: 23-29; Schweizer 1970: 272; Theissen 1992: 157-65; Such 1999: 53-79.

41. Beasley-Murray 1956: 255-58; 1957: 69-72; Ford 1979: 166-72. Also see Maier 1969 on the subject.

move that was particularly controversial given Phanias' connections with the Zealots in Jerusalem and the fact that his priesthood represented a significant power shift in the prevailing political interests of the day.

What should we make of such a bewildering array of interpretative suggestions and historical reconstructions? It is obvious that there is no unanimity as to exactly what historical event is meant by 'the desolating sacrilege' in Mk 13.14, but one thing is generally agreed upon. This is the fact that the offence somehow involved the Roman army (and by impli- cation, the imperial cultus) in actions that were deemed idolatrous in the eyes of the Jews and Christian onlookers.[42] Whether or not this offensive action on the part of the Romans was tied up with early ideas about an Antichrist depends largely on the importance accorded to 2 Thess. 2.1- 10—a matter about which there is still considerable debate (Ford 1979: 193-242). In any event, it is the oppressive force of the Roman Empire, as exemplified by the actions of its army and legions, which is suggested by the 'abominating horror'.

In short, the phrase 'abominating horror' in Mk 13.14 stands as a summary of the apocalyptic horror that fell upon Jerusalem as Roman armies marched in and laid waste to the city, destroying its temple. The description of such an invasion as an 'abomination' (βδέλυγμα) is striking, and leads us to consider another key passage where similar language is used, namely in Rev. 17.4-5 as part of the description of the Whore of Babylon:

> The woman was arrayed in purple and scarlet, and bedecked with gold and jewels and pearls, holding in her hand a golden cup full of abominations (βδελυγμάτων) and the impurities of her fornication, and on her forehead was written a name of mystery: 'Babylon the great, mother of harlots and of earth's abominations (βδελυγμάτων)'.[43]

The 'Whore of Babylon' (Revelation 17.1-18)
The second apocalyptic motif that is relevant to our discussion of Conrad's *Heart of Darkness* is that of the Whore of Babylon. Most scholars agree that within the Apocalypse John contrasts the figure of the Whore of

42. Only occasionally does a commentator disassociate the 'abomination of desola- tion' from historical events involving the Roman army. A good example is Hengel (1985: 16-20), who takes the phrase to refer to an indeterminate future event prophe- sied before the events of 66–70 CE.

43. Ford (1979: 248) describes the 'Whore of Babylon' as 'another allusion to the Old Testament saga of Antiochus Epiphanes'.

Babylon in Rev. 17.1–19.10 with that of the Woman Clothed with the Sun in Rev. 12.1-17, and that this contrast between the forces of evil and the righteous saints of God is fundamental to the work as a whole.[44] The image of the Whore of Babylon has yielded a rich harvest in terms of English literature, particularly as an expression of the oppressive and corrupt political powers of the day (Bond 1992). Given that these matters are central to the thematic concerns of Conrad's *Heart of Darkness*, it should come as no surprise that Conrad's novella could be said to yield a bumper crop of such apocalyptic images. Nowhere is this more clear than in his use of 'the sepulchral city' (Brussels?) as a representative symbol of the exploitative forces of civilization which, driven by greed, penetrate into the jungle, into the heart of darkness itself. In this sense the 'sepulchral city' serves as Conrad's equivalent of the city of Babylon in John's Apocalypse.

Prior to Rev. 17.1-18 John has already had occasion to include mention of the city of Babylon twice (in 14.8 and 16.19), but in 17.1-18 he gives it a much more elaborate treatment, mixing it with the imagery of a harlot or whore. The vision of the Whore of Babylon here is part of a much larger section of Revelation given over to a description of Imperial Rome and its judgment by God (17.1–19.10). The section not only describes the Whore of Babylon herself in language rich in its suggestiveness of decadence and immorality as she rides on a scarlet beast having seven heads and ten horns (17.1-18), but goes on to relate a song of lament for the Whore after she is attacked by the beast (18.1 24), as well as a song of praise to God for his judgment of her (19.1-10). It is fairly unanimously agreed that the Whore of Babylon described in John's vision is, at some level, a symbol of both the city of Rome and the Roman Empire which extended outwards from the city to engulf most of the ancient world.[45] This is the case even

---

44. Farrer 1949: 141-47; Bruns 1964; Humphrey 1995: 106-109, 115.

45. The majority of commentators proceed along these lines. Included are Caird (1966: 215-21); Beasley-Murray (1978: 260-21); Court (1979: 122-53); Blevins (1984: 85-91); A.Y. Collins (1984: 121-24); Mounce (1984: 306-44); Bauckham (1989: 91-94); Boring (1989: 179-80); Krodel (1989: 291-317); Kraybill (1996: 149-52); Aune (1998: 905-1040); Murphy (1998: 348-85) and Beale (1999: 847-971). Ladd (1972: 228) argues that while Rome may have been the first-century embodiment of the wicked city, the Apocalypse of John also suggests a future 'eschatological Babylon' which cannot be simply equated with any single historical city. Also see Swete 1909: 226; Lohmeyer 1926: 135-44; Niles 1962: 86-87; Farrer 1964: 187-88; Minear 1968: 246; M. Wilcox 1975: 163; Ellul 1977: 189; Ford 1979: 269-72; Sweet 1979: 254, 271; Morris 1983: 213-14; Laws 1988: 37-38; Wall 1991: 202-203, 207-208 and Rowland 1993: 24; 1998: 683-85 for similar comments about how Rome serves for John as a

though no consensus has been arrived at as to what time period of Roman imperial history is being intimated by means of the vision, nor which particular emperor is being symbolized as the 'Beast' (commonly taken to symbolize the emperor himself and the imperial cult attached to him). Nero (54–68 CE)[46] and Domitian (96–98 CE) are the two emperors most commonly invoked in this regard, but others are frequently suggested. In one sense, it does not matter a great deal which Emperor we implicate as the 'Beast' of Rome as long as it is recognized that John's purpose in producing his Apocalypse is not so much an attempt to pull back the curtain on a concrete historical situation of persecution of Christians by the Roman state as it is an attempt to meet the needs of his readers by addressing the crisis within the social world of Roman Asia in which they lived.[47]

Occasionally some commentators have challenged the assumption that the Whore of Babylon is an image of the city of Rome at all and have suggested that the city of Jerusalem is what John has in mind.[48] To my mind this is something of a forced interpretation of the text of Revelation as a whole, especially given the fact that the beast upon which the Whore is seated is specifically said in 17.9 to be seven hills, commonly taken to be the seven hills upon which Rome was built.[49] The mention in 17.18 that the Whore of Babylon is 'the great city which has dominion over the kings of the earth' also points unmistakably in this direction. In short, we can be

contemporary representation of a symbol of evil, the ancient city of Babylon, without either suggesting a simple equation of the two or exhausting its power as a mythic symbol. Schussler Fiorenza (1985: 183-86) summarizes some of the debate about the mythopoetic language of Revelation in connection with the identity of Rome/Babylon.

46.   Robinson (1976: 249), for example, argues that the details contained in Rev. 18.17-18 are an allusion to the great fire of Rome which took place in 64 CE during the reign of Nero.

47.   See A.Y. Collins 1984: 84-110 and L. Thompson 1990: 171-210 for more on the social setting of the Apocalypse.

48.   Ford 1975: 283-86; Beagley 1987: 92-108; Malina 1995: 206-20; Provan 1996: 90-96. Generally the reference in 11.8 to 'the great city in which the Lord was crucified' figures in such interpretations.

49.   Rome is frequently said to occupy seven hills in ancient sources; see Swete 1909: 220; Caird 1966: 216; Aune 1998: 944-45 and Beale 1999: 870 for brief listings. Roman imperial coinage from the reign of Vespasian is also sometimes cited as confirmation of Rome as the city in view here. The so-called 'Dea Roma' coin reverse type of a sestertius from 71 CE shows the goddess Roma seated amidst a number of rocks representing the seven hills of Rome. See Beauvery 1983 and Aune 1998: 920-22 for details.

fairly confident that the reference to the 'Whore of Babylon' is indeed a symbol of the city of Rome.[50] It seems likely that the phrase was first used by Jewish and Christian writers in response to the destruction of Jerusalem and the temple by the Romans in 70 CE; just as Babylon was responsible for the destruction of the temple in 587 BCE, so Rome is responsible for the destruction of the Herodian temple in 70 CE and thus worthy of description as the new Babylon.[51] We see precisely such a description in *4 Ezra* 3.1-2, 28, 31; *2 Bar.* 11.1; 67.7, *Sib. Or.* 5.143, 159 and 1 Pet. 5.13. This is not to say that the imagery is new, for there is much to suggest that John is drawing upon a rich heritage of Old Testament material which equated harlotry with idolatry and (by extension) the economic exploitation of the poor by the wealthy and prosperous.[52] In fact, much of the complex imagery contained in Rev. 17.1–19.10 is a reflection upon, and interweaving of, such texts as Jer. 2.20; 3.6; 51.7-8, 13; Hos. 4.12-14; Nah. 3.4; Ezek. 26–28; and, most importantly, Isa. 23.15-18 (a judgment oracle about the city of Tyre playing the harlot to the nations of the world).[53] What is most intriguing here is the way in which the idolatrous activities of the godless city (whether it be Babylon, Nineveh, Tyre, or whatever) are often intimately bound up with its trade and commercial activities on the world scene.[54] Several recent studies on Revelation have called attention to the importance of this theme. Three in particular are worth mentioning briefly.

The first is Richard Bauckham's thought-provoking chapter on 'The Fallen City' in his *The Bible in Politics* (1989).[55] Bauckham concentrates his discussion on the vision of the destruction of Babylon contained in

50. Bruns (1964: 461-63) suggests that the historical figure of Valeria Messalina, wife of the Emperor Claudius, stands behind the imagery of the harlot. He cites Juvenal, *Satires* 6.116-24 and Tacitus, *Annals* 11.31 in support of such an identification. Also see Barclay 1976: II, 144. Stauffer (1955: 58, 188-89) suggests Cleopatra is the historical model.

51. Hunzinger (1965) argues that Christians took over the practice of describing Rome as Babylon from Jewish writers following the events of 70 CE.

52. Court 1979: 139-42; Rowland 1993: 129-41; Beale 1999: 849-57, 904-925.

53. Fekkes (1994: 210-23); Moyise (1995: 72-77); Beale (1998: 268-70, 311-17) and Royalty (1998: 59-65, 188-97) are some of the recent commentators who have summary discussions of the Old Testament texts alluded to in Rev. 17.1–19.10.

54. So Kuhn 1964: I, 515; Beasley-Murray 1978: 266-69; Court 1979: 140-41; 1994: 63-65; Wengst 1987: 122-27.

55. Also see Bauckham 1991; 1993a: 338-83 which are expansions of the chapter. Bauckham 1993b: 17-18, 35-37 also continues the ideas.

Revelation 18,[56] but applies his discussion in such a way as to illuminate the meaning of the Whore of Babylon image found in Revelation 17. He suggests that John uses two complementary images of the evil of Roman imperial rule, the 'Beast from the sea' and 'the great city of Babylon' (including her portrayal as a harlot). Commenting on the fact that in Rev. 17.3, 9-10 the two images are brought together in that the harlot is enthroned on the seven heads of the beast, Bauckham remarks:

> Roman civilization, as a corrupting influence, rides on the back of Roman military power. The city of Rome grew great through military conquest, which brought wealth and power to the city, and its economic and cultural influence spread through the world in the wake of imperial armies (Bauckham 1989: 88).

In short, the point is that many of the political and economic benefits which the so-called *Pax Romana* brought to the ancient world were bought at a high price. Such things are idolatrous, abominations of the Whore of Babylon, and those who sought after them are likened to men who have committed fornication with a prostitute. In other words, according to Bauckham, the image of the great Whore of Babylon is primarily an economic one. The list in Rev. 18.12-13 of eighteen items representative of the wealth flowing into the capital city of Rome from the far-flung reaches of the empire points powerfully in this direction.[57] At the same time, the economic exploitation that Rome thrived on was sustained by the Roman state religion, including the imperial cultus which elevated the emperor to the status of god and demanded that worship be accorded to him. It is the heady concoction of economics and politics, the exploitation of the poor by the rich, conducted under the auspices of a state religion which glorified the state and worshipped the emperor, that John finds so objectionable.

A similar point about John's overriding critique of the injustices of the Roman economic system is contained in J. Nelson Kraybill's *Imperial Cult and Commerce in John's Apocalypse* (1996). Understandably, it is Revelation 18 which forms the focal point for the discussion here, although much attention is given to what is known about commerce and trading in the first-century Roman world. However, Kraybill advances the

56. A.Y. Collins (1980) offers an important discussion of the form and structure of the chapter. Also see C.R. Smith 1990.

57. Bauckham (1993a: 350-71) discusses these verses in detail. It is not to be overlooked that included within the list is 'all types of ivory' (καὶ πᾶν σκεῦος ἐλεφάντινον), so central to the plot of Conrad's *Heart of Darkness*.

argument a stage further by suggesting that John went so far as to call for Christian believers to sever all economic and political ties with Rome and align themselves with the alternative society that God was forming in Christ, his vision of the New Jerusalem. It was in the complex nature of commercial trade within the Roman world that the danger lay. As Kraybill says:

> [I]n the realm of harbors, guild halls, trade offices and banks we find mundane expression of what John saw as Roman arrogance, greed and idolatry. In the sphere of economic activity John found a virulent hybrid of materialism, social pressure and imperial cult that threatened the very essence of Christian faith (Kraybill 1996: 102).

A slightly different approach is adopted by Robert M. Royalty in his *The Streets of Heaven* (1998), where there is a greater sensitivity to the way in which wealth as an idea functions within the book of Revelation. The key point here, Royalty asserts, is that it is too easy to adopt a negative view about the role that wealth and prosperity play in the descriptions of the various visions contained within John's book. Indeed, it may well be that the focus on Revelation 18 has led us somewhat astray in this regard. As Royalty puts it:

> There is no reason, however, to let Revelation 18 speak for the entire narrative world of the Apocalypse; what of God's jewels and Christ's gold? Money talks, and all of Revelation should be listened to when reading for the imagery of wealth in the text, even if the idea of a wealthy God disturbs modern sensibilities.[58]

At this point Royalty's interpretation takes a rather unorthodox direction, one that is based upon a different reconstruction from the one that most interpreters adopt concerning the social setting of the community to which the Apocalypse is directed. Royalty suggests that the 'battle' being waged within Revelation is not to be understood simply as one between the faithful Christians and the unbelieving Roman state, but one that also reflects struggles between factions within the Christian communities of Asia itself. More to the point, according to Royalty, the teaching on wealth and prosperity must also be read as an essential feature of the internal disputes among the Christian groups of the province of Asia. Thus the 'crisis' which occasions the writing of the Apocalypse is one within the Christian communities of Asia. This raises a question as to the place that

58. Royalty 1998: 4. Royalty is critical of Bauckham's work on Rev. 18, describing it as 'a Marxist critique of Roman economic oppression and injustice'.

opposition to Rome has within the work overall. Royalty's approach is to suggest that the Apocalypse forges a synthesis of opposition wherein all of John's opponents (Roman, Jewish and Christian) are brought together and treated as if they were part of a single, satanic force. As Royalty summarizes: 'John makes the Christian church the battleground for his fight with Rome. When attacking Rome, the author also attacks other Christian teachers, apostles, and prophets whom John claims are allied with Rome and Satan (1998: 245)'. Thus, it seems clear that the wealth imagery in the book of Revelation can actually serve to lend support to, as well as subvert, the author's narrative world; it is the rhetorical strategy of the work which needs to be kept uppermost in mind. Imagery associated with wealth and economic prosperity is, paradoxically, both good and evil: positive insofar as it is applied to God, his rule and purposes, and the New Jerusalem, negative insofar as it is applied to Satan, his rule and designs, and the city of Babylon/Rome.

There is much to be gained from a careful assessment of the teaching on wealth and commerce found within the Apocalypse of John. Yet such 'economic' readings of Revelation are not without their difficulties, not least because of the way in which they assume that it is possible to determine with any degree of certainty the social settings out of which a given text arises on the basis of that text itself. In other words, we cannot assume that the symbolic world of a written document bears any resemblance to the social or historical setting of the writer who created it. It must always be kept in mind that an unavoidable gap exists between the symbolic world of a literary text and the real world of the author of that text. As Iain Provan puts it:

> The problem, it should be stressed, is not that the social world outside the author's head cannot be presumed to exist. It is that the precise way in which analogical, symbolic, liturgical prose refers to that world is in essence uncertain. Reading social situations out of biblical texts like Revelation is therefore a perilous undertaking.[59]

Finally, it is worth noting briefly that some feminist readings of Revelation have called attention to the way in which the work embodies an essentially androcentric perspective which makes it difficult for women

---

59. Provan 1996: 97. His comments are specifically geared to Bauckham's work, although they might also be extended to Kraybill's interpretation just as readily. Harland (2000: 116-20) also offers some relevant thoughts about the social world of John's readers in Asia Minor.

to appropriate. As Pippin puts it: 'The Apocalypse is not a tale for women. The misogyny which underlies this narrative is extreme'.[60]

We turn now to consider Conrad's *Heart of Darkness*, which had has similar charges of misogyny levelled against it based upon the negative portrayal of women within the story-line. However, as we shall see, there is a much more significant connection between *Heart of Darkness* and the Apocalypse of John. This focuses on the figure of Kurtz's Intended and the way in which she comes to represent the oppressive forces of imperial power.

Reassessing Kurtz's Intended: The Abominating Horror/Whore

The variety of interpretations of *Heart of Darkness* on offer stands as a testimony to the immense richness of the work. The novella has been seen as a re-working of Virgil's *Aeneid* in which the language and symbolism of the descent to Hades is employed;[61] or similarly, as a re-telling of Dante's *Inferno*.[62] Others detect a hint of Coleridge's *The Ancient Mariner* in the way the story is narrated (Ober 1965), or see the journey to the heart of darkness as a modernized version of a knight's quest for the Holy Grail, with Marlow's desire to journey up-river with his companions (described as 'pilgrims') to meet the enigmatic Kurtz providing an intriguing parallel (Thale 1960). Others trace a Faustian theme through the work (Watts 1977: 114-16; 1984: 74-82), or even point to other famous literary tales of river journeys, such as Mark Twain's *The Adventures of Tom Sawyer* (1876) or *The Adventures of Huckleberry Finn* (1884), for parallels (Karl 1960: 133-34).

Conrad's *Heart of Darkness* is extraordinarily simple in terms of its basic plot, but exceedingly complex in terms of its execution. The use of first-person narration has long been an object of discussion, particularly as it relates to the interweaving perspectives of Marlow and Kurtz.[63] The

---

60. Pippin 1992: 78. S.R. Garrett (1992: 381) remarks: 'The objection that 'Baby-lon' is only a metaphor, a symbol, does not eliminate the problem that the text creates for women readers'. Also see Pippin 1992: 50-86.

61. Feder 1960; Yarrison 1975; Watts 1977: 55-59; Cleary and Sherwood 1984: 183-88. Watts (1977: 53) associates the two knitting women who guard the door of darkness with the Sibyl who guards the entrance to the underworld.

62. Evans 1960; Cleary and Sherwood 1984: 188-92; Saha 1987.

63. Watt (1980: 211-14) offers an important perspective on this. Also see Morrissey 1981.

elaborate use of multiple narrators also creates distance between the reader and the character of Kurtz; he is encountered primarily through the impression he makes upon others.[64] In this sense Kurtz never really becomes a character in the story; he remains a phantom of the imagination, a 'voice' to be heard more than a person to be encountered.[65] Kurtz is frequently described as being gifted with 'eloquence', but there is precious little of this in what we actually hear Kurtz himself *say* in the story. Much of what he does say, or is reported to have said, comes in the form of carefully structured rhetorical dialogues with Marlow involving the idea of moral and ethical restraint.[66] In any event, it is all channelled through Marlow himself, a fact which inevitably raises questions about the identification of Kurtz's perspective with Marlow's.[67] Little wonder, given the complex narrative techniques used within the story, that Cedric Watts has warned that Conrad's 'techniques may lead the reader to be ambushed by the text'.[68] On the same score, it is hardly surprising that Conrad has been an important focal point for critical discussion about the rise of English modernist fiction.[69]

Perhaps the most discussed paragraph of *Heart of Darkness* comes in the third section of the novella as Marlow goes to Kurtz's pilot cabin as the steamer lies moored along the banks of the impenetrable river. He is carrying a candle, but notices that Kurtz is incapable of seeing the light of the flame. Then we read:

64.   The suggestion that impressionism and symbolism are backdrops against which to understand Conrad's work is frequently made within the critical literature. See Watt 1976.

65.   Maud (1971) attempts to reconstruct Kurtz's own story through the veiled hints and allusions contained within the novella.

66.   McClure 1977. Benson (1971: 215-16) is also worth consulting on this point

67.   As Gibson (1997: 128) puts it: 'Everything that Kurtz says in the story is in double quotation marks. It is speech incorporated into Marlow's speech'.

68.   Watts 1993: 130. Also see Watts 1984: 21 for a similar remark. The issues of voice, narration and dialogue in *Heart of Darkness* have been discussed at great length. Recent studies include those of Cox (1981: 11-13); J.H. Miller (1985); Reeves (1985); Seidel (1985); Knight (1987); Meisel (1987: 235-47); Murray (1987); Lothe (1989: 21-44) and Ambrosini (1991: 84-115). Of special note is Brooks (1996), who perceptively notes how the narrative framework of *Heart of Darkness* does not conform to patterns usually found in fiction (he compares it to Mary Shelley's *Frankenstein*, for example). Lothe (1989: 22-24) assesses Brooks' interpretation.

69.   As Lodge (1984) asserts.

Anything approaching the change that came over his features I have never seen before, and hope never to see again. Oh, I wasn't touched. I was fascinated. It was as though a veil had been rent. I saw on that ivory face the expression of sombre pride, of ruthless power, of craven terror—of an intense and hopeless despair. Did he live his life again in every detail of desire, temptation, and surrender during that supreme moment of complete knowledge? He cried in a whisper at some image, at some vision—he cried out twice, a cry that was no more than a breath—'The horror! The horror!' (*HD* 111).

In fact, Kurtz's final cry 'The horror! The horror!' is mentioned twice more in the third part of the novel. The first of these occurs shortly after the description of Kurtz's death as Marlow, ostensibly still on the steam boat, reminisces about the remarkable man. In this case the doubled final words are contracted in Marlow's memory to a single expression of the enigmatic phrase.[70]

This is the reason why I affirm that Kurtz was a remarkable man. He had something to say. He said it. Since I had peeped over the edge myself, I understand better the meaning of his stare, that could not see the flame of the candle, but was wide enough to embrace the whole universe, piercing enough to penetrate all the hearts that beat in the darkness. He had summed up—he had judged. 'The horror!' He was a remarkable man (*HD* 112-13).

The second of these references to Kurtz's final words occurs towards the end of the tale as Marlow recalls his visit to Kurtz's fiancée, the Intended. As he stands before the door to her house wondering what to say to the woman, his thoughts go back to his encounter with Kurtz in the jungle:

It was a moment of triumph for the wilderness, an invading and vengeful rush which, it seemed to me, I would have to keep back alone for the salvation of another soul. And the memory of what I had heard him say afar there, with the horned shapes stirring at my back, in the glow of fires, within the patient woods, those broken phrases came back to me, were heard again in their ominous and terrifying simplicity. I remembered his abject pleading, his abject threats, the colossal scale of his vile desires, the meanness, the torment, the tempestuous anguish of his soul. And later on I seemed to see his collected languid manner, when he said one day, 'This lot of ivory now is really mine. The Company did not pay for it. I collected it myself at a very great personal risk. I am afraid they will try to claim it as theirs though. H'm. It is a difficult case. What do you think I ought to do—

70. The manuscript of the novella has 'Oh! the horror!' in all three instances that the phrase occurs. See Kimbrough 1971: 136 for a reproduction of the actual page concerned.

resist? Eh? I want no more than justice'… He wanted no more than
justice—no more than justice. I rang the bell before a mahogany door on
the first floor, and while I waited he seemed to stare at me out of the glassy
panel—stare with that wide and immense stare embracing, condemning,
loathing all the universe. I seemed to hear the whispered cry, 'The horror!
The horror!' (*HD* 116-17).

The range of interpretations offered of 'The horror!' is astonishing[71] and
stands as testimony to the multivalent nature of much of Conrad's writing.
One of the most common ways of understanding it is to see 'the horror' as
Kurtz's pronouncement of judgment on the depravity of humanity and a cry
about the hopelessness of the human condition, particularly as it has been
experienced in the jungle wilderness. In short, it is an indictment of human
civilization as a whole, a recognition that the 'progress' of civilization has
all gone horribly wrong.[72] As one commentator put it:

> The imperialists could use their power to illuminate and ennoble or to
> develop a beneficial presence, but they do not. Marlow recognizes in Kurtz
> a paradoxical duality in which the darker element has taken control. Dark-
> ness, being enacted behind a facade of light, makes European depredations
> on the Congo an abomination (Neilsen 1987: 41).

Such a reading of the meaning of Kurtz's cry can also be projected upon
Marlow himself as he hears it, and realizes for himself the ring of authen-
ticity and honesty in Kurtz's words. This is the kind of interpretation
offered by Jeremy Hawthorne when he links the passage to what he
identifies as the novella's overall theme, namely the clash between
idealism and imperialism:

> A very brief, summary answer as to why Marlow admires Kurtz for his
> despairing cry might be that Marlow remains convinced of the need for
> ideals even in the face of their manifest powerlessness or of the self-
> deception which they involve. However much Kurtz's ideals fail him, they
> provide our only hope of making the world better, or moderating the
> behaviour of those freed from external restraints.[73]

71. Hawthorne (1990: 195) describes it as 'the best-known critical crux in *Heart of
Darkness*'.
72. T.S. Eliot is quite attracted to this reading of the passage. See Watt 1980: 236.
Dowden (1957) offers a much-cited discussion of how light/darkness imagery is used
along these lines within the novel.
73. Hawthorne 1990: 195-96. He also suggests (1990: 196) that a desire to spare
women from entering into the dark clash between ideals and imperialism is precisely
the reason why Marlow lies to the Intended, or at least that is how Marlow justifies the
lie to himself.

On the other hand, many critics see Kurtz's 'horror' in more personal terms and take it to be a cry of repentance, or an expression of sorrow, over the evil things that he has done in his life. This appears to be the way in which Marlow himself understands Kurtz's dying whisper, for he describes it as a 'paradoxical victory' over all that Kurtz was before, now surrendered up in a self-condemnatory confession by the man as he looks back over his life and realizes the folly of his Faustian pact. As Frederick R. Karl puts it:

> As Marlow understands the scream, it represents a moral victory; that is, on the threshold of death, Kurtz has reviewed his life with all its horror and in some dying part of him has repented. Marlow hears the words as a victory of moral sensibility over a life of brutality and prostituted ideals.[74]

Is Kurtz to be regarded as a hero to be emulated,[75] or as a villain to be despised? It is difficult to decide. At one point in the novel he is called 'the emissary of light' and as such represents the best of an enlightened Europe, an idealist with a passion for bringing civilization to the dark continent. And yet through him the myth of empire is destroyed, for Kurtz himself degenerates morally and finds that his idealism fades into nothingness.[76] He is corrupted by his own lack of restraint, a Nietzschean superman with an awesome will to power that knows no bounds.

At some level 'the horror' is Kurtz's realization of an inadequacy or moral weakness within himself, an inadequacy that is recognized in the face of the vast wilderness which confronts him. 'The horror' is the woe-fully inadequate summary of his experience of truth gleaned in the wilderness. The wilderness 'speaks' to him, as indeed it speaks to Marlow and the reader, with a voice that is part of the complex mechanism of narration set up within the story.[77]

---

74. Karl 1968: 151. Hampson (1992: 111) similarly remarks about Kurtz's final cry: 'Whatever its exact significance, Kurtz's statement is in the realm of moral discourse'. Also see Moser 1957: 24; J.I.M. Stewart 1968: 79-84; O'Prey 1973: 21; McLauchlan 1978: 120; 1983: 9-10; Batchelor 1994: 91-93.

75. Trilling 1966: 20-21; Ruthven 1968; Berthoud 1978: 60-61.

76. On the failure of idealism in Conrad's work, see Watt 1980: 147-68; Hawthorne 1990: 12-182. Eagleton (1976: 135) also discusses the struggle between commercialism and a Romantic idealism as the centre of *Heart of Darkness*. More recently, Goodheart (1991: 23-43) argues that *Heart of Darkness* can be read as an 'allegory of Enlightenment' in which the traditional juxtaposition of reason and desire is challenged.

77. For more on the matter of narration within the work, see Vitoux 1975; Watt 1978–79: 164-65; Fogel 1983: 134; Elliott 1985.

However, others suggest that Kurtz's repentance may not be all that it first appears, that we should not automatically assume that Marlow's interpretation of Kurtz's death cry is what Kurtz himself meant when the words were uttered.[78] Thus, Osborn Andreas remarks:

> His last words, as he contemplates his life with the savages, are 'The horror—the horror'. This, however, is not exactly a recantation. It expresses not only his disgust with what he has discovered about himself, his desire to be a deity, but also his powerlessness before the intensity of this pleasure. It expresses the intensity of his happiness in Africa (Andreas 1962: 52).

Little wonder then that some commentators simply admit defeat in the face of an impossibly ambiguous passage, one which intertwines the perspectives of Kurtz, Marlow, and Conrad (not to mention the contemporary reader!). As Lionel Trilling remarks: 'For me it is still ambiguous whether Kurtz's famous deathbed cry, "The horror! The horror!" refers to the approach of death or to his experience of savage life' (Trilling 1966: 20). Yet there remain many attempts to interpret the passage in terms of its philosophical or epistemological implications (including Pecora 1985). In other words, how does Conrad intend his readers to understand the story as a whole, and this passage in particular, in terms of what it might reveal about human life and its attendant experiences? James Guetti, in an influential study from 1965, suggested that Conrad was addressing the idea of the 'failure of the imagination', and as such was attempting to illustrate the limitations of expressing human experience. Guetti comments on Kurtz's last utterance:

> As a summation of the literary experiences of 'Heart of Darkness', 'The horror!' can have but one meaning: all hearts are in darkness; the morality and meaning with which man surrounds himself and his experiences is unreal; the reality of experience lies beyond language and the processes of the human imagination.[79]

---

78. Thus, Guerard (1958: 36) remarks: 'A little too much has been made, I think, of the redemptive value of those two words—'The horror!'' Karl (1968: 151-52) also questions whether Marlow's interpretation is to be taken at face value. Singh (1988: 277) ties together 'The horror!' with the colonialism that Marlow hypocritically ascribes to: 'I would suggest that contrary to Marlow's implication the 'horror' refers first to what Kurtz has done to the blacks and only secondarily to what he has done to himself, since the latter is only the effect, and not the cause of the former. Consequently, the full application of Kurtz's last words would not only be to himself but also to men like Marlow who seemed to hate colonialism but really lived by its values and associated the practices of the blacks with the road to perdition'.

79. Guetti 1965: 501. Also see Sugg 1975.

For many critics, the interpretative waters are muddied even further, for it is impossible to know exactly how much Conrad's *own* ideas as to the meaning of 'The horror!' are communicated through the character of Marlow. Watts suggests that Marlow's confusion as to Kurtz's meaning is tied up with Conrad's own confusion on the matter. Conrad, he suggests, was resistant to the resolution of the dramatic paradoxes he had created:

> So what he offers is a pseudo-resolution: a dramatic statement by Kurtz which seems to promise that grand *finale* of revelation but which, on closer examination, proves to be itself a compressed paradox, an oxymoron: a statement which mirrors, and does not reduce, the extreme ambiguity of the characterisation (Watts 1993: 136).

Other critics of Conrad's *Heart of Darkness* have noted the significance of the encounter between Marlow and Kurtz's Intended, particularly the way in which it brings to a dramatic climax the struggle within Marlow himself.[80] Should he tell the truth, and answer the Intended's question about Kurtz's last words? Or should he tell her a 'white' lie and allow her to retain some sense of dignity and a will to live,[81] however falsely conceived and self-delusory such an existence might prove to be? In the end Marlow lies to the Intended and tells her that Kurtz's last spoken utterance was her name, when in fact (as we all know) it was 'The horror! The horror!'.[82] Of course, it could be argued that at one level Marlow does not

---

80. Dilworth 1987. Also see Dowden 1957: 49-50; S.C. Wilcox 1960: 12-13; Bruffee 1971: 236; Boyle 1971: 241-44; Stark 1974–75. Not all critics, however, feel that the final encounter between Marlow and the Intended is the literary high point of the story, and some have objected to the style of the dialogue between the two. Mudrick (1971: 188), for example, describes it as 'cheaply ironic double-talk' and 'a jumble of melodramatic tricks'. Brown (1964: 137) similarly describes the ending as 'sentimental heroics', while Daleski (1977: 76) asserts that Conrad 'bungled the scene'.

81. Daleski (1977: 75) describes Marlow's lie to the Intended as 'an ordinary white lie, a humane expression of compassion without devious moral implications'. Stewart (1980: 327-28) discusses this interpretation of Marlow's deceit. Said (1966: 148) contrasts Kurtz's death (in the face of truth) with Marlow's life (in the face of a lie). For more on Marlow's lie to the Intended, see Moser 1957: 79-81; Baines 1960: 229-30; Kauvar 1971; Whitehead 1975: 131-32; Ong 1977; Berthoud 1978: 61-63; Thumboo 1981; McLauchlan 1983; Parry 1983: 36-39; Staten 1986: 720-22; Hoeppner 1988; Batchelor 1994: 91-93.

82. Leavis (1993: 209) likens this passage to 'the melodramatic intensities of Edgar Allen Poe'.

lie at all, but paradoxically tells her the truth: she *is* 'the horror' of which Kurtz spoke.[83]

This leads us on to consider one of the most intriguing interpretations of 'The horror! The horror!', an interpretation which lends itself readily to a comparison with the apocalyptic imagery from Mk 13.14 and Revelation 17–18 outlined above. We begin with the study offered by Kenneth Lincoln, who focuses upon the encounter between Marlow and Kurtz's Intended at the end of the novel and sees this as holding the key to understanding the meaning of Kurtz's death-cry. Lincoln suggests that Conrad is deliberately injecting an element of humour into the story at this point, but that he does it in such a way that it is easily overlooked.[84] Lincoln explains using the conclusion of Shakespeare's *Antony and Cleopatra* (V.ii), where Cleopatra is described as both a 'horror' and a 'whore', as a backdrop for under-standing Conrad's playfulness:

> 'The last word he pronounced was—your name', Marlow reassures Kurtz's Intended. In fact, the last word uttered by Kurtz was 'the horror!' We can read the conclusion to *Heart of Darkness* hearing echoes of Dr. Johnson's comments on the 'quibble' in Shakespeare. A pun on the words 'horror' and 'whore' may well be the fatal Cleopatra for which Conrad lost the world, general audience and literary critics alike (Lincoln 1972: 186).

In short, the suggestion is that the meaning of 'the horror!' is bound up with Kurtz's Intended herself; she is 'the horror/whore', and insofar as Marlow informs her that Kurtz's last word was 'your name' he is not lying at all, but is speaking the truth, albeit in a highly ironical fashion. Thus, Lincoln continues: '[Conrad] has played one of the most shadowy jokes in prose fiction. It is a hidden but audacious pun, which triggers a network of images whispering of whoredom throughout'.[85] In other words, insofar as the Intended is the embodiment of the cruel system of colonial exploitation, living in a tomb-like house at the centre of the sepulchral city (presumably, Brussels),[86] she is indeed 'the horror' of which Kurtz speaks.[87]

---

83. Otten 1982: 92-93. Ong (1977: 153) remarks: 'The name of the Intended remains a permanent blank in the story, a blank which can only be filled in by "The horror! The horror!"'.

84. Lincoln builds upon the work of Hoffman (1965) in making this suggestion.

85. 1972: 188. Kahane (1989: 145) argues that the switch from 'horror' to its homonym 'whore' suggests Freudian preoccupations. She also notes (152) how Shake-speare also makes use of the phoneme 'whore' in *Othello* (IV.ii.161-62).

86. So Watts (1977: 50); in contrast, Bradbury (1988: 87) thinks it is London. At one level, it matters little whether Conrad intends us to think of Brussels or London,

This is a fascinating angle on what has long been a *crux interpretum* in Conradian fiction, but will it stand up to closer scrutiny? There are some indications, notably within some letters that Conrad wrote at the time, that it does. For example, a letter from Conrad to his friend Cunningham Graham seems to point in this general direction. In the letter Conrad playfully suggests that the ending of *Heart of Darkness* was so cleverly written that one of the key ideas within it might go unrecognized, even by his closest friends:

> I am simply in the seventh heaven to find you like the 'H. of D'. so far. You bless me indeed. Mind you don't curse me by and by for the very same thing. There are two more instalments in which the idea is so wrapped up in secondary notions that you,—even you!—may miss it.[88]

Several features of the story come together when this suggestion that the Intended was 'the horror/whore' is kept in mind. For example, the connection between Kurtz's final cry and the subsequent encounter between Marlow and the Intended makes much better sense (Baines 1960: 229). Some early commentators dismissed the encounter as an afterthought, or an epilogue.[89] But this hardly seems justified, and misses the importance that Conrad himself apparently attributed to the episode. We get an indication of this in a letter written to his Edinburgh publisher William Blackwood on 31 May 1902. Within the letter Conrad mentions the ending of *Heart of Darkness*, offering a rare opinion as to the function of the encounter between Marlow and the Intended as a means of tying together the story as a whole. Conrad suggests that:

> [in] the last pages of *Heart of Darkness* […] the interview of the man and the girl locks in—as it were—the whole 30000 words of narrative description into one suggestive view of a whole phase of life, and makes of that story something quite on another plane than an anecdote of a man who went mad in the Centre of Africa (cited in Blackburn [ed.] 1958: 154).

just as it matters little whether in Rev. 17 John intends us to think of Rome or Jerusalem as the city represented by the Whore of Babylon.

87. Stark (1974–75) offers a fascinating study along these lines. It should be noted that his interpretation assumes that Kurtz's final cry 'The horror! The horror!' represents a rejection of all of his original, noble intentions in coming to the darkness of the jungle.

88. See Jean-Aubry 1927: I, 268-70) for the full text of the letter which is dated 8 February 1899. The letter is discussed by Baines (1960: 202); Cox (1974: 16); Ambrosini (1991: 86-87) and Murfin (1996b: 100).

89. Baines (1960: 229).

If Lincoln's creative suggestion about the word play on 'horror/whore' is correct, then we have a possible answer to the playful question posed by John Sutherland at the beginning of our study. Sutherland asks why it is that Kurtz speaks English instead of French, especially in an area of central Africa where one would naturally expect French to be used. The answer, quite simply, is that it is to facilitate the pun on the homonyms 'the horror/the whore'.[90]

Film Interpretations of Heart of Darkness

Conrad's fortunes within the popular market saw something of a revival of interest in 1998 following the television airing of Alastair Reid's adaptation of his *Nostromo* in 1996. Yet Conrad's fictional work has had several appearances within the cinematic world, although not always in the most predictable of ways. For example, this self-same novel *Nostromo* (1904) is perhaps best known to science-fiction enthusiasts because of its connection to the classic *Alien* cycle of films: the mining ship upon which the heroine Ripley and crew were travelling was named the *Nostromo* in *Alien* (1979), while in *Aliens* (1984) the transport ship which carried Ripley and the marines to the planet Acheron was named the *Sulaco,* after the name of the port city in the novel *Nostromo* (Billy 1989). At one level the symbolic naming of the ships is entirely appropriate, for both films have as a prominent subtext the exploitation of space colonies by a faceless and uncaring Corporation, where self-seeking greed wins out over a crew which is expendable and an even greater threat is revealed. A connection between the *Alien* cycle and *Heart of Darkness* is not all that difficult to forge, for it is in space, the new heart of darkness, where the intrepid miners encounter the unspeakable 'horror' to end all horrors, the Alien herself.[91] And we all know that one of the reasons why *Alien* is such a powerful film is precisely because we are never allowed to see the monster clearly or for very long. In cinematic terms this is the equivalent of making the horror *unspeakable,* something incapable of being pinned down, lending itself to endless adaptation and re-adaptation within the imagination of the viewer.

Without doubt, however, it is Francis Ford Coppola's *Apocalypse Now* (1979) that is most frequently associated with Conrad's *Heart of Darkness,*

90. Hampson (1990: 15-22) discusses the hierarchy of languages contained within *Heart of Darkness*.

91. See Pippin 1999: 78-99 for an interesting discussion of the relationship between Revelation and horror films.

and for good reason. Coppola deliberately intended the Vietnam war epic to be a reworking of Conrad's novel, and even went so far as to require all of the actors and crew involved with the project to read *Heart of Darkness* on location during the filming of the movie.[92] I shall discuss Coppola's master-piece more fully below, but before I do so it is appropriate to note that two other celebrated directors have turned their attentions to Conrad's novella over the years. The first of these is no less a figure than Orson Welles, who had planned to film the story in 1939 and even went so far as to produce a full shooting script.[93] Sadly, the project was never brought to completion, although many *aficionados* of Welles' work are quick to point out that his classic *Citizen Kane* (1941) does contain many features reminiscent of *Heart of Darkness*.[94] The most striking of these is, of course, the fact that both of the central characters die with an impossibly cryptic utterance on their lips: Kurtz's 'The horror!' has its counterpart in the form of Kane's 'Rosebud!'.[95]

The second director to have produced a film version of *Heart of Darkness* is Nicolas Roeg, who has offered a more straightforward adaptation of Conrad's novel. We turn now to consider his film in more detail

Nicolas Roeg's Heart of Darkness *(1993)*
It takes a brave film-maker to attempt to tackle something as structurally complex and symbolically resplendent as Conrad's *Heart of Darkness*. The

92. Coppola 1995: 17. According to Eleanor Coppola (1995: 128), Marlon Brando admitted to Francis Coppola in the midst of filming that he never read the novella as requested. Also see Manso 1994: 838-42; Moore 1997: 15.

93. See Rosenbaum 1972; DeBona 1994; Chatman 1997: 207-208, 222 and Watson 1981; 1997 for details. Welles remained fascinated by Conrad's story, as his two radio plays based on *Heart of Darkness* testify. The first of these was broadcast on *The Mercury Theatre on the Air* on 6 November 1938 and the second was aired on 13 March 1945 as part of the short-lived *This Is My Best* series of half-hour programmes. See Spadoni 1997 for a fine discussion. One of the most interesting things that Welles suggested in the radio plays was an association between Kurtz and the megalomaniac of his (Welles') own day, Adolf Hitler. See Rosenbaum 1972: 29-30; Laskowsky 1982 and Higham 1985: 136-40 for more along these lines.

94. Cohen 1972. Welles significantly expands the role of the Kurtz's Intended within the proposed script, giving her the name Elsa Gruner and having her travel part of the journey up the river with Marlow. Marlow, who falls in love with her, sends her back before she comes to any harm on the dangerous journey. See Carringer 1985: 3-15 for a full discussion.

95. As Cohen (1972: 16, 21-22) and Sinyard (1986: 112) note.

novel just does not lend itself readily to a simple screenplay adaptation, particularly given all of the narrative complexities that it contains. But director Nicolas Roeg has long had something of a reputation as an *avant-garde* film-maker, and he has applied himself admirably to the task at hand. His film *Heart of Darkness* (1993) was originally aired in the USA on the Turner Television Network on 13 March 1994 and was subsequently put on general video release; the video version, distributed by Turner Pictures Worldwide, lasts 101 minutes and carries a '15' certificate. The film is explicitly said to be based on Conrad's novella, with the very imaginative screenplay coming from Benedict Fitzgerald. The promotional poster of the film summarizes it as 'A Journey from the Edge of Civilization into an Evil Beyond Imagination' (see Figure 1)

The film stars Tim Roth as Charlie Marlow and John Malkovich as Kurtz, with Phoebe Nicholls as The Intended and the Somalian actress Iman as Kurtz's native mistress (described in the film credits as The Black Beauty). Other characters to note include James Fox as John Gabriel Gosse, Peter Vaughan as the Director, Michael Fitzgerald as Gustave Harou, Patrick Ryecart as Alphonse De Griffe, Geoffrey Hutchings as Jacques Delcommune, Morten Faldaas as the Russian Harlequin, and Isaach de Bankole as Mfumu. Several of the characters in the novel (who are known only by their titles) are given further definition, generally in the form of being given the actual names of the persons upon whom Conrad based them from his own trip up the Congo river in 1890. Thus, the Company's Chief Accountant at the Outer Station is named in the film as Jacques Delcommune, the Company agent who accompanies Marlow to the Central Station is named as Gustav Harou, and the novel's anonymous General Manager of the Central Station is identified as Mr Gosse. Even the novel's anonymous helmsman/boilerman, who is killed in the attack on the steamer as it travels up-river, is given a name, Mfumu. Another way in which Conrad's own experiences in his trip up the Congo are made explicit in the film involves the name of the steamer that carries him from Kinchassa to Stanley Falls (modern Kisangani). In real life this ship was named *Roi de Belges* (*King of the Belgians*), and in the film the steamer that Marlow skippers from the Central Station to Kurtz's Inner Station is given precisely this name.

In addition, the ambiguous geographical locations of several places within Conrad's novella are made explicit. Not only is the location of the 'heart of darkness' said to be the Congo in central Africa, but the Company Station is identified as Matadi, and the Inner Station is specified

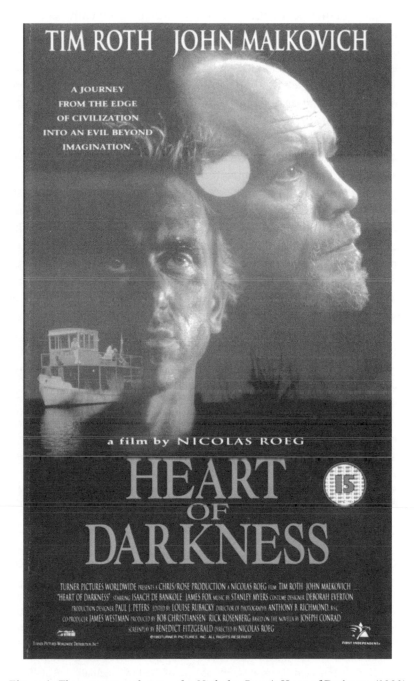

Figure 1. *The promotional poster for Nicholas Roeg's* Heart of Darkness *(1993)*

as Stanley Pool (the Central Station is never specifically said to be Kinchassa, but it is clear that this is the case). Somewhat surprisingly, the European city in which the Intended lives is not the Belgian city of Brussels, as most critics identify it in the novella. Rather, in the film it is the city of London itself (the English accent of the Intended can be taken as secondary confirmation of this).[96] Some of the scenes were shot on location in the docks along the Thames in London while the jungle scenes were, for the most part, shot on location in Belize in Central America. There are several visually striking images within the film which testify to the abilities of Anthony B. Richmond, the director of photography. The film opens and closes, for example, with the camera slowly panning over the wrinkled skin of an elephant, which lies dying on the ground, obviously the victim of ivory hunters. The elephant's tear-filled eye, closing slowly with death, is an extreme image of pathos not easily forgotten.

Interestingly, several lines from Conrad's letters and published essays are incorporated within the film, effectively bringing together Conrad's own experiences and the fictional world of *Heart of Darkness.* In this sense, the film serves as a bridge between the two, allowing the world of fiction and the world of historical reminiscence to mingle creatively. The best example of this occurs at the beginning of the film as the image of the dying elephant, stripped of its ivory tusks, fills the screen. Here the voice of Marlow is heard to say:

> It was one of the dark places of the earth—the vilest scramble for loot that ever disfigured the history of human conscience and geographical exploration. Just bones, death...and ivory.

This is clearly an adaptation of Conrad's famous words from his *Last Essays* (1926) in which he recalled his visit to Stanley Falls in September of 1890:

96. This is similar to the adaptation of Conrad's *Heart of Darkness* by director Adam Low for the BBC programme *Bookmark* (first broadcast on 22 July 1995). The adaptation consists of contemporary visual images of London (the 'sepulchral city') and Zaire (the 'heart of darkness') which are set against a narrator's voice-over (given by actor Alfred Molina). Here the city of London, with its network of investment banking as embodied in Lloyd's of London, becomes identified with the Company contained in Conrad's novel. Interestingly, in this adaptation there is no mention whatsoever of Kurtz's Intended. Thus, it stands as one of the few cinematic adaptations of *Heart of Darkness* which completely removes the climactic encounter between Marlow and the Intended from the story-line.

[T]here was no shadowy friend to stand by my side in the night of the enormous wilderness, no great haunting memory, but only the unholy recollection of a prosaic newspaper 'stunt' and the distasteful knowledge of the vilest scramble for loot that ever disfigured the history of human conscience and geographical exploration.[97]

Having noted some of the ways in which Conrad's own life experiences inform the story as it is presented within the film, it is fair to say that it does nevertheless follow the basic structure of the novella quite closely. This includes the use of a framing narration at the beginning and end of the story. Thus, at the beginning and at the conclusion of the film Marlow is shown on board a small sailing ship talking with his three companions, the lawyer, the accountant and a representative from the Company (who is named as Mr Yeager, the Company Director). One clever thing that the film does in this regard is to identify these characters with the various representatives who come to Marlow towards the end of the novella and ask to be given Kurtz's surviving papers (in the novella these visitations to Marlow take place *before* he goes to see the Intended, whereas in the film this order is reversed). Other continuities between the novella and the film are also to be found. The extreme fastidiousness of the accountant Delcommune is portrayed, notably his irritation at having an agent dying of malaria in his office, making it impossible for him to keep his account books in order. The cannibalism of the helmsman Mfumu is also brought out as a significant sub-theme; at one point it is juxtaposed with what we later recognize as an image of the shrouded body of the dead Kurtz as he is being buried by natives. The senseless dynamiting of the hills surrounding the Outer Station at Matadi is well presented in the film, as is the misery of many of the chained labourers working to the point of exhaustion and then collapsing in a grove of death. It is somewhat disappointing that the evocative scene of the French gun-ship senselessly shelling the jungle bush is not depicted, perhaps because of the enormous costs involved in presenting a nineteenth-century man-o'-war.[98] The famous words 'Mistah Kurtz …he dead' are

97. Conrad 1926: 17. The 'stunt' is an allusion to the fact that Henry Stanley, a newspaper reporter for the *New York Herald* was, sent to Africa in 1871 to track down David Livingstone and write about the discovery of the missionary who had not been heard of since 1856 and was presumed dead.

98. Pinsker (1981: 56) notes how some writers equated Conrad's image here with images of American warships off the coast of Vietnam bombarding the jungles. See Herzog 1992: 216-17 as a case in point. M. Wood (1979: 17) likens Conrad's image to

also included within the film, although they are uttered by one of the native carriers as Marlow leaves Kurtz's house after the latter's death and *not* on board the boat (as occurs in the novella).

The portrayal of Kurtz by actor John Malkovich is striking, and earned him nominations in 1995 for Best Actor in a TV movie or mini-series in both the Golden Globe and Screen Actors Guild Awards (neither of which he won). Malkovich's Kurtz appears ill and exhausted, on the verge of death as he shuffles wearily from place to place. One intimation of his impending death is the white gauze cloth which he wears over his red dressing gown, making him look every bit like a king with a stately robe which has been wrapped up in a burial shroud.

I noted above that many critics of the novella have identified an underlying Faustian theme as foundational to Conrad's purposes. At one point Kurtz is made to give explicit voice to this Faustian theme. Following Marlow's arrival at the Inner Station, and after the two men have conversed about the nature of life, Kurtz picks up a book from his shelves in his house and reads aloud from Goethe's *Faust,* citing the German and then offering his own translation and commentary: ' "Zwei Seelen wohnen, Ach, in meiner Brust—Alas, two souls dwell in my breast". Goethe…long gone. Neither good nor evil. Dead.' This is immediately followed by a shot of a decapitated head of one of Marlow's carrier boys which has been affixed to the tree outside his house (Kurtz has bartered half of his ivory stockpile for the young boy, had him killed and added his head to his infamous 'trophy' tree). Thus, one of the most gruesome passages from the novella is given explicit visual expression in the film.

Most important for our considerations within this study is the way in which Kurtz's Intended is portrayed in the film. True to the novella, we do not actually see her on screen until the end of the story as Marlow goes to visit her following Kurtz's death and his return from the heart of darkness at the centre of Africa. However, in the novella there are intimations of her presence in the story-line, most prominently in the form of portraits which Kurtz is said to have painted of her. There are three such paintings of the Intended which appear in the film, and together they serve to illustrate her role as a symbol of Kurtz's 'horror'. The first is seen as Marlow shares a drink with De Griffe at the latter's cabin in the Central Station at Stanley Pool. De Griffe explains that the painting was done by Kurtz, 'right here in this room', he says. The painting shows the Intended in a three-quarters

that of a formation of American fighters dropping napalm on an empty tropical landscape, the opening scenes in *Apocalypse Now.*

profile and facing to the right; she looks coldly off into the distance and wears a black evening gown which contrasts with her ivory-like bare shoulders and arms. As the two men share a drink, De Griffe explains his feelings about Kurtz to Marlow:

> The same people who sent him also sent you. You belong to the new gang, the moral gang. Both of you. I've seen the evidence. Don't say 'No!' Kurtz is the ethical genius of your new band—spreads virtue and culture wherever he goes. The blazing comet of shining good will. The lily-white protector of the dark hordes. This is not to say that I have any apprehensions about him. I have never been haunted by the fear of God or the devil, let alone of a man.

What is interesting about this sequence is that the camera shifts to a close-up of the painting just as De Griffe utters the words 'the devil' within his speech, suggesting to the audience a connection between the Intended and some devilish, malevolent force.

The second painting is found in Kurtz's house within the Inner Station and is clearly of the same woman, although in this case she is presented in a full frontal pose with her breasts bare and tribal markings running down the length of her chest. The Intended is presented here as if she is a white version of the Black Beauty (we first see the painting in two scenes with Kurtz's native mistress). Clearly there is a deliberate visual similarity between the two women, both in terms of their general physique and the poses they adopt. The Intended is surrounded by jungle vegetation, as if to suggest that she is a natural part of the Congo and belongs there.

The third painting in the film is the one that we might expect, in that it is mentioned within the novella and depicts the Intended as a blindfolded woman carrying a lamp or lighted candle. Marlow discovers the painting in Kurtz's house at the Inner Station and is admiring it as Kurtz enters the room and offers an explanation:

> She is a memory of a past with no history…like Africa. She was intended to be my wife. You are too close to it. You mustn't look at the picture in sections—a hand, candle, nose, a dress. You might conclude that a painting is nothing more than a heap of smudges. Guess at the painter before you study his picture.

We do well to recall the passage within Conrad's *Heart of Darkness* in which this image of the painting of the Intended is mentioned:

> Then I noticed a small sketch in oils, on a panel, representing a woman, draped and blindfolded, carrying a lighted torch. The background was

somber—almost black. The movement of the woman was stately, and the effect of the torchlight on the face was sinister.[99]

This is the most idealized of the three paintings, commonly understood to depict the Intended as brandishing the torch of civilization for the places of the world which live in darkness but blind to the disastrous effects of her missionary enterprise.

How do the three paintings fit together and how are we meant to interpret their significance within the story-line? Clearly they are all meant to depict in some way Kurtz's Intended, or at least to represent how he feels about her and her place in his life as he lives in the midst of the jungle wilderness (we can safely assume that they were all painted during Kurtz's stay in the Congo). A good case can be made, I think, for suggesting that the three paintings are meant to illustrate the development of the relationship between Kurtz and his Intended, and as such they provide a subtle but all-important indication of Kurtz's state of mind. I would like to propose two different ways of interpreting the three paintings and what they might represent. There is nothing to indicate that one is a *better* interpretation than the other, although there is a common thread between the two interpretations which unites them, namely the presentation of the Intended as a demonic force in Kurtz's life. The first of these interpretations of the paintings we can call 'the presented order' in that it suggests that the order in which we first see the paintings is the order in which they were painted by Kurtz; the second I shall call 'the inverted order' in that it suggests that the order in which we first see the paintings is exactly the opposite of the order in which Kurtz painted them. Let us examine briefly what interpretative possibilities these two suggestions present.

The implication of the 'presented order' interpretation is that Kurtz's Intended is the cold and foreboding woman we see in the first painting. She lives in London and comes across as somehow detached from Kurtz and his ambitions in the Congo, looking far off into the distance. This first painting is executed, as De Griffe tells us, when Kurtz is staying at the Central Station at Stanley Pool, presumably before he makes his way further up the Congo river and establishes himself at the Inner Station. In this sense, the Intended is remembered by Kurtz, but not lovingly portrayed by him. It is perhaps no accident, then, that the camera cuts to this painting just as De

99. Conrad 1973: 54. Todorov (1989: 167) remarks: 'As one might have guessed, when Kurtz paints, it is in chiaroscuro'. This supports Todorov's contention that Kurtz himself is the heart of darkness, the dramatic centre of intrigue and movement throughout the novel.

Griffe utters the word 'devil', as I have already mentioned. We might even conclude that the Intended was the reason why Kurtz travelled to the heart of the jungle in the Congo in the first place; that he went there to get away from her and all that she represented in terms of an oppressive society. The second painting is deliberately contrasted with this and depicts the Intended as everything that Kurtz wishes her to be. No doubt his relationship with the Black Beauty is largely responsible for the transformation of the 'devilish' Intended into a white native beauty who fits naturally into the jungle setting with all of its vibrancy and suggestive sexuality (she is, after all, depicted as bare-breasted). The third painting, the one in which the Intended is depicted with the candle of civilization, represents a further extrapolation in Kurtz's mind. The Intended is here so idealized as to become almost unrecognizable as a person, perhaps suggesting that Kurtz has resolved the tensions illustrated in the first two paintings and effected a reconciliation between them. He has forsaken the 'devilish' Intended of London, and realized that no matter how hard he tries he cannot fashion her after the likeness of the Black Beauty and make her a part of the Congo in which he now lives. So he creates an idealized portrait of her in which she blindly carries the torch of civilization.

However, there is one difficulty with this particular way of reading the paintings, and it has to do with the way in which Kurtz in several scenes is shown to stand alongside his native mistress and next to the second painting. He gazes longingly at it, and is even made to caress the tribal markings on the breasts of the painting of his Intended. In other words, there is some difficulty in interpreting the third painting as representing a resolution in Kurtz's mind about the Intended and all that she stands for when there remains this preoccupation with fashioning the Intended into a white version of his native mistress. Therefore, let us look at an alternative way of interpreting the paintings.

The interpretation I have called 'the inverted order' suggests that the third of the paintings (the one in which the Intended bears the torch of civilization) is the earliest of the three and that it was painted when Kurtz still viewed her with some love and affection (hence her classic lines of beauty and idealized form). At the same time, he is not oblivious to the blindness that she embodies, living back in London with no comprehension of what the Western civilization (which she represents) has meant to the Congo in the heart of Africa. Thus Kurtz depicts her as blindfolded—a well-intentioned, but ultimately naive woman. The next stage in Kurtz's assessment of his Intended is depicted in the second painting, the one which presents her as closely resembling his native mistress, the Black Beauty. Here we get an indication that Kurtz is attempting to integrate the Intended within his new jungle home, and that reality has somehow begun to be blurred for him. The lines of separation between the Intended and the Black Beauty are no longer clear for Kurtz and he paints her as if she is a paler, whiter version of his native mistress. However, the integration proves to be impossible and Kurtz finds that at the end of the day the Intended is a force irreconcilable with life in the Congo within the heart of darkness. Therefore he paints the first portrait we saw of the Intended, the one in which she is depicted as a rather aloof and detached figure, looking coldly off into the distance. He comes to view her as his 'devil' (to use De Griffe's term), a demonic figure that represents the evil and oppressive forces of imperialism in the midst of the Congo. This way of viewing the significance of the paintings is given additional validity by the handling of Kurtz's final death speech in the film.

As Kurtz lies dying on his bed in his house he beckons to Marlow to come and sit by him and hold his hand. Kurtz is supported by two native servants who flank him on either side. Kurtz's speech is laboured and halting; his final words are directed to Marlow:

> All that you are now…have been…and hold dear…is not…really you. Remember! There is no more empty…and detestable creature…in nature than the man…who runs away…from his demon. No faith…no fear…*[A shot of the first painting of the Intended is seen as Kurtz finishes his death speech.]* The horror!…The horror![100]

In other words, the viewer is left with the strong impression that Kurtz's 'horror' is the Intended herself. She is his demon, his horror, and Kurtz can only view himself as a vile and detestable creature for having run away from her. In this sense, he repents of having failed to stand up to the brutalizing forces of imperialism that she represents. Such an interpretation makes sense of the film's final sequence which shows the visit of Marlow to the house of the Intended in London. The following exchange takes place between the two:

> The Intended: I've lived so long in silence I can't help feeling his loneliness. Nobody near him to understand. No one to hear him as I could and did. You were there, Captain Marlow, when he died? Did you hear him speak?

100. Chatman (1997: 207-208) discusses the intonation of 'The horror!' by Malkovich, comparing it to Marlon Brando's whispered cry in *Apocalypse Now* and the two radio-play versions by Orson Welles.

Marlow: I did, on several occasions, listen to him as he spoke.

The Intended: You were present when he died?

Marlow: I was nearby. I'm not sure anyone is ever present in another's death, Ma'am.

The Intended: Were you near enough to have heard his last words, Captain Marlow?

Marlow: His last words, Ma'am, are the reason I came to see you. His last words told me how to find you. *[The camera focuses in on the Intended and pans down the length of her black dress, complete with its panel of contrasting black-and-white lace and brightly coloured feather brooch.]* His last words gave me your name.

The Intended: Poor Henri! *[Marlow departs from the Intended's house and returns to his ship. As he walks on the deck we hear the familiar words of Kurtz in a voice-over.]*

Kurtz: Remember! There is no more empty nor detestable creature in nature than the man who runs away from his demon.

Remarkably, the final words of Kurtz which are heard by the viewers of the film are not 'The horror! The horror!', as we anticipate will be the case because of our familiarity with the novella. In fact his last words are a voice-over in which a curtailed version of his earlier death speech is (re-)heard. And yet, the point is not lost, for Kurtz's very last word in the film is 'demon', and a powerful association between 'demon' and 'the horror' is forged in our minds as viewers. We anticipate that Kurtz's last words in the film voice-over are going to be 'The horror! The horror!' (we have even heard them once already as we watched Kurtz die). But what we hear in their place is 'demon', alongside the declaration that this was the name of the Intended that was given to Marlow by Kurtz. It is clear throughout the film that in many ways the Intended is the demon with which Kurtz wrestles. She is an embodiment of 'the horror' that he should have faced and from which he fled; she is a modern version of the Roman imperial forces, the Horror/Whore of Babylon, spoken of by the early Gospel writers and the first generations of Christians.

We turn now to the most celebrated film adaptation of Conrad's novella and again seek to point out some of the intriguing parallels between it and the apocalyptic motifs from Mk 13.14 and Revelation 17–18 outlined above.

Francis Ford Coppola's Apocalypse Now *(1979)*

Few films can match either the acclaim or the criticism heaped upon *Apocalypse Now* (1979), Francis Ford Coppola's nightmarish exploration of

the madness of the American involvement in Vietnam.[101] The film boasted a
big-name cast, with a very overweight Marlon Brando playing the role of
Colonel Kurtz, Martin Sheen as the Marlow character Captain Benjamin
Willard, and Robert Duvall as Lieutenant-Colonel Kilgore. It was the
subject of a considerable campaign of media hype, much of it focused either
on Brando's $3.5 million fee, or on the ominous delays in filming. The
extent to which the production of the film itself serves as an illustration of
the American experience in Vietnam has been hugely debated. To a certain
extent, Coppola himself set up this debate through a press release issued to
film critics at advance screenings of the film. He stated:

> The process of making the film becomes very much like the story of the
> film. I found that many of the ideas and images with which I was working
> as a film director began to coincide with the realities of my own life, and
> that I, like Captain Willard, was moving up a river in a faraway jungle,
> looking for answers and hoping for some kind of catharsis.[102]

The production of the film was fraught with difficulties. Not only was
Coppola engaged in a long and complicated wrangle with United Artists
about the financing arrangements of the film,[103] but the actual filming on
location in the Philippines was plagued by a series of disasters.[104] A
tropical storm destroyed many of the props, an attempted coup meant that
much of the military equipment (rented from the government of President
Ferdinand Marcos) was called away at crucial moments. At the end of the
day, the film took 238 days of shooting on location, during which 1.5
million feet of negative were exposed; the cost was $31 million. Indeed,
the process of filming *Apocalypse Now* was itself the subject of an award-
winning documentary by Fax Bahr and George Jickenlooper entitled
Hearts of Darkness: A Filmmaker's Apocalypse (1991). The documentary

101. McInerney (1979–80: 31) describes *Apocalypse Now* as 'a prolonged hallucina-
tion' about the Vietnam war.
102. Cited in Grenier 1979: 67-68. Wilmington (1988: 286) describes the film as 'the
great 'obsessional' movie project of our time'. Fitzgerald (1996: 284) describes *Apocalypse Now* as a failure insofar as its attempts to re-create Conrad's *Heart of Darkness*
against the backdrop of Vietnam are concerned, but notes that Coppola's failure 'is
actually the perfect metaphor for the whole Vietnam experience'. Baudrillard (1994: 59-
60) notes the 'inspired irony' of Coppola's film, suggesting that 'the war in Vietnam
and this film are cut from the same cloth, that nothing separates them, that this film is
part of the war'. Cowie (1989: 116-41) remains the best source for a discussion of
Coppola's efforts to bring the project to the big screen.
103. J. Lewis (1995: 40-45, 50-52) discusses this.
104. Bergan (1998: 53-59) offers a brief summary.

is based on the work of Coppola's wife, Eleanor, who travelled to the Philippines in March of 1976 and produced a journal of the experience there published as *Notes: On the Making of* Apocalypse Now (1979).[105] In the end, *Apocalypse Now* premiered in New York in August of 1979 and proved to be a box-office success, earning over $150 million world-wide. It was also critically acclaimed, sharing the prestigious Palme D'Or prize at the 1979 Cannes Film Festival, as well as going on in 1980 to win two Oscars (for Best Cinematography and Best Sound), three Golden Globe Awards (for Best Director, Best Supporting Actor [Duvall], and Best Original Score), and two BAFTA awards (for Best Direction and for Best Supporting Actor [Duvall]).

The basic plot of the film is straightforward, and its reliance upon Conrad's novella is easily seen, although, ironically, Conrad himself is never mentioned in the film credits.[106] Captain Benjamin Willard (played by Martin Sheen) is an Army assassin sent up-river in a PBR (a Navy patrol boat designed for river travel) to find and kill a US Special Forces Colonel named Walter Kurtz. Kurtz has gathered around himself a band of soldiers, both native Montagnards and US deserters, and has begun to conduct a campaign of intimidation and terror along the Vietnamese-Cambodian border. Most of the film is given over to chronicling Willard's trip up the Nung river (a cipher for the Mekong river), with the four-man crew of the PBR.[107] As they proceed towards Cambodia some of the lunacies of war are exposed and two of the crew are killed. Eventually Willard arrives at Kurtz's camp in the depths of the jungle and a fateful confrontation ensues between the two men. Kurtz is killed by Willard who, like a modern-day version of the beast of Rev. 13.1, rises ominously from the sea and moves inexorably to face him in the temple-complex (see Figure 2). As Kurtz is struck with his fatal wound he falls to the floor and

---

105. For a discussion of the documentary see Worthy 1992; Elsaesser and Wedel 1997: 151-52; Rosenbaum 1997: 134-39. The Coppolas' marriage was under severe pressure during the making of the film, notably due to an intense extra-marital affair that Francis had with one of the junior screenwriters (Melissa Mathieson). See Breskin 1992: 18-20, 46-49 for Francis Ford Coppola's later reflections on the matter.

106. But see Hagen 1988: 295-97 where the various stages of the production of a screenplay, dependent upon and yet distanced from Conrad's novella, are discussed. Also see Riley 1979; Cahir 1992; Phillips 1995: 133-37; Schumacher 1999: 192-96.

107. Greiff (1992) has a very interesting discussion of the four crewman and their relationship to Conrad's story-line.

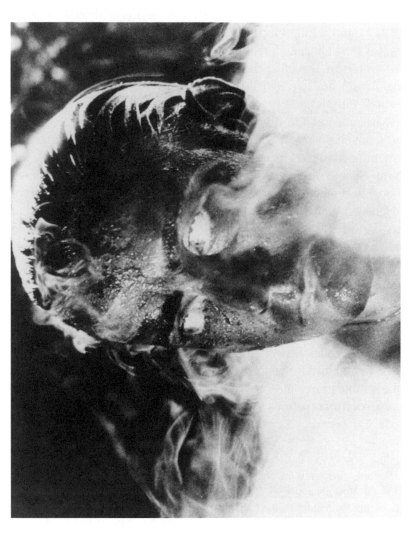

Figure 2. *Captain Willard (Martin Sheen) as the beast rising from the sea in Francis Ford Coppola's Apocalypse Now (1979)*

utters his last words in true Conradian fashion: 'The horror! The horror!'[108]

There has been endless discussion of how well the film follows the basic story-line of Conrad's *Heart of Darkness*.[109] To what extent is it a legitimate recasting of Conrad's novella? Or is it the case that the film takes such a different direction that the influence of Conrad's vision of a journey into the heart of human darkness becomes somewhat tangential at best? Indeed, the appropriateness of using Conrad's tale as a vehicle for exploring the horrors of war has been questioned by some,[110] although many Vietnam veterans have found *Heart of Darkness* to be an important mirror of their experiences in the war.[111] In any event, the film does succeed in some respects as an artistic reworking of *Heart of Darkness*, although at least one critic has likened the lack of substance within the film to E.M. Forster's famous quip about the secret genius of Conrad, that it 'contains a vapour rather than a jewel' (Canby 1979b: 1). Not surprisingly, *Apocalypse Now* works best in those scenes given over to the journey up-river itself.[112] Perhaps the best example of this is the depiction of the attack on the patrol boat as it approaches Kurtz's compound. In Conrad's novella the natives attack from the wilds of the jungle with what Marlow first identifies as 'sticks'. He realizes quickly that they are arrows, and they are quite deadly; the attack culminates in the loss of Marlow's black helmsman who is killed with a spear. In Coppola's version the attack on the boat is remarkably faithful to Conrad's original, with wave after wave of short wooden arrows

108. Bergan (1998: 59) suggests that this is an echo of the final utterance of *The Bridge on the River Kwai*—'Madness! Madness!'.

109. Kinder 1979–80; Pym 1979–80; Langman 1980; Bogue 1981; Pinsker 1981; Stewart 1980–81; W.J. Palmer 1987: 211-29; Coupe 1997: 20-21, 29, 63-65, 75, 82-89.

110. Grenier (1979: 72) remarks: '*Heart of Darkness*, after all, is the study of gradual reversion to savagery. But war is organized cruelty from the start. There is no way around it. In war it doesn't take years in the 'bush' or months of slow travel on a jungle steamer to strip off the veneer of civilization. In combat it happens in minutes'. Also see Selig 1993: 5.

111. Herr 1978: 15; Just 1979; Herzog 1992: 24-31.

112. Although it is by no means the first film to visualize such a journey into the unknown. Indeed, it appears that Coppola is indebted to Werner Herzog's classic *Aguirre: The Wrath of God* (1972) for much of the imagery. Kael (1987: 402) suggests that Coppola gives a visual gesture of acknowledgment of this when he gives us a shot of a Huey helicopter burning in a tree, an image which is reminiscent of a similar scene in *Aguirre: The Wrath of God* of a boat lodged high in the treetops.

being launched from the deadly jungle,[113] and one fateful spear striking Chief, the Navy officer Phillips who is in command of the boat.[114] The depiction of the photojournalist at Kurtz's temple-compound at Nu Mung Ba, the Russian harlequin figure from Conrad's novella,[115] is also a point of great similarity between the film and the book. Much of the dialogue spoken by Dennis Hopper, who portrays the burned-out photojournalist, comes straight from the novel. The film opens and closes with music from Jim Morrison and the Doors, namely 'The End', which serves as an equivalent to the frame-narrator of Conrad's novel (Greiff 1992: 188-89). So some important similarities are to be found. But what are some of the differences between Conrad's novel and Coppola's film?

Clearly the resetting of the story to Vietnam and Cambodia in the year 1969 is a major change. The lack of geographical precision about Marlow's journey up-river is one of the features of *Heart of Darkness* that enables it transcends time and space. Ironically, this is precisely one of the points at which *Apocalypse Now* breaks most with the spirit of Conrad's novella. By so identifying the refashioning of the story with a specific time and place (the Vietnam war in the 1960s–70s), the ability of the film to sustain the same level of transcendence that the story conveys so brilliantly is severely impaired.[116]

The ending of the film is another place at which there is a significant departure from Conrad's novel. Most critics agree that the ending of the film is something of a disappointment, and it is frequently noted that Coppola himself struggled with the question of how to bring the film to a suitable conclusion.[117] Several different endings were shot, including one which was shown with the initial 70mm release of the film; this version has been described as the 'anti-war' ending, given its rather non-violent nature. It closes with scenes of Willard dropping the machete with which he has killed Kurtz and making his way through the temple compound

113. Hagen (1983: 238-40) discusses the way in which the film portrays the jungle wilderness as a mysterious and unconquerable force.

114. Dempsey (1979–80: 6) remarks: 'the skewering of the captain by a spear gains extra irony now that it happens during an overwhelmingly technological modern war'.

115. Verleun (1981) discusses the importance of the Russian harlequin within the story, particularly as the figure represents, at some level, Conrad himself. Also see Whitehead 1975: 129-30 on this point.

116. This point is well presented in Sutherland 1998: 12-13.

117. Not the least of Coppola's problems with the film's ending were the difficulties he had in persuading Marlon Brando to adhere to the script at hand. See G. Marcus 1979: 54; LaBrasca 1988: 291-93.

with Lance (the sole surviving crewmember) back to the patrol boat. The final image is of the patrol boat drifting away from the shore, with Willard and Lance on board. Radio contact with air-base command is made, although Willard switches the radio off, and (presumably) delays calling in an air-strike to destroy Kurtz's compound. Yet a suggestive hint of this imminent destruction is given, in the form of a complex montage of images including Willard's camouflaged face, a stone statue of a Buddha from Kurtz's temple-compound in Nu Mung Ba,[118] a circling helicopter gun-ship and an eruption of flames, all of which is punctuated by a repetition of Kurtz's breathy final words 'The horror! The horror!'. The suggestion is that the compound has been levelled by an air-strike which brings to fulfilment Kurtz's prophetic instructions (which Willard had earlier discovered scrawled in red ink on a page of a typed manuscript in Kurtz's room within the temple-complex): 'Drop the Bomb. Exterminate them all'.[119]

Alternatively, the 'pro-war' ending of the 35mm version of the film[120] closes with the film credits running against the backdrop of scenes of the destruction of Kurtz's temple-complex. The destruction itself is a fantastic pyrotechnic display which makes the famous sequence of the napalm air-strike at the beginning of the film seem minor by comparison.[121]

118. The temple complex was modelled on the famous Angor Wat ruins. W.J. Palmer (1987: 224) suggests that the stone idol physically resembles the CIA agent at the beginning of the film whose solitary line in the film gives the Army assassin Willard the parameters of his mission up-river: 'Terminate with extreme prejudice'. Coppola (1995: 23) notes that the model for the statue was a beautiful young Filipina maid from a nearby boardinghouse.

119. G. Stewart (1980–81: 458-59) suggests that Conrad's line 'Exterminate all the brutes!' has become 'transposed into a nuclear key'.

120. Tomasulo (1990: 155-56) discusses the two endings and their implications for interpreting the film as a whole. Chatman (1997: 219), echoing the words of T.S. Eliot at the conclusion of *The Hollow Men*, calls the two endings the 'whimper ending' and the 'bang ending'. Burden (1991: 80-81) says of the ending of the film: 'The film ends, as does the world it represents, not with a whimper but with a bang. The film is not framed with the civilised company of men listening to the storyteller. It is framed by the flames of napalm... Conrad allows some light, albeit dimmed to appear at the end of the darkness. The only light from Coppola's film is from the napalm strike'. Also see G. Marcus 1979: 56-57; Dempsey 1979–80: 7-8; Adair 1981: 166; Cowie 1989: 122-23; Lewis 1995: 48-53; French 1998: 68-71.

121. This footage can be viewed on the (1999) DVD version of the film available from American Zoetrope in San Francisco, California. This extra six-minute sequence is entitled 'Destruction of Kurtz's Compound' and includes a commentary by Coppola

Part of the difficulty of the ending of the film involved Coppola finding a way visually to depict the significance of Kurtz's 'horror', and yet to do so in a way that topped what is for many the most memorable sequence of the film, namely the attack on a Vietnamese village by Lieutenant-Colonel Kilgore's helicopter gun-ships with Wagner's *Ride of the Valkyries* blaring forth from loudspeakers attached to them.[122] For many this sequence is the real heart of the film, and everything else which follows is simply anti-climactic.[123] As one critic comments about Kilgore's character: 'Robert Duvall's bold thumbnail sketch of paranoia at ease with itself is far and away the movie's best performance'.[124] In short, dramatically the film does not manage to hammer out an acceptable balance between Kilgore and Kurtz. This stands as a central weakness in the story-line, particularly when it is Kurtz's 'horror!' which has such a place of prominence in Conrad's novella, as well as the throaty exclamation of Brando's Kurtz with which the film concludes. As one film critic states: 'The film succeeds in forcing us to experience the horror of the war and to acknowledge our own complicity in it, but it fails to illuminate the nature of Kurtz's horror' (Kinder 1979–80: 13).

Not surprisingly, much has been written about the controversial ending of the film that was eventually issued on general release, with its juxtaposition of images of the ritual slaughter of a sacrificial water-buffalo by the Montagnards with those depicting Willard's execution of Kurtz in the temple with a machete. The idea of incorporating images of the ritual sacrifice came from Coppola's wife, Eleanor, who had witnessed an animal being so slaughtered by local Ifugao natives from Luzon in the northern

himself. On 20 November 2001 Francis Ford Coppola released an extended version of the film on DVD which was entitled *Apocalypse Now Redux*. This version lasts 202 minutes and includes many scenes deleted from the original, including the famous 'French plantation' sequence and extra footage involving the Playboy bunnys. Unfortunately, this version was not available for viewing in time to be considered within this study.

122. Michaels (1979) makes this point. Sundelson (1981: 43) similarly comments on the character of Kilgore in the film: 'Here, not in the Brando character, with his quotations from T.S. Eliot, is Coppola's version of the perverse but impressive purpose that Marlow finds in Kurtz'.

123. M. Wood 1979; Canby 1979a: 15; 1979b: 1, 15; Rich 1979; Kael 1987: 244; Scott 1994: 175-81. Kinder (1979–80: 20) offers a slightly different perspective.

124. Adair 1981: 153. Also see DeFuria 1980: 87; Schumacher 1999: 265.

part of the Philippines during the shooting of the film.[125] There is clearly an attempt to relate such a ritual killing to the assassination of Kurtz, and thus give visual expression to the mythical tales of a dying-and-rising god made popular in books such as Sir James Frazer's *The Golden Bough* (1922) and Jessie L. Weston's *From Ritual to Romance* (1920).[126] It is no accident that both of these books, along with the Bible, works by Goethe, and T.S. Eliot's *Collected Poems* (1963), from which Kurtz reads, all form part of Kurtz's library in his temple-compound.[127] The significance of the ritual slaying of the water-buffalo is suggested earlier in the film at the conclusion of the helicopter battle sequence. This is the most overtly religious scene in the film and is set against the backdrop of a half-finished church in front of which a few soldiers are tossing a football back and forth. Here we are given a scene in which a Catholic military chaplain is conducting a Holy Communion service for some soldiers and, just as he invites the assembled soldiers to join in the recitation of the Lord's Prayer, we see a shot of a water-buffalo being lifted by a helicopter from the battlefield. The very next sequence is of Lieutenant-Colonel Kilgore and his victorious men dining on the animal which has been roasted over an open fire. Clearly an association is intended between the sacrifice of Christ commemorated in the Mass, including the elevation of the sacred host, and the lifting up of the animal (Dorall 1988: 307).

It is at this point that we have the clearest connection between *Apocalypse Now* and the 'abominating horror' from Mk 13.14 discussed

125. Coppola 1995. 131-35, 167, 282; Schumacher 1999: 219-20. A total of 264 Ifugao aborigines were used to portray Montagnards in the film.

126. May (1982: 168) remarks: 'Coppola's great gamble with *Apocalypse Now* is to have given his work a mythic dimension not shared by its literary source; from Sir James Frazer's *The Golden Bough*…he has appropriated the mythic ritual of the killing of the divine king'. For more on the way in which *Apocalypse Now* explores dimensions of mythology contained within the work of Frazer and Weston, see G. Marcus 1979: 55; Tessitore 1979: 21; Bogue 1981: 620-21; Holstmark 1991: 75-77; Detweiler 1996: 163-64; Coupe 1997. Gillespie (1985) also discusses these matters, particularly concentrating on the importance of T.S. Eliot's *The Waste Land* for Coppola's film.

127. The connection between Joseph Conrad and T.S. Eliot is easily made, especially when it is remembered that Eliot clearly had Conrad's *Heart of Darkness* in mind when he wrote both *The Waste Land* and *The Hollow Men* (see McConnell 1962 for more on this). In fact, Eliot cites the famous words uttered by the manager's servant in Conrad's novel ('Mistah Kurtz—he dead') as an epilogue to the latter of these works, as if to suggest that all that remained following the death of Kurtz were 'hollow men' (as Ruthven [1968: 43] notes).

above. This has to do with the sacrilege which takes place in the temple. For Mark's readership this sacrilege was tied up with the tradition of the desecrating actions of Antiochus IV Epiphanes and those who followed in his path, including the Romans. If the Jewish historian Josephus is to be believed, the desecration involved the slaughter of a pig on the temple altar. In *Apocalypse Now* we have a fresh reworking of that motif wherein the modern successors of the oppressive Seleucids/Romans, the United States of America, ritually slaughter their own version of a swine in the temple-complex. Willard's killing of Kurtz in the temple is the film's 'abominating horror', with Kurtz's final words, 'The horror! The horror!', echoing in our ears to this effect. Now I do not for a moment believe that Francis Ford Coppola was aware of the traditions involving Antiochus IV Epiphanes which lay behind the phrase 'the abominating horror', or that he deliberately set out to film the ritualistic killing of Kurtz as a modern equivalent of Mk 13.14. Nevertheless, his film does offer some fascinating parallels along these lines, and one cannot help but feel that both stories and their cryptic temple-based expressions (Mark's 'abominating horror' on the one hand, and Coppola's 'The horror! The horror!' on the other) have much in common.

So what are we to make of the other New Testament apocalyptic motif, that of the Whore of Babylon from Revelation 17–18? What is its equivalent in *Apocalypse Now*? Here the key lies in the way that the wives of Kurtz and Willard are presented in the film. Most important for our considerations in this regard is the fact that Captain Willard does not return to Kurtz's wife (his 'Intended') with news of how he died—or at least he does not do so in the film as it was eventually released to the public. However, there is a suggestion at one crucial point in the film of how Willard *might* carry out Kurtz's wishes along these lines. This occurs in a scene in which Willard spends time with Kurtz within the temple-compound, learning more about the man he has been sent to 'terminate with extreme prejudice'. In an important moment of self-revelation by Kurtz, we learn of his concern about his loved ones back in the States, in this case his wife *and his son*.[128] Kurtz says to Willard:

128. We learn from Kurtz's dossier (which Willard reads on the boat as he journeys up-river) that Kurtz's wife is named Janet Anderson and that they married on 14 June 1951. She is never further identified in the film, although photographs of her and the (unnamed) son appear at key points. According to the 1975 draft screenplay of the film by John Milius and Francis Ford Coppola, the son was named Jeff.

I worry that my son might not understand what I've tried to be. And if I were to be killed, Willard, I would want someone to go to my home and tell my son everything. Everything I did, everything you saw. Because there is nothing I detest more than the stench of lies. And if you understand me, Willard, you'll do this for me.

This links to an earlier scene in which Willard reads from a letter contained in his dossier on Kurtz. It is a letter from Kurtz to his son, explaining why it is that he has not written recently. In it Kurtz says that he has been officially accused by the Army of committing murder and describes his actions in executing four Vietnamese double-agents. The full text of the letter reads:

Dear Son,

I'm afraid that both you and your mother would have been worried for not hearing from me these past weeks. But my situation here has become a difficult one. I've been officially accused of murder by the Army. The alleged victims were four Vietnamese double agents. We spent months uncovering and accumulating evidence. When absolute proof was completed, we acted. We acted like soldiers. The charges are unjustified. They are in fact, under the circumstances of this conflict quite completely insane.

In a war there are many moments for compassion and tender action. There are many moments for ruthless action, for what is often called ruthless, what may in many circumstances be the only clarity—seeing clearly what there is to be done and doing it directly, quickly, aware, looking at it.

I would trust you to tell your mother what you choose about this letter. As for the charges, I'm unconcerned. I'm beyond their timid, lying morality. And so, I am beyond caring. You have all my faith.

Your loving,
Father.

The care and concern that Kurtz has for his wife and son stands in marked contrast to Willard's own family situation, which we learn about largely through the voice-over narration offered by Willard.[129] The voice-over narration forms something of a link between Willard and the character of Marlow in Conrad's novella, especially given the fact that both men are offering a retrospective view of their encounter with the

---

129. The script for Willard's voice-over narration was written by Michael Herr, whose book *Dispatches* (1978) is generally regarded to be one of the best to come out of the Vietnam war.

mysterious Kurtz.[130] The voice-overs are delivered by Martin Sheen in a flat monotone, probably in part due to his poor state of health (he had suffered a heart attack during the course of filming).[131] Through them we learn that Willard has already served one tour of duty in Vietnam, and that his return to the States was not a triumphant one. There are several hints about Willard's family relationships, and they all suggest difficulties, and an eventual marital break-up. For example, within Willard's opening voice-over, as he wakes up in a drunken stupor in a Saigon hotel room and looks through the Venetian blinds to the street outside, we hear him say:

> Saigon. Shit! I'm still only in Saigon. Every time I think I'm going to wake up back in the jungle. When I was home after my first tour, it was worse. I'd wake up and there'd be nothing. I hardly said a word to my wife until I said yes to a divorce. When I was here I wanted to be there. When I was there, all I could think of was getting back into the jungle.

The haunting spectre of Willard's wife is to be noted here, even if she makes only a brief, fleeting appearance. As we hear Willard's voice-over we are also given an image of him lying on his bed, smoking a cigarette. He reaches across the bedside table and picks up a black-and-white photograph of his wife which is on top of some hand-written letters. As he says the word 'divorce' in the voice-over noted above he moves the photograph to the tip of his cigarette, as if to ignite it and obliterate her from his memory.

One other voice-over comment Willard makes also sheds light on his disastrous return to the States and to his family. Following the helicopter gun-ship attack on the Vietnamese village, Kilgore's troops throw a big surfing party on the beach. Willard remarks: 'They were looking for a way home, but I had been there and it just didn't exist any more'. In short, the image is of a man who lives a tortured existence, someone who is in agony of spirit and is in search of himself. The world that Willard left behind in the States and the nightmare that he faces in his second tour of duty in Vietnam are not as far apart as he might hope. As one perceptive critic of the film puts it, commenting on the opening scenes of the film as the

---

130. The voice-over narration is discussed by Watson (1981); Hagen (1983: 236-37); W. Palmer (1987: 216-19, 225-27) and Chatman (1997: 209-210). Geng (1979), Adair (1981: 148) and Hellmann (1984: 429-32) discuss the suggestion that Willard's voice-over narration is a parody of the cinematic adaptations of Raymond Chandler's detective novels in which the fictional private eye Philip Marlowe offers similar sardonic comments about his cases.

131. Kinder (1979–80: 15) discusses this. Also see Cowie 1989: 122.

drunken would-be assassin awakens in a Saigon hotel room amidst a montage of images of a broken family and the destructiveness of war:

> Coppola superimposes the image of one world over another…[he] seems to be suggesting that the world of Vietnam is not a startling contrast from what we consider to be normal life; it is not an aberration but an extension of our society: this is why Willard slips so easily from 'the real world' to 'in country' (Larsen 1988: 354).

The domestic difficulties of Willard set up an interesting twist in the narrative, particularly if, as is frequently noted, there is clearly a level of identification between the characters of Willard and Kurtz (just as there is between the characters of Marlow and Kurtz in Conrad's novella) (Tomasulo 1990: 150-51). Indeed, it is not without significance that the photographic image of Willard's ex-wife and those of Kurtz's estranged wife (seen later in scenes where Willard examines Kurtz's dossier on the boat up-river and in a scene showing Kurtz's quarters in the temple-compound) are remarkably similar.[132] We hear something about the psychic identity of the two men from Willard himself in another voice-over shortly after he has been told to report to ComSec Intelligence in Nha Trang. Willard says:

> It was no accident that I got to be the caretaker of Colonel Walter E. Kurtz's memory, any more than being back in Saigon was an accident. There is no way to tell his story without telling my own. And if his story is really a confession, then so is mine.

Interestingly, in the 1973 draft screenplay of the film by John Milius and Francis Ford Coppola, Willard does indeed return to the States and seek out Kurtz's widow. In this sense he does fulfil his role as the caretaker of Kurtz's memory, just as Marlow does in the novella. The sequence is set in a scrubbed-clean suburban neighbourhood in California, on a clear, sunny day. Willard enters the home of Mrs Kurtz carrying a folder under his arm and the following dialogue takes place as the two sit together on a sofa.

Kurtz's wife:	Did you know him very well?
Willard:	You get to know each other pretty well out there.
Kurtz's wife:	And you admired him?
Willard:	He was a remarkable man. It was impossible not to …
Kurtz's wife:	Love him? Yes, it is true. That's the hard part for me…I knew him better than anyone…I knew him best.
Willard:	You knew him best.

132. Cowie (1989: 137) states: 'Women for these men, exist only in photographs'.

Kurtz's wife:	You were his friend. You must have been, if he had given you this...*[the packet is indicated]* If he sent you to his home. He was the best this country had... He was...
Willard:	Yes. I know...
Kurtz's wife:	I'll never get over it. But I'll always remember him.
Willard:	Both of us...
Kurtz's wife:	Men looked up to him. *[She loses herself in a thought.]* He died as he lived.
Willard:	His death was... Yes, he died as he lived.
Kurtz's wife:	Were you with him when...
Willard:	Yes, I was. He said his last words to me.
Kurtz's wife:	What were they? Tell me. *[Close-up on Willard remembering the incredible day moving down the river.]*
Kurtz:	*[In a voice-over]* The horror! The horror!
Willard:	He spoke of you, ma'am.

What is intriguing about this exchange is the way in which it sets up an association, at least as far as Willard's memory is concerned, between Kurtz's last words ('The horror! The horror!') and the person of Kurtz's wife. The dialogue goes a step further in this direction than Conrad's novella does, where Kurtz's final words are said to be associated with *the name* of the Intended. By slightly altering this to 'He spoke of you, ma'am', Kurtz's wife can be more directly equated with his 'horror' than is possible in the novella. Kurtz's 'horror' is not just a name—it is a person, a woman, his wife. And as he says at one point in the middle of his 'diamond bullet' soliloquy, 'I know horror...Horror has a face'.

All in all, *Apocalypse Now* is not a film in which women fare very well. In the few scenes in which they do appear, they are either accidentally killed (such as the peasant woman on the sampan), or portrayed as cunning killers who must be tracked down and executed without mercy (such as the Viet Cong woman who blows up the helicopter with a bomb concealed in her hat). Western women are predominantly portrayed as objects of male fantasies, as the passing remark made by Chef about Raquel Welch as he goes searching for mangoes illustrates. Chef fantasizes about an Eden-like existence which takes him far away from the war.[133] 'I'm not here. I'm walking through the jungle gathering mangoes I meet Raquel Welch. I make a nice mango cream pudding. Kinda spread it around us'.

By far the most extended sequence involving women is that depicting the United Service Organization (USO) show in which a helicopter sporting the

---

133. Greiff (1992: 192) discusses this point.

Playboy bunny logo lands on a stage at the base camp of Hau Phat and three scantily clad beauties emerge to perform in front of a raucous audience of sex-starved soldiers. Not surprisingly, the three Playmates[134] are all Western (American) women, as their costuming as 'cowboys and Indians' indicates.[135] More importantly, their suggestive cavorting on stage can be read as an indication of the moral ambiguities of life with wives and girlfriends back in the 'good ole USA'. Thus, one critic comments on the way in which the American women are represented:

> The white female is interpolated by means of family pictures, especially the sober and proper ones of Mrs. Kurtz, symbolizing civilized order and respectability, who almost seems part of a lost past, as Willard peruses the assignment dossier on the trip up the river. However, Coppola also takes due note of the underlying female role as earth-mother and lure of the life-force, when Willard sardonically watches the beautiful, lewd dancers in a U.S.O. entertainment whip the troops into sexual frenzy.[136]

134. The three women were Cyndi Wood (who plays Playmate of the Year Carrie Foster, dressed in a blue cowboy outfit), Colleen Camp (who plays May Playmate Teri Teray, dressed in a Native American buckskin outfit and wearing a brown headband), and Linda Carpenter (who plays August Playmate Sandra Beatty, similarly dressed in a Native American loincloth and a blue US Cavalry top—complete with yellow chevrons!—and wearing a white scarf around her neck). Two of the women had in fact posed for *Playboy* and thus were somewhat typecast in their roles. Cyndi Wood was Playmate of the Month for February of 1973 and Playmate of the Year 1974; Linda Carpenter (under the name of Linda Beatty) was Playmate of the Month for August of 1976. Their centrefolds are among those shown as being on sale for $1.00 each in one of the opening scenes of the sequence. In addition, an imitation centrefold for Colleen Camp was created for the film and it too is on sale at the Hau Phat supply depot; it is also visible in several scenes on board the PBR as Willard and the crew head further up-river, just as the Linda Carpenter centrefold is to be seen in the trench occupied by the two soldiers manning the 50-caliber machine-gun at the Do Long bridge. The Colleen Camp centrefold is contained in the October 1979 issue of *Playboy* (pp. 118-19) where it forms part of a larger review article about the film (see Williamson 1979).

135. Detweiler (1996: 158) discusses the use of the 'cowboys and Indians' motif here, and argues that *Apocalypse Now* can be viewed against the historical backdrop of similar atrocities committed against Native Americans. Coupe (1997: 29) suggests that the three Playmates serve at some level as the fertility goddess figure within the overall 'myth and ritual' structure of the film's story-line. John Milius, whose screenplay was reworked by Coppola into the film, is on record as suggesting that the Playboy bunnies were akin to the Sirens in the Greek myths of the journeys of Odysseus, with Willard in the role of Odysseus and Kilgore in the role of the Cyclops (see R. Thompson 1976: 15; French 1998: 175-76).

136. Gillespie 1985: 73. Gillespie suggests that the relatively safe area of the Nung

The 'bump-and-grind' routine of the Playmates includes scenes suggesting masturbation with M-16s. Little wonder that the USO entertainment for the troops ends in chaos as a number of soldiers invade the stage in an attempt to get the Playmates to sign pictures that the soldiers have of them. The women are quickly herded back into the Playboy helicopter, which lifts off, even though some desperate soldiers are hanging on to the skids. This is an image which is strikingly reminiscent of the similar chaos surrounding the evacuation of the American Embassy during the fall of Saigon in April of 1975 when desperate Vietnamese clung to the helicopters which represented their last chance of escape from the advancing Communist forces.

One other sequence within the 1973 screenplay is also worth mentioning here in that it sheds further light on how the relationship between Kurtz and his wife was being portrayed as one of severe strain. This is seen as Willard reads some letters from the dossier on Kurtz while the patrol-boat is travelling up-river. First he reads a letter from Kurtz's wife to Kurtz in which she says that she cannot stand the strain of separation any longer, that she has gone against his wishes and that she has asked a friend in the military to try to find out more information about her husband's mission. She explains that their son Jeff has been involved in fights at school (presumably because he is defending his father's honour), and that the boy has become preoccupied with Vietnam and has covered his bedroom walls with maps of the country. Next Willard takes another letter from the dossier, one marked 'TOP SECRET' with a stencilled date on it and an explanatory note stating that this is the last correspondence to leave Nu Mung Ba. It is a letter addressed to Kurtz's wife, one written in a scrawled, savage hand. The letter reads:

> Sell the house
> Sell the car
> Sell the kids
> Find someone else
> Forget it
> I'm never coming ~~home~~ back
> Forget it!!

In the final version of the film this letter does appear, but it is not one from Kurtz to his estranged wife. Rather, it is a letter from a Captain

---

river where this sequence takes place is the equivalent to Conrad's Central Station in the novella. The whole sequence is the equivalent to the wild, intoxicating dance of the natives in Conrad's novella. For more on the presentation of women within *Apocalypse Now* see Showalter 1991: 95-104; Worthy 1996: 160-61.

Richard Colby to his wife, and Willard learns of it at the Do Lung bridge as he is given his final communication from his superiors in Nha Trang. Willard reads the covering note from Headquarters which explains that Captain Colby had been sent on an identical mission to assassinate Kurtz some months before, but that he had now joined Kurtz's renegade army. The letter from Colby to his wife had been intercepted and was being relayed to Willard to let him know what the latest developments in the situation were. In short, it seems clear that the 1975 screenplay suggested that the relationship between Kurtz and his wife had broken down altogether. In the 1979 film, however, this breakdown is not explicitly put forward, and some of the essentials of it have become applied to another character, namely Captain Colby. Nevertheless, the letter does serve as a further indication that within the 1975 screenplay Kurtz's 'horror' is in some way associated with his estranged wife and all that she represented. In this respect Kurtz's wife functions as the equivalent of the Intended in Conrad's *Heart of Darkness*.

Conclusion

I began this chapter by noting the way in which biblical categories of parable and apocalyptic have been applied recently to an assessment of Joseph Conrad's *Heart of Darkness*. This is an approach which invites further exploration, and I have sought to do precisely that by a careful study of both Conrad's novel and two of the film adaptations of it, namely Nicolas Roeg's *Heart of Darkness* (1994) and Francis Ford Coppola's *Apocalypse Now* (1979). To this end two particular apocalyptic motifs were selected and discussed at some length: the cryptic idea of the 'abominating horror' from Mk 13.14 and the provocative image of the 'Whore of Babylon' from Revelation 17–18. Each of these biblical motifs provides in its own way a fresh angle on Conrad's novella, particularly as it is concerned with matters of colonialism and imperial oppression for the sake of economic interests.

Most importantly, I suggested that it is Conrad's playful use of the homonym pairing of 'horror/whore' that drives us to put the two apocalyptic images of Mk 13.14 and Revelation 17–18 together in a new and constructive way. One would not necessarily make a connection between the 'abominating horror' and the 'Whore of Babylon', beyond the fact that they are both somehow vaguely associated with the Roman Empire. However, the way in which Conrad's novella sets up an intimate relationship between his equivalents of the two apocalyptic images ('The horror! The horror!' and 'the Intended') alerts us to the possibilities of a deeper association between them than is generally recognized. Thus, the 'abominating horror' and the 'Whore of Babylon' are mutually reinforcing images of the oppressive political and economic forces of Roman imperialism in the first-century world.

Conrad's *Heart of Darkness* has prompted us to reconsider the meaning of the biblical materials. Far from taking *Heart of Darkness* simply to be a modern reworking of apocalyptic themes contained in the New Testament, viewing it as merely a literary work which shows the influence of the Bible, we can view the novella rather as a work in which the flow of hermeneutical influence is reversed. A careful study of *Heart of Darkness* and the film adaptations of it means that we go back to the biblical materials with fresh eyes, and are able to see layers of meaning and significance not previously visible.

Chapter 3

THE DECISIVE HOUR OF JUDGMENT:
GOOD CONFRONTS EVIL IN *HIGH NOON* AND *OUTLAND*

One of the most important novels by the late Arthur Koestler was the evocatively titled *Darkness at Noon* (1940).[1] It was the first part of a trilogy of stories whose common theme was an exploration of revolutionary and political ethics, and whether the end always justified the means used to achieve it.[2] The novel tells the story of an old Bolshevik named Nicolas Salmanovich Rubashov as he awaits his execution in the GPU prison. It is a stinging indictment of the excesses of the Russian Revolution, and, beyond that, of all revolutionary dictatorships which sap the life out of people who foolishly dedicate their lives to them. Rubashov selflessly gives forty years of his life to the Party, only to find that he has become entangled in a web of deceit and senseless in-fighting which can only result in his death. In the end, Rubashov is shot and the meaninglessness of his death, the sheer inconceivability of there being any purpose for his execution within the larger scheme of things, strikes the reader powerfully. Here indeed is a tale in which the message of the title's central symbol, of darkness at the very hour of the day when there should have been the most light, is powerfully communicated by Koestler. It is a good example of an evocative image ('darkness at noon') being creatively adapted to produce a modern work of art which both stimulates the imagination and challenges the will.

The task within this chapter is an examination of the image that Koestler used as the title for his gripping novel. More precisely, I shall explore the biblical idea of 'darkness at noon', an essential feature of the apocalyptic

1. According to Ward (1998–99: 134), the title for the book comes not from the Gospel accounts of the passion of Christ (as one might expect), but from a line in Milton's *Samson Agonistes,* 'O dark, dark, dark, amid the blaze of noon'.
2. The other two parts of the trilogy were *Arrival and Departure* (1943) and *The Gladiators* (1949).

imagery that is used within the gospel accounts of the crucifixion of Jesus Christ. I shall also look at how the idea of 'darkness at noon' has been creatively reworked in three films, namely Fred Zinnemann's classic Western *High Noon* (1952), the recent remake of that classic, Rod Hardy's *High Noon* (2000), and a science-fiction adaptation of the same Western by Peter Hyams entitled *Outland* (1981).

Darkness at Noon: Apocalyptic Confrontation in the Crucifixion of Jesus

All of the Synoptic Gospels portray the death of Jesus against a highly stylized, and theologically significant, chronological framework. According to Mk 15.25 the crucifixion takes place 'at the third hour' (ἦν δὲ ὥρα τρίτη), that is to say, at 9.00 a.m. In addition, all three Synoptic Gospels record that at about the sixth hour, that is, at 12.00 noon, a darkness came over the land which lasted until the ninth hour, which is to say, until 3.00 p.m. (see Mt. 27.45/Mk 15.33/Lk. 23.44).[3] In short, the Synoptic Gospels are agreed in portraying 12.00 noon (the sixth hour) as a decisive moment within the apocalyptic timetable of God, for it is then that the penultimate scenes of the great drama of redemption unfold; it is here that darkness covers the land as the Son of God is crucified.[4]

This is not to say that the three Synopticists are without their own particular emphases, however. While the basic outline of events surrounding the crucifixion appears to be based upon Mark's account, Matthew and Luke add distinctive features to their portrayal of the death of

---

3.   Gos. Pet. 5.15, 18 similarly records: 'Now it was midday and a darkness covered all Judaea. And they became anxious and uneasy lest the sun had already set, since he was still alive. <For> it stands written for them: the sun should not set on one that has been put to death… And many went about with lamps, since they supposed that it was night, <and> they stumbled' (see Maurer 1991: 223-24). The explicit identification of Judaea with 'the whole land' (ὅλην τὴν γῆν) referred to in Lk. 23.44 remains one of the most interesting developments of earlier tradition within The Gospel of Peter.

4.   Jn 19.14 similarly records that 'it was about the sixth hour' (ὥρα ἦν ὡς ἕκτη) that the actual death of Jesus takes place. It is generally acknowledged that John deliberately altered the timing of the crucifixion to reflect his own particular theological perspective. According to John, Jesus dies on Thursday (the Day of Preparation), as opposed to Friday (the Passover festival). Thus, John presents Jesus as the sacrificial lamb of God who is slain at the very moment that the lambs were being slaughtered for the Jewish celebrations of Passover.

the Messiah. There is much to suggest that each of the Gospel writers presents the crucifixion in such a way as to highlight his own understanding of the nature of the event, and that each does this for specific reasons. For his part, Mark concentrates much of the drama on the death of Jesus at the ninth hour (3.00 p.m.), stressing the utter desolation that is involved by recording in 15.34 that Jesus quotes Ps. 22.1 in Aramaic just before he dies: 'My God, my God, why have you forsaken me?' This is followed in v. 38 by a declaration that the curtain of the temple was torn from top to bottom, as if to suggest that a supernatural portent accompanies the death of Jesus on the cross and punctuates its significance. In other words, Jesus' death is presented as having tremendous theological weight and this is signalled by the event involving the temple curtain. But how are we to understand this tearing of the temple curtain? Does Mark intend his readers to accept the circumstances surrounding the death of Jesus as literal, historical facts? There is a great deal of debate over this point. The ripping of the temple curtain in Mk 15.38 is probably meant as a figurative event, perhaps representing the coming destruction of Jerusalem, along with the cessation of the cultic activities associated with Herod's temple located there. Some interpreters suggest that it symbolizes the bridging of the gap between God and humankind in the act of redemption, in that the temple curtain which hitherto served as a boundary-marker and barrier is now put aside. The fact that (according to Mark) this temple curtain is torn 'from top to bottom' could even hint at the divine initiative in this act of redemption. In this sense, Jesus' death has somehow destroyed the temple curtain and set up a new basis for understanding the relationship between God and humankind. If this is correct, then Mark's point is not all that different from that of the writer of Hebrews, who declares in 10.19-20 that Jesus 'has inaugurated a new and living way for us through the curtain' (ἐνεκαίνισεν ἡμῖν ὁδὸν πρόσφατον καὶ ζῶσαν διὰ τοῦ καταπετάσματος). In any event, the fact that Jesus' death is associated so closely with a figurative, supernatural event (the tearing of the temple veil) is a key feature in Mark's crucifixion narrative (see Motyer 1987; Ulansey 1991).

What is also interesting at this point is that both Matthew and Luke keep the tearing of the temple curtain as an essential part of their crucifixion narratives, although each builds upon it and adds additional supernatural events to the story. As G.B. Caird puts it:

> [Matthew and Luke] have detached the rending of the curtain from the centurion's confession and have linked it instead, the one with the earthquake, the other with an eclipse. It would appear that what began as a figurative

statement has ended in a literal one: interpretation has been taken as actuality. [5]

Thus, Matthew follows mention of the tearing of the temple curtain in 27.51a by reference to an accompanying earthquake in v. 51b. Even more astonishingly, he follows this up with mention in vv. 52-53 of the opening of tombs and the resurrection of many deceased saints who go into Jerusalem. Such an expansion using traditional ideas contained within apocalyptic literature is unique to Matthew.[6]

For his part, Luke does *not* include any mention of the earthquake or the general resurrection of the dead, although he too mentions some supernatural signs which accompany the death of Jesus on the cross. Luke's way of doing this is stylistically distinctive, however. For one thing, he moves the reference to the tearing of the temple curtain in 23.45 to an earlier point in the crucifixion narrative, thus making it *precede* the actual death of Jesus (which is recorded in 23.46).[7] At the same time, Luke expounds the meaning of the darkness which is said to come over the whole of the land from the sixth to the ninth hours (23.44) by adding an explanatory note about the sun (in 23.45a). In the words of Joseph

---

5.   Caird 1980: 214. Also see Caird 1963: 253; Daube 1956: 23-26. Moule (1959: 176) similarly comments: 'The one point in the Synoptists where all attempt at historical narrative seems to be abandoned is in the reference to *the rending of the veil*. This is surely symbolical *in intention*'. Sylva (1986) also discusses the various interpretative possibilities. He argues that the tearing of the temple curtain is much more intimately associated in Luke's mind with Jesus' death than is commonly recognized. One of the indications of this, according to Sylva, is the reference in 23.44c to the death of Jesus taking place at the ninth hour, and the fact that according to Acts 3.1 (and 10.30?) the ninth hour was the time of prayer within the temple in Jerusalem. In other words, Jesus' final words in 23.46 ('Father, into your hands I commit my spirit') are a prayer addressed to God in the temple, the very temple to which access has been gained by the rending of the dividing curtain. Luke thus moves the reference to the tearing of the temple curtain to a position in the narrative *prior* to Jesus' death in order to present the final moment of the Messiah's life as one of intimate communion with God in the temple. For additional discussion on Luke's presentation of the tearing of the temple curtain motif, see Weinert 1982; Matera 1985; J.B. Green 1988: 95-99; 1994.

6.   An extended discussion of Mt. 27.51-53 is beyond the focus of this study. However, for a recent discussion of the passage see Hagner 1995: 846-53 and the literature cited there. Hagner stresses the symbolic significance of the resurrection of the saints.

7.   Although it is worth noting that the text of Luke in the fifth–sixth century *Codex Bezae Cantabrigiensis* (D) follows the Markan order on this point and gives the description of the tearing of the veil *after* the death of Jesus.

Fitzmyer, 'He creates a symbolic backdrop for the death by the reference to two cataclysmic events that accompanied it: darkness over the whole land (of Palestine) and the rending of the Temple veil (in Jerusalem)' (1985: 1513).

It is in connection with 'darkness over the whole land' that we have one of the most interesting debates over the actual text of Luke's account, for it is by no means clear what the words mean, or even what the original text of 23.45a was. Two major variants are extant for 23.45a: καὶ ἐσκοτίσθη ὁ ἥλιος (translated 'the sun was darkened'), or τοῦ ἡλίου ἐκλίποντος (translated either as 'the sun's light failed' or 'the sun was eclipsed').[8] The former variant is generally regarded to be the easier reading theologically and was probably substituted by copyists in order to avoid the difficulties associated with the idea of a solar eclipse (which seems to be hinted at by the genitive absolute τοῦ ἡλίου ἐκλίποντος).[9]

The verb ἐκλείπειν is somewhat rare within the New Testament. It occurs a total of four times, three of which are within the Gospel of Luke (the final occurrence is in Heb. 1.12 which cites the LXX of Ps. 101.28). Significantly, the verb is never used in the LXX to refer unambiguously to an eclipse of the sun.[10] Moreover, on the other two occasions that the term is used within the Gospel of Luke it clearly means 'to fail' or 'to lack'; it appears in 16.9 and 22.32 in precisely this sense. The first reference is found within the so-called parable of the unjust steward where it is applied to the mammon of unrighteousness which will eventually *fail*, and the second refers to the faith of Simon Peter which is to be found sadly *lacking* when the critical moment arrives. Thus, neither of these two earlier references in Luke lends itself to a cosmic interpretation as does the use of ἐκλείπειν in 23.45. So what are we to make of the unusual phrase which is contained in this verse? On the surface, at first reading, it appears

8.   Some manuscripts have the present participle ἐκλείποντος instead of the aorist ἐκλιπόντος. Patella (1999: 97-99) discusses the various textual variants of the verse.

9.   Occasionally the unusual phrase is taken to be a corruption of a hypothetical marginal note to Lk. 23.45 which would have read τοῦ Ἠλείου ἐκλείποντος. The suggestion here is that the words explained the omission of the reference to Elijah which appears in the parallels in Mt. 27.46-49/Mk 15.34-36. See Plummer 1901: 545 for details. Marshall (1978: 285) dismisses the idea as completely unnecessary.

10.   The verb appears over 175 times in the LXX, frequently with reference to the 'failing of life' in old age as death approaches. One of the most interesting examples occurs in *Sir.* 22.11 where the dead are described as those for whom 'the light has gone out' (ἐξέλιπε γὰρ φῶς).

that Luke has the crucifixion of Jesus accompanied by a 'failing' of the sun's light, a description which has often been taken to indicate an eclipse of the sun. It is at this point that the difficulties commence, for it appears that the scientific world clashes head on with the theological world.

To be more specific, there is a severe complication here, in that a solar eclipse is astronomically impossible during the Passover when there would have been a full moon. Eclipses only occur during a new moon, a fact which was recognized long ago, as the intriguing reference in Thucydides *History* 2.28 relates:

> The same summer, at the beginning of a new lunar month (which seems to be the only time when such a thing is possible), there was an eclipse of the sun after midday. The sun took on the appearance of a crescent and some of the stars became visible before it returned to its normal shape.

> Τοῦ δ' αὐτοῦ θέρους νουμηνίᾳ καὶ σελήνην, ὥσπερ καὶ μόνον δοκεῖ εἶναι γίγνεσθαι δυνατόν, ὁ ἥλιος ἐξέλιπε μετὰ μεσημβρίαν καὶ πάλιν ἀνεπληρώθη, γενόμενος μηνοειδὴς καὶ ἀστέρων τινῶν ἐκφανέντων.

Moreover, the maximum length of time that a solar eclipse can last in any given area is 7 minutes and 40 seconds[11]—a far cry from the three hours of darkness suggested by the Gospel accounts. And beyond that, astronomical calculations by scientists confirm that there was no solar eclipse observable in Jerusalem during the first century CE.[12] Given these scientific difficulties, it is little wonder that some manuscripts replace the awkward phrase in Lk. 23.45 with 'and the sun was darkened' (καὶ ἐσκοτίσθη ὁ ἥλιος)! Indeed, some of the early Christian apologists engaged in heated debate with pagan opponents to the faith over precisely this issue. For example, Julius Africanus (c. 220 CE) challenged the pagan historian Thallus on the matter, and the eclipse is alluded to by Tertullian (150–222 CE) in a context which indicates an awareness of the astronomical impossibilities concerned: *Apology* 21.19 makes mention of the difficulties that the unusual darkness at the crucifixion presented to those opponents of Christ who did not know that such a phenomenon had been predicted by the Lord himself, and thought

---

11. See Driver 1965: 333 on this point.

12. There was, however, a partial eclipse of the moon observable in Jerusalem on 3 April 33. Some scholars have argued that this is what is alluded to in Acts 2.20 where Peter quotes Joel 2.31 and refers to 'the sun being turned to darkness and the moon to blood'. See Fotheringham 1934; Maier 1968; Humphreys and Waddington 1983; 1989; Kokkinos 1989 and Brown 1994: 1041-42 for further discussion.

(quite naturally) that what they were witnessing was simply a solar eclipse.[13]

More recently, scholars have sought to explain the unusual darkness which fell over the land during the crucifixion as due to some other natural phenomenon, such as a dust storm caused by a searing Mediterranean wind (known as a sirocco),[14] or some other meteorological condition that is perhaps inexplicable in terms of natural science but which was nonetheless real in terms of history.[15] Yet despite the obvious scientific and astronomical difficulties associated with what might be called 'the eclipse hypothesis', there are many interpreters who argue that this is indeed precisely how the writer of the Gospel intends us to understand the meaning of the 'darkness' motif in Lk. 23.44-45a.

Further exploration as to why Luke (apparently) associates the death of Jesus with the timing of a solar eclipse is needed. We have space to consider three different, but overlapping, ways in which scholars have sought to interpret the eclipse within Luke's account of the crucifixion. Common to each of these three ways of understanding the 'darkness' motif in Luke's Gospel is the assumption that the writer has deliberately included reference to a solar eclipse, or at least hinted at one, as a constituent element within his story-line.

The Lukan Eclipse as Portent of History
First, it is important to remember that within the ancient world great historical events were often thought to be accompanied by supernatural portents, including eclipses or unnatural darkening of both the sun and the moon. Several examples of this are known within the writings of antiquity. For instance, Lucan (*The Civil Wars* 7.199-204) discusses the battle of Pharsalia (48 BCE), in which the armies of Pompey and Julius Caesar clashed, in language along these lines. Lucan states that any augur who perceived the importance of the battle might describe it in terms of cosmic signs. Thus, Lucan describes the augur, whose insight into the meaning of the battle is beyond human abilities and therefore reflects a divine perspective, with these words:

13. Tertullian states: 'Deliquium utique putauerunt qui id quoque super Christo praedicatum non scierunt'.
14. Especially see Driver 1965 on this point. The idea is taken up by Marshall (1978: 875).
15. Nolland (1993: 1156) and Bock (1996: 1859-60) argue that the darkness is intended to be both literal and historical.

Either he observed the thunder and the warning bolts of Jupiter; or he saw that all the firmament and the poles were at strife with the warring sky; or else the sorrowing deity in heaven signified the battle by the dimness and obscurity of the sun. At least it is certain that Nature made the day of Pharsalia pass unlike all other days which she reveals; if human intelligence, by means of skilled augurs, had observed all the strange signs in heaven, then the battle might have been watched all the world over.

Seu tonitrus ac tela Iovis praesaga notavit,
Aethera seu totum discordi obsistere caelo
Perspexitque polos, seu numen in aethere maestum
Solis in obscuro pugnam pallore notavit.
Dissimilem certe cunctis quos explicat egit
Thessalicum natura diem: si cuncta perito
Augure mens hominum caeli nova signa notasset,
Spectari toto potuit Pharsalia mundo.[16]

The deaths of legendary figures and prominent people within the ancient world were also thought to be accompanied by unusual astronomical signs and wonders.[17] An often-cited case in point is found in an interesting work by Aelius Aristides (c. 117-181 CE), namely, a funeral oration for Alexander of Cotiaetum (a city about 200 miles east of Smyrna). In *Oration* 32, Aristides makes a passing reference to a fragment of Aristophanes (fragment 643K) which describes the death of the Greek playwright Aeschylus:

What Aristophanes says about Aeschylus, 'that there was darkness when he died', ought to be said now about this man in regard to education.

ὃ δέ φησιν Ἀριστοφάνης περὶ Αἰσχύλου σκότον ἐῖναι τεθνηκότος, τοῦτ᾽ ἄξιον καὶ περὶ τούτου νῦν εἰπεῖν εἰς παιδείας λόγου.[18]

Unfortunately, the passage does not *explicitly* state that the death of Aeschylus was accompanied by an eclipse as such, and in this sense it is not as clear as one would perhaps wish. The 'darkness' concerned could be entirely metaphorical. However, a clearer example is contained in the

16. Also see *Civil Wars* 1.540-43 for a similar comment about the sun hiding its face.

17. Grández (1989) and Danker (1988: 379) list examples from antiquity of the deaths of people of exceptional merit being accompanied by unusual natural phenomena. Included is a comment contained in Pseudo-Callisthenes 3.33.26 concerning the death of Alexander the Great in 323 BCE.

18. See Aristides 1981: 164. The oration dates to c. 150 CE. Danker (1988: 379) wrongly associates this oration with Alexander the Great.

writings of Ovid (43 BCE–17 CE). His *Fasti* 2.493-94 records the natural world's reaction to the death of Romulus, legendary founder of Rome:

> The sun vanished and rising clouds obscured the heaven,
> and there fell a heavy shower of rain in torrents.

> sol fugit, et removent subeuntia nubila caelum,
> et gravis effusis decidit imber aquis.

A similar remark is contained in the Greek writer Plutarch (c. 50–120 CE). He records in *Romulus* 27.6 that at his death the legendary king of Rome was holding an assembly of the people, when suddenly

> The light of the sun failed, and night came down upon them, not with peace and quiet, but with awful peals of thunder and furious blasts driving rain from every quarter.

> τοῦ μὲν γὰρ ἡλίου τὸ φῶς ἐκλιπεῖν, νύκτα δὲ κατασχεῖν, οὐ πραεῖαν, οὐδὲ ἥσυχον, ἀλλὰ βροντάς τε δεινὰς καὶ πνοὰς ἀνέμων ζάλην ἐλαυνόντων πανταχόθεν ἔχουσαν

The Latin writer Cicero (106–43 BCE) also contains a brief mention of eclipses associated with the passing of Romulus. He says in *On the Republic* 6.24.3:

> The sun appeared to men to be eclipsed and blotted out, at the time when the soul of Romulus entered these [heavenly] regions.

> Namque ut olim deficere sol hominibus exstinguique visus est, cum Romuli animus haec ipsa in templa penetravit.[19]

The death of Julius Caesar is described by the poet Virgil (70–19 BCE) in language which clearly has a solar eclipse in mind. We read in *Georgics* 1: 466-68 of the sun's reaction to the assassination of the dictator:

> Nay, he had pity for Rome, when, after Caesar sank from sight, he veiled his shining face in dusky gloom, and a godless age feared everlasting night.

> ille etiam exstincto miseratus Caesare Romam, cum caput obscura nitidum ferrugine texit impiaque aeternam timuerant saecula noctem.

Similarly, Plutarch (*Caesar* 69.3) writes of some of the astronomical events which occurred in the heavens following the assassination. He says:

---

19. The association of an eclipse with the death of Romulus is also mentioned in *On the Republic* 1.25.4 and 2.17. Dionysius Halicarnassus, *Roman Antiquities* 2.56 also has a note on Romulus along these lines.

Among events of divine ordering, there was the great comet, which showed itself in great splendour for seven nights after Caesar's murder, and then disappeared; also, the obscuration of the sun's rays.

Τῶν δὲ θείων ὅ τε μέγας κομήτης (ἐφάνη γὰρ ἐπὶ νύκτας ἑπτὰ μωτὰ τὴν Καίσαρος σφαγὴν διαπρεπής, εἶτα ἠφανίσθη) καὶ τὸ περὶ τὸν ἥλιον ἀμαύρωμα τῆς αὐγῆς.[20]

Pliny the Elder (23/24–79 CE) and Petronius (d. 66[?] CE) also contain some interesting lines which illustrate how readily connections were made between astronomical events and social upheaval such as the civil wars of 49–45 BCE and the death of a figure of such stature as Julius Caesar in 44 BCE. Petronius (*Satyricon* 122.128-30) describes the sun's (Titan's) reaction to these things:

For Titan was disfigured and dabbled in blood, and veiled his face in darkness: thou hadst thought that even then he gazed on civil strife.

Namque ore cruento
deformis Titan vultam caligine texit:
civiles acies iam tum spectare putares.

Pliny similarly relates in *Natural History* 2.30:

Portentous and protracted eclipses of the sun occur such as the one after the murder of Caesar the dictator and during the Antonine war which caused almost a whole year's continuous gloom.

Fiunt prodigiosi et longiores solis defectus, qualis occiso dictatore Caesare et Antoniano bello totius paene anni pallore continuo.

Brief mention should also be made of the work of the Jewish writer Josephus (c. 37–100 CE), whose *Ant.* 14.12.3 also refers to the dimming of the sun at the death of Julius Caesar. This passage occurs in the midst of a letter purported to be from Caesar's heir Mark Antony to the Jewish high priest Hyrcanus II and written in 42 BCE. It is perhaps also worth noting that the only explicit reference within Josephus to an eclipse *per se* (as opposed to the sun's dimming) occurs in *Ant.* 17.6.4. This records the death of Herod the Great as having taken place shortly after a *lunar* eclipse.[21]

---

20. The appearance of the comet in the skies over Rome was used to great effect in the coinage issued by Julius Caesar's successor Octavian. See Kreitzer 1996: 84-86.

21. This probably refers to the lunar eclipse which took place on the night of 12–13 March 4 BCE, although the eclipse of 29–30 December 1 BCE also fits a reconstructed chronology. For more on the question of the date of Herod's death, see Filmer 1966; Barnes 1968; Van Bruggen 1978; Edwards 1982; Bernegger 1983; E.L. Martin 1989; Johnson 1989; Hoehner 1989 and Maier 1989.

It is beyond doubt that many writers of antiquity associated eclipses of the sun with important historical events, including the deaths of legendary figures or great political leaders. This offers a partial explanation as to why Luke chooses to include reference to the eclipse of the sun at the crucifixion of Jesus of Nazareth; it confirms his place within the tradition of Graeco-Roman historiography. Yet there is another intriguing possibility which also needs to be considered, one that focuses not so much on the way in which eclipses were viewed as portents of history, but on the experience of the writer of the Gospel himself.

The Lukan Eclipse in Personal Experience
Assuming that the reference to the darkening of the sun's light in Lk. 23.45a is intended to indicate an actual solar eclipse, we need to consider *why* it is that Luke makes such a statement when it is quite clear that such an event could not have taken place in Jerusalem at the time of Jesus' crucifixion. What drove him to incorporate such an idea within his Gospel account, when by his own claims (in 1.1-4) the work was supposed to have been meticulously researched? Some scholars have simply suggested that Luke was just not aware of the impossibility of there being an eclipse at the time of the Passover.[22] Others have more sophisticated solutions to what remains an awkwardness within the Gospel record.

For example, John F.A. Sawyer offers a tantalizing explanation of how Luke might have come to include an allusion to an actual solar eclipse within his Gospel. He notes that the only total solar eclipse that would have occurred in the ancient Near East during the first century CE took place on 24 November 29 CE. This eclipse would have been visible in Greece as well as parts of Asia Minor and Syria and would have begun at about 11.15 a.m., lasting for about 90 seconds. Sawyer builds upon the early tradition associating Luke with the church at Antioch, and suggests that Luke himself may have been an eyewitness to this solar eclipse when he was a young man, presumably living in Asia Minor or even within the city of Antioch itself. In short, Sawyer argues that Luke incorporated his memory of this unforgettable experience into his description of the crucifixion of Jesus Christ in 23.45a.[23] There is much within this suggestion that makes sense, given what is known about the eclipse itself.

22. So Creed 1960: 288. Others concur, including Brown (1994: 1041).
23. Sawyer 1972: 124-28. Similarly, Stephenson (1969) discusses the reference to lunar and solar eclipses in Joel 2.31 and concludes that the writer of Joel was in all likelihood an eyewitness to a total eclipse of the sun, either on 29 February 357 BCE or

This particular eclipse of 29 CE is briefly alluded to in other ancient writers, namely Origen (c. 185–254 CE) and Eusebius (c. 260–340 CE). Both discuss the eclipse in connection with a certain Greek historian from Asia Minor named Phlegon who mentions an eclipse (accompanied by an earthquake) in his work entitled *Chronicles*.[24] Thus, Origen in *Against Celsus* notes some of the arguments put forward by his opponent Celsus and challenges them, in part, by referring to the independent witness of Phlegon. Note the following two brief mentions of Phlegon:

> And concerning the eclipse in the time of Tiberius Caesar, during whose reign Jesus appears to have been crucified, and about the great earthquakes that happened at that time, Phlegon has also made a record in the thirteenth or fourteenth book, I think, of his *Chronicles* (2.33).

> Περὶ δὲ τῆς ἐπὶ Τιβερίου Καίσαρος ἐκλείψεως, οὗ βασιλεύοντους καὶ ὁ Ἰησοῦς ἔοικεν ἐσταυρῶσθαι, καὶ περὶ τῶν μεγάλων τότε γενομένων σεισμῶν τῆς γῆς ἀνέγραψε καὶ Φλέγων ἐν τῷ τρισκαιδεκάτῳ ἢ τεσσαρεσκαιδεκάτῳ οἶμαι Χρονικῶν.

> [Celsus] thinks that the earthquake and the darkness are a fantastic tale. We defended these as well as we could earlier, quoting Phlegon who related that these events happened at the time of the Saviour's passion. (2.59)[25]

> Οἴεται δὲ τερατείαν εἶναι καὶ τὸν σεισμὸν καὶ τὸν σκότον. περὶ ὧν κατὰ τὸ δυνατὸν ἐν τοῖς ἀνωτέρω ἀπελογησάμεθα, παραθέμενοι τὸν Φλέγοντα ἱστορήσαντα, κατὰ τὸν χρόνον τοῦ πάθους τοῦ σωτῆρος τοιαῦτα ἀπηντηκέναι.

If Sawyer's reading of Lk. 23.45a is correct, it means that Luke is creatively reworking his own personal experience of this same solar eclipse into the Gospel narrative. Apparently he does this in the full knowledge that the historical chronology is not strictly accurate. In other words, the writer's experience of a rare astronomical phenomenon such as a solar eclipse is put into the service of his theological aims. How likely is this to be the case?

on 4 July 336 BCE. Also see Holladay 1968 and Sawyer 1972 for a related discussion about another problematic passage from the Old Testament which is sometimes associated with a solar eclipse.

24. Phlegon lived during the reign of the Emperor Hadrian (117–138 CE). For more on this see Brown 1994: 1041-42.

25. Chadwick 1953: 94 and 112. Elsewhere Origen tends to accept the variant reading καὶ ἐσκοτίσθη ὁ ἥλιος for Lk. 23.45a and thereby avoid the thorny problems associated with a naturally impossible eclipse. For more on this matter, see Metzger 1963: 86-87; Brown 1994: 1040.

The creative rewriting of history associated with eclipses is by no means unique. There is one particular parallel from antiquity which is worth noting in this regard, especially since it involves a reworking of history in such a way that an eclipse is made to underline the significance of the events concerned. Herodotus (*History* 7.37.2) mentions a total eclipse that (allegedly) took place in Sardis as Xerxes and his army prepared to march to Abydos. The passage states:

> When they had set forth, the sun left his place in the heaven and was unseen, albeit the sky was without clouds and very clear, and the day was turned to night.

> ὁρμημένῳ δὲ οἱ ὁ ἥλιος ἐκλιπὼν τὴν ἐκ τοῦ οὐρανοῦ ἕδρην ἀφανὴς ἦν οὔτι ἐπινεφέλων ἐόντων αἰθρίης τε τὰ μάλιστα, ἀντὶ ἡμέρης τε νὺξ ἐγένετο.

Interestingly, although the march of Xerxes' army is almost certainly dated to April of 480 BCE, the only total eclipse visible in Sardis is known to have taken place on 16 February 478 BCE.[26] In other words, *History* 7.37.2 may be another example of a creative re-dating of an eclipse so as to make it coincide with an historical event which is deemed to be of special significance (in this case, the starting of the expedition to Abydos). What makes the connection between this ancient piece of historiography and the Gospel of Luke even more fascinating is the way that the story-line continues in Herodotus. Xerxes is worried about the meaning of the eclipse and consults some magi who offer an explanation which he finds soothing. They say that through the solar phenomenon

> God meant to foretell to the Greeks the eclipse of their cities—for it was the sun which gave warning of the future to Greece, just as the moon did to Persia.

> ὡς Ἕλλησι προδεικνύει ὁ θεὸς ἔκλειψιν τῶν πολίων, λέγοντες ἥλιον εἶναι Ἑλλήνων προδέκτορα, σελήνην δὲ σφέων.

It appears that Herodotus specifically included within his story the magi's interpretation of the solar eclipse as a portent for the coming destruction of the Greek cities. This is precisely how many New Testament scholars interpret the significance of the eclipse within the Gospel of Luke, viewing it as intimately connected with the destruction of the city of Jerusalem. Is it coincidental that both Herodotus and Luke present a solar eclipse as a symbol of the 'eclipse' of cities? The parallelism on this point

---

26. See Macan 1908: 57 and How and Wells 1928: 144-45 for further discussion. Herodotus also mentions eclipses in 1.74.2 and 9.10.3.

is striking, even if it has not been generally recognized.[27] The idea of an eclipse somehow symbolizing the judgment and destruction which can befall a city is also contained in a number of other ancient texts. A good example of this is found in Philo of Alexandria (c. 20 BCE–50 CE). In his treatise *On Providence* he discusses some of the effects of natural phenomena, including rainbows and eclipses. Philo states in 2.50:

> Much the same may be said about eclipses as about the rainbow. The sun and moon are natural divinities, and so these eclipses are concomitant circumstances, yet eclipses announce the death of kings and the destruction of cities.
>
> οἷός γ᾽ οὖν ἐπὶ τῆς Ἴριδος, τοιοῦτος καὶ ἐπὶ τῶν ἐκλείψεων ὁ λόγος. θείαις γὰρ φύσεσιν ἡλίου καὶ σελήνης ἐπακολουθοῦσιν ἐκλείψεις. αἱ δὲ μηνύματά εἰσιν ἢ βασιλέων τελευτῆς, ἢ πόλεων φθορᾶς.

In addition, both Diodorus Siculus (c. 80–20 BCE) and Plutarch describe a celebrated incident in which a solar eclipse was said to have come over the city of Thebes. This occurs just as the Theban general Pelopidas prepares to withdraw his army from the city and wage war against his rival Alexander of Pherae. Diodorus Siculus (*Library of History* 15.80.2) relates:

> Many were superstitious about the phenomenon and some of the soothsayers declared that because of the withdrawal of the soldiers, the city's 'sun' had been eclipsed.
>
> πολλῶν δὲ τὸ γεγονὸς ὑποπτευσάμενων τῶν μάντεων τινες ἀπεφήσαντο διὰ τὴν γενομένην ἔξοδον τῶν στρατιωτῶν ἐκλιπεῖν τὸν τῆς πόλεως ἥλιον.

Plutarch (*Pelopidas* 31.2-3) similarly remarks about the incident (commonly connected with an eclipse which occurred on 13 July 364 BCE):

> The eclipse was thought to be a great sign from heaven, and to regard a conspicuous man.
>
> μέγα γὰρ ἐδόκει καὶ πρὸς ἄνδρα λαμπρὸν ἐξ οὐρανοῦ γεγονέναι σημεῖον.

In short, it is entirely possible that one of the reasons Luke chooses to include an explicit reference to a solar eclipse in his crucifixion narrative has to do with his own personal experience of such a rare and unforgettable event. At the same time, there was a widespread association of eclipses

---

27. Few commentators point to the passage in Herodotus, *History* 7.37.2 as a background text for the idea of eclipses. Beyond that, never (as far as I can determine) are the implications considered of the rest of the passage for Luke's presentation of the solar eclipse as a portent for the destruction of the temple in Jerusalem in 70 CE.

with the divine destruction of cities, and this may have fitted well within Luke's overall theological purposes. We move now to consider this possibility more closely.

The Lukan Eclipse as Theological Metaphor
'Darkness' is used as a spiritual metaphor for human sinfulness within the Gospel of Luke, as 22.53 clearly indicates. As Jesus is arrested he says to Judas and the crowd: 'When I was with you day after day in the temple, you did not lay hands on me. But this is your hour, and the power of darkness'. Thus, it seems that the reference to the darkness that takes place during the crucifixion of Jesus is very much part and parcel of Luke's theological perspective.[28] Darkness is presented as the opposite of spiritual perception (as can be seen in 11.35-36), and as such it is an essential motif within his apocalyptic understanding of the Christ event. Yet the darkness is something that is essentially metaphorical and thus spiritually perceived (see Lk. 1.78-79; Acts 2.20; 26.18 for other good hints in this direction). Clearly, astronomical signs and portents are integral to the coming of the apocalyptic Day of the Lord that Jesus himself predicted, as Lk. 21.25-27 states (perhaps building on imagery contained in Amos 5.18). Yet it appears that even here Luke's apocalyptic perspective is subtly different from those of Mark and Matthew, both of whom present the death of Jesus as the beginning of the end of the age, the fulfilment of eschatological expectations. For one thing, Luke omits *explicit* reference to the darkening of the sun and the moon within Jesus' great eschatological discourse. Both Mk 13.24 and Mt. 24.29 make mention of this darkness motif, whereas Luke is content to state the point in a much more open-ended fashion Thus, Lk. 21.25 reads: 'And there will be signs in sun and moon and stars', with any mention of a darkness or an eclipse carefully omitted in the process. It is as if Luke wishes to hold back the darkness motif until the climactic event of Jesus' death on the cross, associating it with explicit mention of the eclipse in 23.45a.

Such a metaphorical understanding of the 'darkness' motif may help us better appreciate another unusual feature of Luke's depiction of the crucifixion of Jesus. In 23.44 we see that Luke has moved the mention of the

---

28. Tannehill (1996: 345) comments: 'As Jesus' death approaches, the darkness at midday suggests that Satan is fully in control'. Nolland (1993: 1156) similarly links the references to darkness in 22.53 and 23.45 when he remarks: 'Luke thinks of the Satanic onslaught that stands behind the cruel deed that comes now to its fruition'.

tearing of the veil in Herod's temple[29] to a position earlier in his narrative, perhaps as a way of associating it more closely with the darkness motif. This is in stark contrast to Mt. 27.51 and Mk 15.38 where the tearing of the temple curtain occurs *after* Jesus' final words and death.[30] Why does Luke do this?

One possible explanation is that 'darkness' for Luke is an indicator of divine displeasure; it is a symbol of the anger of God at the rejection and crucifixion of his son. Another more likely reason is that Luke deliberately forges a conceptual connection between the darkening of the sun and the rending of the veil in order to focus attention on the guilt of the Jewish leaders for their part in the unjust death of Jesus. In other words, the tearing of the veil of the temple is meant to symbolize the destruction of the temple (from Luke's perspective, an historical event which had already taken place in 70 CE). This destruction ultimately comes about because of the darkness of human hearts which rejected the Messiah. This is the way in which J. Bradley Chance understands the passage, arguing that 22.53 should be determinative for our understanding of how the darkness motif functions in Luke. Chance says that the verse suggests that 'darkness' has an essentially satanic character about it, and that Jesus' opponents, including the Jewish leaders who come to arrest Jesus, are operating as instruments of Satan.[31] And yet (Chance continues), Luke wants to assert that the darkness mentioned in 23.44 was a literal phenomenon, for he goes on to state in 23.45a that 'the sun's light failed'.

In other words, given that eclipses were commonly understood to be signs of great events in history, and were particularly associated with the deaths of great rulers, and given the possibility that Luke's own personal experiences of having witnessed a solar eclipse in Antioch in 29 CE is what drives him to incorporate reference to one in his account of Jesus' death, we are nevertheless faced with the fact that the eclipse suggested in Lk. 23.45a is part and parcel of the apocalyptic imagery in which he couches his account of Christ's crucifixion. The eclipse motif, with its attendant darkness at noon, highlights the apocalyptic confrontation which takes place at Jesus' death. It stresses the confrontation between the forces of

---

29. Debate about which temple curtain is meant need not detain us. The question is a contentious one and much hinges on the evidence contained in Josephus, *War* 5.5.4.

30. See Sylva 1986 and J.B. Green 1994 for further discussion of this point.

31. Chance 1988: 118-19. Also see Tinsley 1969: 202 and Allison 1987: 74-75 for similar interpretations along these lines.

evil and darkness, which connive to bring about Jesus' death, and the divine power of God, who, paradoxically, will effect salvation through it.

Before we move on to consider how the films *High Noon* and *Outland* present their own unique vision of an apocalyptic confrontation, it is worth recording how some cinematic portrayals of the life of Jesus Christ handle the crucifixion scene. Interestingly, the way in which the 'darkness' motif is handled by film directors often parallels the range of interpretations offered by commentators. Perhaps the most common means of depicting the darkness within films is to have a violent thunderstorm take place just as Jesus dies. This is the explanation used by director Franco Zeffirelli in his reverential *Jesus of Nazareth* (1977), for example. The same thunder-storm imagery was used to even greater effect within William Wyler's *Ben-Hur* (1959), where the accompanying rain cascades down from the cross of Christ on Calvary hill and pours into the surrounding countryside below. This rain brings health and healing to people below, notably the leprous relatives of Judah Ben-Hur who cower in fear in an isolated cave. Other means of explaining the darkness are also to be found in cinematic interpretations of the life of Jesus Christ. For example, the 1979 movie entitled *Jesus*, directed by Peter Sykes and John Krish, is a conscious attempt to film the Gospel story as it is found within Luke, and it has a vivid portrayal of the crucifixion which includes a scene depicting the cause of the darkness. This scene is accompanied by a voice-over which reads the text of Lk. 23.44 in the New International Version: 'It was now about the sixth hour, and darkness came over the whole land until the ninth hour'. The textual reading is visually illustrated with a shot of dark clouds moving across the face of what appears to be the sun (or is it the *moon*?—it is difficult to tell); this is then followed by a shot of the crowd at Golgotha being subjected to an unnatural darkening. What is fascinating about this particular depiction of the 'darkness' motif is that it does not show a rainstorm or a solar eclipse as such, nor does the narrator's voice-over extend to the awkward phrase of Lk. 23.45a, rendered by the NIV as 'for the sun stopped shining'. One cannot help but wonder if the diffi-culties presented by a literal rendering of Lk. 23.44-45a proved to be too controversial, and a less contentious depiction was therefore adopted.

On the other hand, occasionally, films depicting the crucifixion of Christ *do* follow (what appears to be) Luke's suggestion in 23.44-45a and portray the 'darkness at the sixth hour' as if it were an actual eclipse of the sun. One of the most creative examples of this occurs in Richard Fleischer's film *Barabbas* (1962), an adaptation of Pär Lagerkvist's award-winning novel of the same name. Within the film the darkness caused by the eclipse becomes a metaphor for the spiritual darkness which hovers over the figure of Barabbas, who struggles to deal with the fact that Christ died on the cross *literally* in his place. What is remarkable about Fleischer's film is the fact that he deliberately chose to shoot the crucifixion scenes during an actual solar eclipse. Fleischer explains:

> This total eclipse took place about sixty or seventy miles north of Rome, where we were, so we had to go there and we only had forty-eight hours or so to organize the thing. We had to build our own section of the hill and put it in the right place, exactly where the sun was going to come up on the day of the eclipse. We took about a hundred people there, technicians and the extras—and the crosses. I don't think such a thing had ever been filmed before and I must say, in all modesty, that it was breathtakingly beautiful.[32]

This leads us on to the second part of this chapter—the world of the cinema, arguably *the* art form of the twentieth century. Indeed, a good case can be made for the claim that nowhere else has the clash between good and evil been presented more powerfully to the general public than in the moving image.

Darkness at the Decisive Hour: The Apocalyptic Timetable is Reworked

Some of the most effective reworkings of the 'darkness at noon' motif are found, somewhat ironically, not within biblical epics which attempt to portray the life of Christ, but rather in films of two very different genres, the Western and science fiction. In each instance the apocalyptic confrontation between good and evil is given a new twist.

Fred Zinnemann's High Noon *(1952)*
John M. Cunningham's short-story 'The Tin Star' first appeared in *Colliers* magazine in the issue dated 6 December 1947. It was a simple story set in the American West, and probably would have been completely forgotten were it not for the fact that a film adaptation was made in 1952, an adaptation that has subsequently proved to be unforgettable.[33]

Cunningham's story served as the basis for the classic film *High Noon,*

---

32. Cited in Cow 1970: 24. For more on the film, see Kreitzer 1993: 67-87.

33. For a discussion of the relationship between the short story and the film, see McDougal 1985: 377-80. The book contains the full text of Cunningham's story (on pp. 382-93).

directed by Fred Zinnemann, a film that is commonly regarded as one of the best Westerns of all time and was the recipient of several Academy Awards. Thus, the film earned Oscars for Gary Cooper for Best Actor in his role as Marshal Will Kane, Harry W. Gerstad II and Elmo Williams for Best Film Editing, Dimitri Tiomkin for Best Musical Score, and Tiomkin (music) and Ned Washington (lyrics) for Best Musical Song (the song in question was 'Do Not Forsake Me Oh My Darlin'...' and was sung by Tex Ritter). In addition, it was nominated for three other Oscars, namely Fred Zinnemann for Best Director,[34] Stanley Kramer for Best Picture, and Carl Foreman for Best Writing of a Screenplay. *High Noon* also served as the launching pad for the film career of Grace Kelly, who played the role of Amy Fowler, a young Quaker who marries Marshal Kane at the beginning of the film. Filming took twenty-eight days, between 5 September and the weekend of 13–14 October 1951, with most of the scenes of the town of Hadleyville shot on the Warner Brothers studio lot in Burbank and the steam locomotive scenes in the town of Sonora some 300 miles north-east of Los Angeles.

One of the most intriguing features of the film is the fact that the screenplay was deliberately written to reflect the political situation of the time (or so Carl Foreman, the screenwriter, claims). The United States was caught up in the phenomenon of McCarthyism, dominated by the so-called 'Red Scare', with fears rife about Communist infiltration of American society. Nowhere was this more visible than in Hollywood, where the witch-hunt for Communist agents meant that many well-established actors, directors and producers were called before tribunals and had their careers cut short as a result of 'blacklisting'. Foreman was subpoenaed to appear before the House Un-American Activities Committee (HUAC), the government body set up to investigate the Communist infiltration of society. He used the events of the time as a backdrop for the screenplay, effectively working his own experience into the character of Will Kane.[35] The pressure was such that eventually Foreman himself abandoned Hollywood and moved to England where he continued as an active force within the world of the media.[36] He was appointed by Queen Elizabeth II an Honorary

34. For more on Zinnemann and the film, see Zinnemann 1952; 1992: 96-110; Giannetti 1981: 354-74; Phillips 1990: 109-124.

35. Behlmer (1989: 269-77) discusses this. Also see Biskind 1983: 44-49; Mitchell 1996: 191-93; Drummond 1997: 19, 37-38.

36. Foreman (1972) offers a sharp spoof of the HUAC activities surrounding the film in the form of a proposed remake.

Commander of the civil division of the Most Excellent Order of the British Empire in recognition of his contribution to the British film industry.

The reaction in some quarters of Hollywood to the film was positively vitriolic. One of the most celebrated reactions was from the actor John Wayne, who personified the myth of the American West on screen for so many years. In short, Wayne thought *High Noon* was an unmitigated disaster. He felt that it undermined all the values and principles that had made America great, and that decency and commitment were deliberately being mocked within the film, particularly in the final scenes where Will Kane throws his Marshal's star in the dust and walks away from an unsympathetic town.[37] Indeed, Wayne was so incensed by what he perceived to be the un-American message of the film that he made a 'corrective' to it, the film *Rio Bravo* (1959), directed by Howard Hanks.[38]

In the intervening years since *High Noon* was released, it has continued to engender a number of interesting political interpretations, both from the liberal left and the conservative right. For example, some have attempted to ground it in the concrete circumstances of the day, and have suggested that it was a political allegory about American involvement in the Korean War of 1950–53,[39] while others point out that the film is infinitely adaptable and can be made to fit virtually any historical or political scenario.

So what is it about *High Noon* that continues to captivate the interests of movie-goers and critics alike? The film has often been praised for its realism, the fact that it presents the central character Will Kane as a flesh-and-blood human being with doubts and weaknesses. In this sense *High Noon* challenges the myth of the invincibility of the Western hero.[40] This has meant that the film has become a focal point for postmodernist discussions about the ways in which cultural values and beliefs are challenged, overturned, and reconstructed. For example, in recent years *High Noon* has been investigated for what it has to say about male–female relationships, the role expectations of men and women, and the possibilities of misunderstanding that can take place between the sexes. This is made all the more sharp by the fact that *High Noon* portrays a high-principled but ageing and

37. See R.W. Lewis 1971: 90; Willis 1997: 273-79. Foreman (1974) has a hilarious assessment of John Wayne and his hypocritical reaction to *High Noon*. For Zinnemann's thoughts on Wayne's reaction, see Levy 1998.

38. R. Wood (1996: 87-89) compares the two films.

39. See P. French 1977: 35 for details.

40. A challenge which has been continued in the form of Clint Eastwood's Oscar-winning *Unforgiven* (1992).

over-the-hill lawman marrying a virginal but strong-minded Quaker. What will be the result when such an ideological clash takes place within a marriage? The film challenges its viewers to contemplate whether such a mismatch of personality and temperament can survive the maelstrom of marriage.[41] Before we move on to consider some of the specifically theological dimensions of the film, it is perhaps worthwhile to familiarize ourselves with the basic plot of the story.

The film is set in the 1860s, in the town of Hadleyville[42] within the territory of New Mexico. Hadleyville is a small community of about 650 people, most of whom are hard-working and decent folk. Hadleyville is on the verge of a new prosperity, brought in part by the railway line which runs through town. The Marshal of Hadleyville is a middle-aged man named Will Kane, but he has resigned his job in order to marry a local Quaker woman named Amy Fowler and start up a new life with her as a storekeeper in a neighbouring town. The story takes place on a Sunday morning, the day of the wedding between the middle-aged Kane and his young bride Amy. The joy of their wedding day is interrupted by the arrival of the master of the train station at the proceedings; he carries with him a telegram containing ominous news. It says that a notorious outlaw named Frank Miller is arriving on the noonday train. Miller had been sent to prison five years before for murder, and had vowed revenge upon Marshal Kane, the man responsible for his capture and conviction. Miller has been released from prison on parole and is now returning to Hadleyville to confront Kane. The stationmaster explains that Miller's brother Ben and two others, Jack Colby and James Pierce, are waiting at the station for the train to arrive. Meanwhile, Kane is persuaded by the friends at his wedding reception to take his bride Amy and leave town, before the trouble arrives (a new Marshal is scheduled to arrive the next day). The couple do so, riding out of town on a buckboard, but not very far out of the town limits Kane has a crisis of conscience, and explains to Amy that he has to return and face his responsibilities. His wife does not understand this and presents him with an ultimatum: he must choose between his responsibilities as Marshal and his role as husband. Her Quaker principles

41. For more along these lines see Warshow 1972; Mellen 1978: 228-31; R.B. Palmer 1984–85; Rapf 1990; Foster 1994; Mitchell 1996: 200-201; Drummond 1997: 73-81.

42. Mark Twain's short story 'The Man Who Corrupted Hadleyburg' (1900) provided inspiration for the name. Twain's story paints a picture of a small town which is filled with its own petty concerns and interests.

assert themselves and she says that if he returns to the town she will leave him on the noon train. Kane is thus faced with the difficult task of balancing what he perceives to be his duties to himself, his wife, and the community.[43]

Much of the film details how Kane goes about the town trying to elicit support in facing Frank Miller and his henchmen. Again and again throughout the film we see Kane asking people in the town to support him (some seventeen scenes in the film are built around this theme). Kane's deputy Harvey Pell abandons him and resigns his position, citing personal differences as his reason. There is a complex background to this resignation, including the fact that Pell's woman 'friend', the half-Mexican Helen Ramirez, was once Kane's lover. Pell wanted to succeed Kane as Marshal and had asked him for his support, but Kane refused; Pell thinks (wrongly) that this is due to jealousy over Helen Ramirez. In any event, Harvey Pell does not assist Kane in his hour of greatest need. Even Kane's long-term friend and predecessor as marshal, Matt Howe, whose hands are crippled with arthritis, begs off, saying that he would be a danger to Kane. The people of the town are unsympathetic and several different reasons for not standing by Kane in his hour of crisis are offered. In the end, Kane is left to face the four gunmen on his own, filled with trepidation and uncertainty about what to do.

The four gunmen advance on the town like the Four Horsemen of the Apocalypse, intent on bringing death and destruction to the representative of law and order. The only person to help Kane is his wife Amy, who hears the gunshots of the final shoot-out and returns from the train station on the outskirts of town. She too has a crisis of conscience which must be faced. Her Quaker principles of non-violence are tested to the limit as she shoots in the back one of the four gunmen (Frank Pierce) intent on killing her husband, before herself being taken hostage by the ringleader Frank Miller (Kane has already by this time dispatched Ben Miller and Jack Colby). In the final confrontation, Amy struggles free from the outlaw, scratching his face, and Kane is able to shoot him dead. The thankful townspeople then begin to gather in the main street, now that the gun battle has ended. They are faced with an exhausted and disillusioned Kane, who takes off his Marshal's badge and drops it into the dirt. He gathers

43. See Prince 1999 for a fine study on how Zinnemann's own sense of ethical decision-making is carried through in the interior drama that we see confronting Will Kane.

Amy into the buckboard and rides away, turning his back on the town which had refused to help him in the hour of his greatest need.

The action of the film is all directed towards this final confrontation at noon between Kane and the Miller gang. The frantic movement of Kane as he goes about the town trying to elicit support is contrasted with scenes of Ben Miller, Jack Colby and James Pierce waiting for the arrival of the noon train. The film builds to a fateful, timed clash between Kane and the Miller gang, offering an intriguing version of an apocalyptic confrontation between good and evil.

At an impressionistic level, there are several ways in which the story-line seems to parallel the biblical story of the life and ministry of Jesus Christ. For example, it seems clear that in the Gospel accounts Jesus is, at some level, in tension with the structures and institutions of the Judaism of his day, particularly the religious leaders. There are signs that Marshal Kane also fits rather uncomfortably within the world of which he is a part, the frontier town of Hadleyville. He is married by the Justice of the Peace in his office, rather than by the minister within the town church (at one point the pastor even admonishes him for his lack of attendance at worship services). His choice of a *Quaker* bride further illustrates his sense of alienation, as she is outside the religious orthodoxy of the town as a whole. In addition, both Kane and Jesus find themselves largely abandoned by their erstwhile supporters; indeed, it is only women who remain faithful and appear at the crucial moment, as illustrated by the women viewing the crucifixion from a distance and Amy's return from the train station. Similarly, a parallel could be drawn between Jesus' doubt-ridden anguish in the garden of Gethsemane and Kane in the marshal's office writing his last will and testament a few minutes before 12.00 noon, fully expecting that he will not survive what is about to take place.[44] The piercing whistle of the train as it arrives at noon can be likened to the cock-crow within the Gospel narratives, marking the transition to the confrontation itself.

Beyond that, the film contains several other interesting features which invite theological reflection. Three such theological 'snapshots' in particular are worth exploring briefly.

Invoking the Old Testament: Malachi 4 and 'Day of the Lord' Imagery. First, we consider the scene in which Kane enters the church and asks for

---

44. Drummond (1997: 52) remarks: 'Instead of identifying with our hero's actions, we identify with the chain of voiceless looks which mark his acceptance of rejection and denial'.

help from the congregation. This is an especially moving sequence, which Philip Drummond calls 'the moral centre of the film' (1997: 47). The minister of the church is speaking from the pulpit, announcing that the text for his sermon will be Malachi 4. He then begins to read v. 1 of the Authorized Version, part of the prophet's description of the apocalyptic Day of the Lord when the Lord of Hosts himself will come in judgment upon the people of Israel:

> For behold the day cometh that shall burn as an oven. And all the proud, yea, all that do wickedly, shall be stubble: and the day that cometh shall burn them up, saith the Lord of hosts, that it shall leave them neither root nor branch.

Although Marshal Kane enters the church and interrupts the reading, one cannot help but wonder if the viewers are intended to complete the passage in their minds. This is an especially interesting question, given that Malachi 4 concludes with a declaration about the sending of the prophet Elijah:

> Behold, I will send you Elijah the prophet before the great and terrible day of the Lord comes. And he will turn the hearts of fathers to their children and the hearts of children to their fathers, lest I come and smite the land with a curse (Mal. 4.5-6).

At one level we can view Kane as the Elijah figure, the one sent before the terrible time of judgment which is rapidly approaching in the form of the noon train. Insofar as he attempts to persuade the townspeople to help him face Frank Miller and his gang, Kane is turning the hearts of the fathers to their children and vice versa. He is trying to get them to face up to the responsibilities that they have to one another and avert the crisis which is about to befall them.

A Musical Counterpoint: Julia Ward Howe and 'The Battle Hymn of the Republic'. The celebrated hymn by Julia Ward Howe (1819–1910) entitled 'The Battle Hymn of the Republic' (1861) figures prominently at one point within the film. This occurs about a third of the way through the film, before Marshal Kane enters the church and asks for help in facing Miller and his gang. The church congregation is heard to sing:

> Mine eyes have seen the glory of the coming of the Lord,
> He is trampling out the vintage where the grapes of wrath are stored.
> He hath loosed the fateful lightning of his terrible swift sword,
> His truth is marching on!
> Glory, glory, Hallelujah! Glory, glory, Hallelujah!
> Glory, glory, Hallelujah! His truth is marching on!

He hath sounded forth the trumpet that shall never call retreat,
He is sifting out the hearts of men before his judgement seat...

The scene then cuts to the Marshal's office where Kane anxiously awaits the arrival of his deputies, those who will stand by him in the impending hour of crisis. The camera focuses on the clock in Kane's office; as its pendulum swings from side to side it is accompanied by a single repeated note in the soundtrack which matches the note on which the hymn itself ended.[45] This serves to link the idea of judgment contained in the hymn to the approach of high noon, inexorably advancing as we watch. Kane himself will never call retreat, for it is not in his character, and it is his heart, as well as the hearts of others within the town, that is being sifted before the judgment seat. Even more striking is the fact that the camera cuts away before the next line of the hymn is sung:

O be swift, my soul, to answer him; be jubilant my feet!

In a sense the trumpet has sounded and sure and certain judgment is coming, but despite the fact that they are singing about it, the members of the congregation are anything but on their feet in jubilation about what awaits them. Kane, in this regard, stands as something of a Christ-figure who calls the others to face judgment by his example; he is both sifted and sifter. Irony reigns supreme in this particular sequence.

Inverting the Eclipse: Timely Confrontation under a Cloudless Sky. One of the most intriguing ways in which the film might be said to echo the crucifixion narratives concerns its use of time. Thus, the crucial moment of confrontation between Marshal Kane and Frank Miller and his gang is set to take place at 12.00 noon,[46] precisely the time, within the Gospel narratives, at which the crucifixion of Jesus reaches a critical juncture and darkness descends upon the land.

The presentation of the passage of time within *High Noon* is one of the most frequently noted features of the film (see for example Combs 1986: 188). The film lasts a mere 84 minutes and this 'real time' is very nearly matched by the 'narrative time' of the story itself. Thus, one of the opening

45. Thus, C. Palmer (1990: 142) notes: 'Tiomkin intuitively realized that the film's thematic *idée fixe*—the deadly approach of "High Noon"—should be complemented and reinforced in the music'. For more on the Ukranian-born Tiomkin and his musical score for the film, see Darby and Du Bois 1990: 246-49.

46. Interestingly, this is a change from Cunningham's story 'The Tin Star', in which the train carrying the outlaw is said to arrive at 4.10 p.m.

scenes of the film is of the town church, its bell ringing for Sunday morning services at 10.30 a.m. The film moves inexorably towards the noon deadline, with the final gunfight lasting twelve minutes or so after the train arrives and Frank Miller and his gunmen enter the town. In other words, there are about 102 minutes of narrative time related through the 84 minutes of actual viewing time. Yet the temporal dimension is not straightforward, for the passage of time is compressed at some points in the story, while at others it is deliberately elongated. In the end the suspense of the film is heightened for the viewer as a result of these innovative uses of a chronological framework for the story. The inevitable confrontation between Kane and the Miller gang, the clash that is to come between good and evil, is marked again and again by scenes in which clocks appear and announce the passing of the minutes.[47] Virtually every major sequence up to the arrival of the noonday train contains a clock to help pace the narrative. There are clocks in the Marshal's office, in the barber's office, at the train station, in the hotel lobby, in Judge Mettrick's office, in Helen Ramirez's room, in the church, at Martin Howe's house, and in the saloon; each contributes to the viewer's perception of the approach of the decisive hour of judgment that is to take place at noon.

A second way in which *High Noon* could be said to parallel the drama of the crucifixion of Jesus as it is recorded in the Gospels, is in its use of light and dark photography. Not only was the film deliberately shot in black and white (at a time when the technological wonders of Cinemascope were being developed and the vast majority of movies were filmed in colour), but many of the scenes were deliberately shot in such a way as to reinforce the contrast between white and black, between light and darkness.

The film is visually striking, presenting a bleak view of life in the American West, with a cloudless sky serving to emphasize the flat and unrelenting landscape. Director Zinnemann explained the rationale behind this:

> We were very careful to omit all clouds in our outdoor shots. In most westerns, beautiful cloud formations are considered *de rigueur*. But we wanted to emphasize the flatness and emptiness of the land, and inertia of

---

47.   An even more overt chronological technique was used in a television episode from M*A*S*H from 1979–80 entitled 'Life Time'. It tells the story of a severely wounded soldier who arrives at the 4077th MASH hospital and needs surgery within 20 minutes if he is to survive and not be paralysed. A real-time clock is superimposed on the screen throughout the episode as a means of heightening the audience's sense of the passage of critical minutes.

everybody and everything. To contrast all that with the movements of the Marshal, we dressed Gary Cooper all in black, so that when his lonely figure issued forth into the stark, bright stillness his destiny seemed even more poignant.[48]

It is as if *High Noon* presents us with a cinematic equivalent of an eclipse in reverse. Here the normal perceptions of light and darkness in an eclipse are deliberately inverted. Instead of an eclipsed sun, seemingly standing still, plunging the landscape into utter darkness, we have a darkened (movie) star, constantly in frantic motion, viewed against the backdrop of a cloudless sky and the brilliantly illuminated streets of the town. This is altogether different in the recent remake of *High Noon,* a colourized version of the film which has lost sight of the black-and-white contrast that was so visually effective.

Rod Hardy's High Noon *(2000)*
The Turner Broadcasting Superstation (TBS) first aired a remake of Zinnemann's *High Noon* in the USA during August 2000. This made-for-television film was directed by Rod Hardy, a director whose main work has concentrated on episodes within established television series. The film stars Tom Skerritt in the role of Marshal Will Kane, Suzanna Thompson as Amy Kane, Reed Diamond as Harvey Pell, Maria Conchito Alonso as Helen Ramirez, and Michael Madsen as Frank Miller. One obvious difference between the original film by Zinnemann and this remake is the fact that the theme song, 'Do Not Forsake Me Oh My Darlin'...', is missing, immediately noticeable to sharp-eared lovers of the 1952 classic.[49] Sadly, this means that one of the connective threads of the overall story line is lost.

In any event, there is a great deal of continuity between this version of the story and that of Zinnemann from 1952, something which is no doubt due in part to the fact that Carl Foreman, who wrote the screenplay for the Zinnemann film, also helped produce the teleplay for this film, along with T.S. Cook. Most of the features of Zinnemann's *High Noon* that made it so memorable are found here, including the desperate attempt by Kane to find

48. Cited in J.H. Reid 1967: 8. Zinnemann is also on record as stating that his intention was to make the film 'look like a documentary, or a newsreel from the period of the 1880s' (see Levy 1998: 173 for this remark). Also see Drummond 1997: 35; Prince 1999: 83-84.
49. Bobbin (2000: 37) reports that the film's producers could not secure the rights to the song for the remake.

support in facing the gunman Miller who is returning on the noon train to wreak his revenge, and the clash of moral values between the duty-driven Kane and his pacifist wife Amy who does her best to uphold her Quaker values. Much more is made of the love-relationships between the principal characters, however, especially that between Will Kane and Helen Ramirez, than was found in the original film. At one point Helen even declares that she still loves the Marshal and asks him to run away from the upcoming confrontation, despite the fact that Kane has only that morning married his Quaker wife Amy. One gets the impression that the film was attempting to pad out a paucity of ideas by injecting romance and sexual intrigue into the story-line.

The attention to the passage of real time, supported by shots of clock faces at critical moments in the story-line, is carried through within the film, although not nearly as deliberately or effectively as in the original. In fact there are seven scenes in which the time of the day is referred to, beginning with a scene at the train station in which the time is given as 11.42 a.m. and including a scene in the Marshal's office as he writes his last will and testament under a loudly ticking clock which shows the time to be 11.57 a.m. In some respects the use made of the timepieces is something of a disappointment, and the slow but relentless build-up to the showdown at noon is not reinforced by shots of the clocks as was the case in Zinnemann's film. The closest thing that we get to such a visual pacing occurs as the noon train whistle blows and we are presented with a montage of images of various scenes and characters in the film all set against a superimposed swinging pendulum. Scenes of Will Kane, Amy Kane and Helen Ramirez, in particular, are all shown in this fast-flowing montage. However, in an attempt (apparently) to compensate for this lack of a visual motif to communicate dramatic power, the film does make one very significant departure from Zinnemann's original. This comes in the form of 'upping the ante' in terms of the number of gunmen that Kane has to face alone. As I noted above, in Zinnemann's film Frank Miller is assisted by three of his buddies, and Kane is forced to face a total of *four* gunmen. However, much more is demanded of the modern Hollywood hero and it is perhaps not altogether surprising to find that in this version of the story Kane has to face a gang of *six* (Miller has rounded up two more buddies while on the train!). This may all be an excellent way to raise the body-count in the film, but it does mean that the associated imagery of Frank Miller and his gang as the Four Horsemen of the Apocalypse is broken. Still, the numbers may have changed but the eventual outcome is the same, with good triumphing over evil. Thus, the film concludes (as did Zinnemann's telling of the tale) with a scene in which Kane climbs into the wagon with his bride, removes his Marshal's badge and throws it into the mud, turning his back on an ungrateful town.

I noted above in my discussion of Zinnemann's film the significance of the singing of Julia Ward Howe's 'The Battle Hymn of the Republic'. Hardy's remake does not include a scene in which the members of the town church are heard singing this hymn. In its place a section of another hymn is sung, namely the well-known 'Rock of Ages' by Augustus Toplady (1740–1778). The congregational singing occurs earlier in the film, however, and sets up a meeting between Helen Ramirez and her business partners (who are inside the church and need to be beckoned outside). As Ramirez moves to sell out her share in the town businesses (at a knock-down price!), we hear the congregation singing:

> Let the water and the blood,
> From Thy wounded side which flowed,
> Be of sin the double-cure,
> Save from wrath and make me pure.

The point here is that the hymn is *not* connected to Kane's request to the congregation for assistance as it was in Zinnemann's film, although it is possible to see the hymn as somehow connected with Kane himself. He is, after all, the one who saves the town from wrath and he is, as the gunfight with Miller's gang will prove, wounded in the side in the process. To what extent the town has been made pure as a result is anyone's guess, although it has at least been purged of the immediate evil.

Mention should also be made of the presentation of the scene in which Kane enters the town church and asks for help. As I noted above, in Zinnemann's film this is connected to Old Testament imagery involving Malachi 4 and prophecies concerning the Day of the Lord. In Hardy's film, in contrast, it is the figure of Jonah who is so invoked. The sequence opens with the minister of the church preaching and relating the essence of the story of Jonah, as found in Jon. 1.4a, 7. The preacher regales his congregation in a mild Scottish accent:

> But the Lord hurled a great wind upon the sea. And the sailors said to one another, 'Let us cast lots that we may know who brought this calamity upon us'. And so they cast. And the lot fell to Jonah.

It is precisely at this moment that Marshal Kane enters the church. Effectively, he is equated with the figure of Jonah in that he has brought calamity upon the town just as Jonah did upon the ship heading to Tarshish. What is most interesting about this use of Jonah is the way in which it forms a juxtaposition with the use made of Malachi 4 in Zinnemannn's film. In one version Will Kane is the embodiment of Elijah, exhorting the people to face the judgment that is on the horizon; in the other he is the embodiment of Jonah, the person who is blamed for the horrors that are soon to appear.

One other minor detail about the remake of *High Noon* is also worth mentioning, insofar it serves to emphasize a motif deliberately made prominent in Zinnemann's original film. This concerns the use of a brilliantly lit town, set against a cloudless sky, to help communicate the notion of an impending collision of the forces of good and evil at 12.00 noon. There is little of such imagery in Hardy's film and much of the scenery is of an overcast sky, or of distant cloud formations. No doubt this is to be explained in part by the fact that the 19-day shoot was done on location in Calgary, Alberta, which is a far cry from the desert-like conditions of southern California in which Zinnemann worked. However, one could argue that the ominous clouds of the Canadian sky are used to precisely the same effect, for at one point in the film they serve to portend the clash between Kane and Miller's gang. This occurs early on in the film as Marshal Kane and his bride are riding out of Hadleyville just after hearing that Miller is returning on the noon train. Kane stops the buggy and engages in an argument with Amy about whether or not he can run away from his responsibilities. In exasperation she says to him, 'You know there will be trouble!' At precisely this moment the camera pulls back and we are presented with a midday sun framed by gathering storm clouds. It is an ominous warning of what is to come, although one can hardly be assured that the imagery was intentional.

We turn now to consider the third of our films, which presents a science-fiction version of an apocalyptic confrontation at a decisive hour. This is generally regarded as a futuristic version of Zinnemann's film—*High Noon* set in space, as it were.

Peter Hyams' Outland *(1981)*

Director Peter Hyams came to the film *Outland* after having established himself as a figure of some weight within the genre of science fiction. His film *Capricorn One* (1978) was a considerable success and helped pave the way for *Outland*, which was acknowledged by Hyams to be a space version of the Western *High Noon* from the outset (Hyams helped write the screenplay for the film as well as directing it). *Outland* has an accomplished cast and stars Sean Connery as Marshal O'Niel, Peter Boyle as Sheppard, Frances Sternhagen as Dr Lazarus, James Sikking as Sergeant Montone, Steven Berkoff as Sagan, and Kika Markham as Carol O'Niel. The film was shot in Pinewood Studios in London, although the shooting schedule was made difficult by Connery's need to fly in and out of the country to avoid the expensive British tax laws.[50] The film did moderately well in the box office, but was not well received by critics. It did, however, receive an Academy Award Nomination for Best Sound.

The plot of *Outland* is quite simple and it is primarily narrated through the perspective of the central character Marshal William T. O'Niel. O'Niel has been assigned by the Federal Security Service as the chief law enforcement officer at a mining installation located on Io, the third moon of the planet Jupiter. He represents law and order in this mining station, a kind of frontier town on the outskirts of civilization; the station has 2144 inhabitants and the tour of duty for personnel is one year. The installation is franchised by the League of Industrial Nations to an earth-based company named Con-Amalgamate, and the General Manager for the mining station (Number 27) is named Sheppard. O'Niel is accompanied on his one-year tour of duty by his wife Carol and their young son Paul. As the film opens we learn that Marshal O'Niel and his family have been at the mining station for two weeks. However, it soon becomes clear that all is not well within the O'Niel household and Carol takes the son and leaves surreptitiously on the weekly transport shuttle. Carol relates her reasons in a videotape 'dear John' message to her husband: she loves him but cannot abide the situation any longer. She cannot bear to see the boy grow up in an oppressive environment like Con-Am 27 and therefore makes arrangements to take him to Earth.

Con-Am 27 is a rough-and-tumble world where the miners are rewarded with financial bonuses for the amount of titanium they produce, and the executives of the company do not care what the human cost is as long as production rates continue to rise and profits come pouring in. There are company prostitutes to keep the miners pacified, and much of the off-duty time is spent drinking and smoking in the Leisure Club, a space-age disco complete with live sexual acts performing on stage under azure lighting. Clearly this is a seedy and soulless world where it is difficult to find anything of nobility and worth. The General Manager Sheppard has

50. On this point see Callan 1993: 220-22; Parker 1993: 213-15; Yule 1993: 236-39.

engineered a scheme whereby an illegal amphetamine, polydichloric-euthinal, is being smuggled into the station and distributed to the miners. It stimulates them to work like demons, doing fourteen hours of work in a mere six hours; unfortunately, after about nine months or so of use the drug begins to affect mental health and the miners become psychopathic, their behaviour becoming violent and unpredictable. Several miners have been killed as a result of such amphetamine abuse, a situation which puts Marshal O'Niel on the trail of the illegal drug trade. O'Niel manages to commandeer and destroy a shipment of amphetamine (which comes in the form of a red injectable liquid), thus setting up a clash of wills between himself and Sheppard.

For his part, Sheppard hires two professional hit-men to eliminate O'Niel so that the lucrative traffic of drugs can continue and the business arrangements of the mining station return to normal. The assassins are due to arrive on Sunday, as passengers on the weekly shuttle from the nearest space station. O'Niel learns that the assassins are on their way and tries to find support among the inhabitants of the mining station. However, the vast majority of the people have a vested interest in Sheppard's scheme of enhanced production and are unwilling to help O'Niel face the gunmen who are arriving on the shuttle. He is isolated and alone, having been abandoned by his wife, and unable to rely on any of the dozen or so law officers under his command. O'Niel does get limited assistance from one of his fellow officers, namely Sergeant Montone, but Montone has already compromised himself to a certain degree by accepting bribes from Sheppard to turn a blind eye to the drug-trafficking. In fact, Montone is himself strangled by one of Sheppard's henchmen on the station, but not before managing to convey to O'Niel an important clue about the drug-smuggling operation. In the end, the only person on the mining station who gives O'Niel any substantial support is the middle-aged medical doctor named Lazarus. Dr Lazarus is crotchety and self-opinionated, with something of a dubious reputation herself, but she is game to lend her weight to anything and anyone willing to challenge the system. Inevitably, the film moves to its climax as the Sunday shuttle arrives bearing the two assassins and O'Niel faces them in a deadly cat-and-mouse showdown through the corridors and passageways of the mining station. In the end, O'Niel survives the attempts on his life (with the assistance of Dr Lazarus), and exposes the evil General Manager Sheppard as the scheming bastard he is, leaving the retribution of the drug-traffickers and the corporate bosses to get what is coming to them. O'Niel is then free to turn his back on the corruption of the mining station, forsaking it for his wife and son as they rendezvous and travel back home to earth. The family is intact once again and right is seen to have prevailed in the face of corruption.

There are many little touches within the film which show the reliance upon the Western film genre in general, and on *High Noon* in particular.[51] For example, the Marshal's office has a set of double-swinging doors so beloved in the depiction of saloons within countless Westerns. It is easy to overlook the fact that both the Marshal of Hadleyville and the Marshal of Con-Am 27 share the same first name—William. It also seems beyond coincidence that the miner who, driven crazy by the amphetamines he has been taking, kills himself by entering an airlock without a pressurized suit is named *Cane*. Clearly this is a subtle allusion to Marshal Kane in *High Noon*. There is also a brief scene in which O'Niel enters the canteen and announces to everyone eating there, 'I could use a little help'. This is an equivalent to the scene in *High Noon* where Marshal Kane enters the church and asks for assistance. Last, but not least, in the closing scenes of the film we see O'Niel in his quarters preparing to leave the mining station and meet up with his wife and son. What is striking here, however, is the way that O'Niel is dressed. He is wearing civilian clothes, having abandoned his blue uniform and its shiny-gold Marshal's badge. For virtually the whole of the film O'Niel is seen wearing his uniform along with the large badge, prominently displayed on his chest (the only exception is when he is in the handball court wearing a sweat-suit). Yet here he is presented out of uniform, as if he has quit his job as Marshal and turned his back on Con-Am 27 and its ungrateful inhabitants. This is the equivalent to the famous scene at the end of *High Noon* where Marshal Kane throws his tin star in the dust and walks away from the townspeople of Hadleyville.

In addition to these rather obvious parallels between *Outland* and *High Noon*, there are several other interesting correspondences worth noting. Above I suggested that *High Noon* has a scene in which the fragility and uncertainty of Marshal Kane are portrayed—a parallel, as it were, to Jesus' episode in the garden of Gethsemane just before his betrayal. This is the scene in *High Noon* where Will Kane sits at the desk in his office writing

---

51. Not all critics agree that *High Noon* has been successfully transported into a space-age setting within *Outland*. Thus, Kael (1987: 219) remarks: 'Hyams is like a guy who saw *High Noon* and didn't get it. It's insane that the workers refuse to help O'Niel—that they don't mind being killed off. The picture would have much more point if it had jettisoned the Western-in-space idea and had one of the miners as the hero who discovered how the company is speeding them to death'.

his last will and testament just as the clock hands come up to mark the twelfth hour. Here as nowhere else we see the doubts and fears of the Marshal rise to the surface. *Outland* has an equivalent scene which takes place in the privacy of a handball court where Marshal O'Niel has been playing a solitary game to pass the hours before the arrival of the Sunday shuttle. Dr Lazarus joins him and seats herself on the floor. After some introductory pleasantries, she engages him in conversation about why he is pursuing the course of action that he is. We catch a glimpse of O'Niel's doubts and self-questioning in the following exchange:

> Lazarus: You know, if you're the kind of guy you're supposed to be, you wouldn't stick around. That's why they sent you here.
> O'Niel: Maybe they made a mistake.
> Lazarus: I was afraid you'd say something like that. Do you *really* think you're making a difference?
> O'Niel: *[Shrugs in a gesture of doubt.]*
> Lazarus: Then *why*, for God's sake?
> O'Niel: Because…maybe they are right. They send me here to this pile of shit because they think I belong here. I want to find out if…well, if they're right. There's a whole machine that works because everybody does what they're supposed to. I found out I was supposed to be something I didn't like. That's what's in the programme. That's my rotten little part in the rotten machine. I don't like it. So…I'm going to find out if they're right.

Another intriguing correspondence has to do with the way that the confrontation between the forces of good and the forces of evil is presented in the two films. There are two specific ways in which *Outland* heightens the confrontation that must take place between Marshal O'Niel and Sheppard and his cronies. Each of them in its own way is an advance upon the story in *High Noon*; each takes an established motif and moves it in a new direction or gives it a new angle.

The Fourfold Threat is Defeated. First, we consider the way in which the conflict between good and evil is presented within the film, particularly as it involves a confrontation between Marshal O'Niel and those who set out to kill him. As in *High Noon* the Marshal must face four figures who plot together to kill him. In this case, however, the four are not all so easily identified, nor are they seen as moving against the Marshal as a unit. Two of the four are hired assassins who arrive in the shuttle and enter the mining station, splitting up as they begin to hunt Marshal O'Niel. This means that the danger they present is heightened and the marshal must fight on two fronts, picking them off one by one as and when the opportunity arises. The ring-leader of the four (the equivalent of Frank Miller within the film) is, of course, Sheppard, the General Manager of Con-Am 27. It is he who has hired the two professional hit-men to kill O'Niel, and it is the arrival of these two assassins on the shuttle which gives the film its race-against-the-clock feel. Sheppard also has a further accomplice, a fourth man on the inside of the mining station, whom Marshal O'Niel must also discover and face. In a nice twist to the story the fourth 'hidden' assassin is a member of O'Niel's own staff, Ballard, a young officer newly promoted to the rank of sergeant following the murder of sergeant Montone. Within the story-line Ballard functions as something of a Judas-figure, a member (allegedly) of the Marshal's own group of disciple-deputies. In some ways he represents the greatest threat, because O'Niel assumes that his opposition is not going to come from one of his inner band. This makes Ballard's betrayal all the more menacing as a result.

The final confrontation between Marshal O'Niel and Sheppard himself is something of an anti-climax, given all the spacesuit acrobatics that we have witnessed with regard to the dispatching of the other three men. When, much to everyone's disbelief, O'Niel returns to the Leisure Club and proves to all concerned that he has managed to 'beat the system' and overcome the threat when the odds were stacked against him, we feel that there is an element of justice in operation. And when O'Niel hits Sheppard in the face and knocks him to the ground we may find ourselves wishing for a greater punishment to be inflicted upon the corrupt general manager. However, we must not forget that Sheppard's own corporate bosses had warned him that if his plan to eliminate the Marshal failed, the next person they were going to come looking for was Sheppard himself. In this sense, the moment that Marshal O'Niel entered the Leisure Club, he signed Sheppard's death warrant. Justice has been served and the supreme embodiment of evil within the film (Sheppard) has been defeated.

The Arrival of the Sunday Shuttle: The Acceleration of Time. Secondly, we note the way in which the timing of the clash between Marshal O'Niel and Sheppard's gunmen is handled within the film. I noted above how the crucifixion of Jesus is set against a chronological framework within the Gospel narratives, a framework which makes 12.00 noon a decisive moment within God's apocalyptic timetable. I also noted how Fred Zinnemann paces the film *High Noon* in such a way as to emphasize again and again the confrontation that will take place at 12.00 noon between Marshal Kane and Frank Miller and his gang. In particular, I noted how *High Noon* creatively uses real time as a near equivalent to narrative time and thereby heightens the impact of the confrontation between good and evil. How does this compare to what Peter Hyams achieves in *Outland*?

Several things are worth noting in this regard. It is clear that the elapsed 'real time' of the film does not correspond to the narrative time of the story-line; in fact the story of the film takes place over several days, if not weeks. However, there are nevertheless some very interesting ways in which the film attempts to create an atmosphere of anticipated confrontation. More to the point, this expected conflict is set within a deliberate chronological framework. Two examples of this come to mind. The first concerns a sequence early in the film where one of the miners, a man named Sagan, takes a dose of the amphetamine and goes berserk. He takes one of the company prostitutes to a leisure compartment and locks himself in with her, threatening her with a knife. An emergency call is made to Marshal O'Niel and he arrives on the scene to find several other law officers anxiously waiting outside wondering how to proceed. O'Niel orders one of his fellow officers, Sergeant Montone, to climb up an air shaft and find a way into the compartment from above. He also gets a maintenance worker with equipment to force open the locks on the room. O'Niel then speaks to the miner through the door and tells him that he is going to force open the door and enter, but that if the miner remains calm and does not hurt the prostitute, he will not be harmed. What is interesting about this sequence is the way in which O'Niel invokes a ten-second countdown before the co-ordinated activity to break into the room is to commence. The camera cuts from scene to scene, inside and outside the compartment, as we hear the ten seconds counted down by O'Niel. The climax of the sequence has Montone drop through the ventilator shaft into the room and shoot the miner dead just as the door to the room is opening and O'Niel enters. The overall effect is to create within the viewer an expectation of a violent and deadly outcome, particularly at the end of a countdown in time. This ten-second countdown thus serves as a brilliant preview of the much more elaborate and extended countdown marking the arrival of the shuttle from the space station.

The time of the arrival of the shuttle is marked by large digital clocks scattered around the mining station (these are the equivalent of the ticking clocks so prominent within *High Noon*). The digital clocks count down the hours, minutes and seconds which remain until the shuttle is scheduled to arrive. In all there are nine shots of these clocks at various points in the countdown. The first we see is one found in the Leisure Club, and it shows that there remains a little over 60 hours before the shuttle is to arrive. We see others at various points of the story as O'Niel tries to prepare his defences, arranging surveillance cameras to track the killers, planting extra weapons in hiding places, and so on. We see clocks announcing 50 hours, 40 hours and 17 minutes, 20 hours, 10 hours, 9 hours and 37 minutes, 1 hour and 32 minutes, 1 hour and 6 minutes, and finally a mere 42 minutes. At this point the film takes an unusual turn. We have been led to believe that the confrontation is following a strict timetable, one that will take place when the shuttle arrives, a moment which digital clocks are relentlessly counting down for us with unerring accuracy. And then, quite unexpectedly, the digital clock suddenly ceases to count time and announces that the shuttle has arrived sooner than expected. A flashing red light proclaims 'Early', and a loud klaxon begins to sound (just as the piercing train whistle signalled the arrival of Frank Miller in *High Noon*). The effect of this is to make the viewer feel as if time to prepare has been stolen from Marshal O'Niel (and the viewer!). The pace increases dramatically and the moment of confrontation is cruelly, but effectively, accelerated. Just as Luke's account of the timing of the crucifixion of Jesus is somewhat vague ('it was now *about* the sixth hour' [Lk. 22.44a]), here the digital clocks are shown to be imprecise. We have been led to believe that they will mark the exact moment of confrontation, but human timepieces prove to be inaccurate measuring devices of apocalyptic moments of confrontation.

Conclusion

I began this chapter by noting that the crucifixion of Jesus is presented as a decisive moment of apocalyptic confrontation within the Gospel accounts. I also observed that one of the ways in which this is highlighted is through the use of the motif of 'darkness at noon', particularly as a means of presenting Jesus' death as taking place within a strict chronological timetable. Within the Gospel of Luke this 'darkness at noon' motif is amplified by means of an unusual expression in Lk. 23.45a (καὶ ἐσκοτίσθη ὁ ἥλιος) which is commonly taken to be a reference to a solar eclipse. I surveyed some of the scholarly discussion about this curious expression and concluded that it is an important feature of Luke's aim of presenting Jesus' death as the critical moment when good confronts evil. Thus, the case was made that the Lukan eclipse stands as a theological metaphor of considerable ingenuity and power.

Having established this as a pattern for the crucifixion narratives I then turned to consider the films *High Noon* (two versions) and *Outland*, and noted how each of them presents a clash between good and evil deliberately set against a chronological timetable. I noted how themes and images contained within the story of the passion and death of Christ are picked up and developed within both films. I also noted some of the points of similarity and divergence between the films themselves.

In the end, the chapter suggests that there is a common thread running through four very different creative works, namely the Gospel of Luke, Fred Zinnemann's *High Noon*, Rod Hardy's remake of *High Noon*, and Peter Hyams' *Outland*. In each of them we find a figure of tremendous courage and integrity, who risks his life to confront the evil of his day. Several things unite Jesus, Marshal Kane and Marshal O'Niel and make them appear not only to be men cut of the same cloth, but men whose destinies have been cast under the same star. For one thing, each has been rejected by the very people they have been trying to help. Thus, all three face the decisive moment of confrontation essentially alone, forsaken by the male colleagues who should have stood by them, and dependent instead upon the help of female supporters who offer assistance at the critical hour of need. Similarly, each of the three heroes is shown to wrestle with fears and doubts about his actions, to question in some way whether what he is doing is the correct way to proceed. Each has a 'Gethsemane experience', so to speak, a crisis of confidence in which the very depths of the soul have to be examined, motives assessed, and the right course of action decided.

At one level we might be tempted to think that the points of commonality are simply necessary components of good drama. On the other hand, we may see them as essential elements in any apocalyptic encounter between the forces of good and evil. In any event, the films *High Noon* and *Outland* provide us with wonderful opportunities to consider afresh the significance of the crucifixion of Jesus Christ which took place at the sixth hour, when the sun was darkened, and something wonderful, beyond the limits of human comprehension, happened within the life of the cosmos.

Chapter 4

THE HANDMAID'S TALE: 'BLESSED ARE THE SILENT'

Margaret Atwood is one of Canada's most respected and talented writers, having distinguished herself first as a poet, then as a novelist and writer of children's books. As a novelist she exhibits an extraordinary range in her work, producing works of science fiction, spy thrillers, Gothic romance, Graeco-Roman myth, and fairy tales.[1] *The Handmaid's Tale*[2] is her sixth novel, in which we see Atwood's well-known interest in political matters combine with her considerable skill as a story-teller.[3] The work quickly became a best-seller and was greeted with a great deal of critical acclaim. It was shortlisted for the Booker Prize in Great Britain,[4] while in Canada it won the General Governor's Prize (Atwood's second award), and in the USA it was the first recipient of the Arthur C. Clarke Science Fiction Prize. It was even nominated for Book of the Year for 1986 by *Time* magazine. In short, *The Handmaid's Tale* holds an enviable place as a poststructuralist feminist work of science fiction and has been widely discussed on this basis.[5] Given all of these dimensions of *The Handmaid's Tale* it is easy to

1.   Atwood discusses her wide interest in literature, including Gothic novels and Grimm's fairy-tales, in a number of published interviews. See Atwood (1996: 46-48, 70-71, 114-15, 147, 152-54). Also see Cooke 1998: 24-26.

2.   The book was first published in Canada by McClelland and Stewart in 1985. Houghton Mifflin in the United States and Jonathan Cape in Great Britain followed suit in 1986. References are to the 1996 Vintage edition throughout.

3.   Fullbrook 1990: 171-93 is a convenient place to see these concerns set out. Howells 1996: 126-47 also contains a good discussion.

4.   The prize was won by Kingsley Amis for *The Old Devils*.

5.   Roberts (1990) offers a good introduction to this. He states (136): 'Drawing on new deconstructive theories about language and paradox, feminist SF writers use both SF concepts and recent cultural theory to challenge patriarchal assumptions'. Roberts discusses Atwood's *The Handmaid's Tale* along with the works of several other female science-fiction writers, notably Ursula LeGuin's *Always Coming Home* (1985). Fitting (1989) is also worth consulting, especially in that he suggests that Atwood's novel is

understand why it is perhaps Atwood's most popular work, and has served as a set text in many schools, colleges and university courses.[6]

The novel has been discussed as a good demonstration of the close connection between fiction and autobiography.[7] Most of Atwood's fiction revolves around imaginative reconstructions of women's lives, with all the inherent trials and vagaries, gaps and misreadings, that memory involves in such matters; *The Handmaid's Tale* is no exception in this regard. The novel deals in a highly creative manner with feminist issues, the relationships between the sexes, and with matters of motherhood and parenting.[8] The fact that the story purports to be based upon the manuscripts of a female character, transcribed and collated through a male academician, raises some interesting questions as to the relationship that the novel has to the epistolary tradition, especially as it suggests that patriarchial attitudes and assumptions control and suppress the voices of women.[9] Various levels of narrative time are creatively interwoven within the story, a feature that adds to the complexity and richness of the story.[10] The shift between the singular and plural 'you' addressed by the narrator in *The Handmaid's Tale* is also a much-discussed feature of Atwood's narrative style.[11]

Structurally, the story is divided into three parts: a one-page Prologue containing three epigrams, 15 numbered sections containing 46 chapters, and a 13-page Epilogue entitled 'Historical Notes'. Seven of the sections in the body of the work are entitled 'Night', for it is in these portions that the central character/narrator, the 33-year-old Offred, gives us her private thoughts and recollections, formed during the only time when she is not

one that helped to mark the end of feminist utopian writing so prevalent in the 1970s. In a slightly different vein, Coupe (1997: 193) describes *The Handmaid's Tale* as 'a mythopoetic novel'.

6. Howells (1998) and Langdon (1998) have produced student 'A-level' study guides to the work. O'Keeffe 1993 contains some interesting observations about teaching the novel to teenagers at a boys' boarding school.

7. Givner 1992: 58-62. Grace (1994) discusses the way in which gender informs autobiography within Atwood's fiction.

8. Palmer (1989: 105-107) offers a helpful introduction along these lines.

9. Kauffman (1989) discusses the tension between 'feminine speech and masculine writing' which the novel embodies. Also see Hutcheon 1988: 156-57.

10. LeBihan (1991: 97) suggests there are four main narrative time strands.

11. See Givner 1992: 71-74 for details. Deer (1992) offers another interesting study, which focuses on the clash between the skill of the story's narrator and the powerlessness of the central character Offred whose voice is being narrated. He notes (225): 'It is as if Atwood's skill as a storyteller keeps possessing her creation of Offred'.

under observation by others (LeBihan 1991: 105). Atwood's affinity for fairy-tales is evident throughout the story, causing one critic to note how the Handmaid Offred and her partner Ofglen, dressed in the red costumes appropriate to their position in society, often travel together to market 'like Red Riding Hood twins'.[12] The Gothic dimensions of the story are frequently identified as another way in which the novel blends a number of formal genres, crossing literary boundaries as the story proceeds (Banerjee 1990: 83-85).

However, it is the religious dimensions of *The Handmaid's Tale* that will concern us here, notably the way in which the novel uses both Old and New Testament imagery. In particular, we will note how the novel, as well as the recent adaptations of the story for film and radio, adapts the words of Jesus in order to present a vision of a futuristic, sci-fi world known as the Republic of Gilead.

The Republic of Gilead: A Christian Fundamentalistic State Gone Awry

The novel, which is set in the not-too-distant future in the Republic of Gilead (a loose cipher for the northeastern part of the United States), is sometimes considered as a critique of American feminism (Hengen 1989: 23). More frequently it has been described as 'a dystopian version of gender relations',[13] as a novel demonstrating 'the corrupting force of institutional Christianity' (Workman 1989: 23), or (with due recognition of the scriptural undertones of the narrative), as a novel portraying a 'terrorist Biblical Patriarchiate in what was once the United States' (Larson 1989: 34). One influential reading of the novel has noted the importance of satire

---

12. Armitt 2000: 211. Also see Banerjee 1990: 83-84 for a discussion of the costuming of the Handmaids as a parody of the fairy-tale of Little Red Riding Hood (the parallel is also drawn by Cowart [1989: 112-14]). Others note the parallels to the fairy-tale of Cinderella, or the Princess awakened by a kiss from the Prince, or Rapunzel, imprisoned in a tower and awaiting her Rescuer (see Bartkowski [1989: 151]; Miner 1991: 165-66; Parrinder 1986: 20). Still others have noted the similarity between Offred and the character of Scheherazade in *The Tales of the Arabian Nights* (see K.F. Stein 1991–92: 269, 276-78 for more along these lines).

13. Lacombe 1986: 8. For more on the dystopian nature of the story, see Malak 1987; Nischik 1987; Kane 1988; Bartkowski 1989: 132-35, 144-58; Ferns 1989; D. Jones 1989; Ketterer 1989; 1992: 147-54; P.D. Murphy 1990; K.F. Stein 1991–92; Coupe 1997: 191-92. Stableford (1987: 97) describes the work as a Book of Lamentations, as opposed to a dystopia.

within the story-line, pointing out that '*Handmaid* boasts what is perhaps the most crucial element of satiric writing, namely, the clear existence of a topical political target, which here is very obviously evangelical Christian fundamentalism'.[14]

In order to spin her tale of a nightmarish future, Atwood creates a scenario which is fairly believable as a vision of the not-too-distant future; this is one of the novel's greatest strengths.[15] Rather than creating a fantasy universe with tangential connections to the world in which we live, Atwood builds upon life as we now experience it, effectively combining what *is* with what *might well be*. She extrapolates from present social tensions and pressures in society, from religious trends and the rise of Christian fundamentalism,[16] from technological expertise and scientific possibilities, to consider how these various forces might come together in a crisis situation and produce an alternative society—the Republic of Gilead. The trigger for the rise of Gilead is thus multifaceted, as we learn bit by bit through the course of the novel. In the words of Victoria Glendinning, 'The reader, mystified at first, picks up what has happened in the world through cracks in the narrative' (1986: 40).

The story postulates that, politically, a power vacuum was created when the President of the United States was assassinated along with most of the members of Congress. In terms of sexuality, the rise of AIDS, together with the appearance of a drug-resistant strain of syphilis and the effects of the use of Agent Orange in Vietnam, meant that the sexual freedom previously enjoyed became positively dangerous. Falling birth-rates brought on by ecological mismanagement, along with an increase in the use of contraception and the practice of abortion, meant that the reproduction level needed to sustain a healthy society was not maintained. Sterility was rife, both in males and females.

14.   Hammer 1990: 39. Also see Keith 1987: 124-26, Foley 1989 and Kaler 1989 on the subject of satire within the novel.

15.   This is not to say that the novel is without its critics as to its historical realism. See Banerjee 1990: 77-80 for a helpful discussion as to the weaknesses in the work, particularly its premise that Christian fundamentalism could lead to a theocracy in the United States. McCarthy (1986: 1, 35), Ehrenreich (1986: 34), and Slonczewski (1986: 122) voice similar reservations about the novel. Ketterer (1989: 215-16) and Hammer (1990: 46) offer something of a rebuttal to such negative criticism.

16.   Miles (1996: 94-103) specifically discusses how Atwood's novel addresses the question of Christian fundamentalism. In Atwood's own words, 'A new regime would not say, "We're fascist". They would say that they were serving God' (cited in C.N. Davidson 1986: 24).

In response, the Republic of Gilead creates a patriarchal system in which key male leaders, known as Commanders, take charge and seek to address the scourge of sterility (always attributing it to the woman in any childless marriage). Most importantly, the resultant system involves Handmaids as the reproductive agents for the preservation of the society. In short, Gilead is essentially a male-dominated society wherein women with viable ovaries are stripped of their identity, dehumanized, and made the private domain of the top-rank males of the society, the Commanders. 'Handmaids' are therefore women who are reduced to their biological function; they are walking wombs, muted breeders for a new society.[17] Effectively, rape has become institutionalized, supported by political and theological rhetoric. The Handmaids are silenced, their names and identities taken away (it is no accident that we never know for certain what Offred's birth-name is, although 'June' seems the most likely).[18] In a novel where names and identity are all-important, the significance of the patronymic designation 'Offred' has been much debated. Is it 'Of Fred', suggesting her dependent relationship to the Commander? Or 'Off-red', suggesting her role as a secret revolutionary who challenges the system and wishes to take off the oppressive clothing which symbolizes her captivity? Perhaps it is 'Off-read', suggesting she has been misread or misunderstood as a person; or 'Off(e)red', suggesting that she has been offered up like a sacrificial victim to the bizarre system of reproduction which the Republic of Gilead has evolved (Wexler 1986: 16; Kaler 1989: 47)? Even the nearly homophonic 'Afraid' has been suggested, summarizing, as it does, so much of the fear and uncertainty that dominates the life of the Handmaid (Parrinder 1986: 20).

In any event, Offred risks telling her story regardless of the consequences, so central is it for the re-establishment of her own identity. Narration and story-telling are symbolic of the dangers inherent for women in the Republic of Gilead where the restriction of speech by the government is the order of the day.[19] The way in which Offred manages to speak out and

17. Rubenstein (1988: 102) summarizes: 'She [Atwood] imagines a world in which women are explicitly defined by their potential fertility (or its absence); procreation and maternity are simultaneously idealized and dehumanized'. Similarly, Wexler (1986: 16) describes the novel as a 'fable of reproductive totalitarianism'.

18. Note McCarthy's comment (1986: 35) about 'textual detective work', based presumably upon the cryptic references on pp. 14, 285. For more on this point see Andriano 1992–93: 90; Bergmann 1989: 853; Ketterer 1989: 214; Miner 1991: 167; Howells 1996: 132-33; and most importantly Rooke 1989: 175-96.

19. The power of language and narration in a postmodern setting is one of the most discussed features of the novel. See Garrett-Petts 1988 and K.F. Stein 1991–92.

communicate her story is one of the key themes of the novel. This is particularly significant given that Gilead is a society in which free speech and written language are forbidden matters.[20] Censorship is the order of the day in Gilead, and the legitimacy of writing as a means of self-expression is undermined. Yet, paradoxically, the paranoia of state censorship in Gilead means that the society is built upon a tissue of lies and half-truths. The novel is deeply disturbing precisely because it presents the central character Offred (with whom the reader is meant to identify) as someone who desperately, but somewhat ineffectually, attempts to discover and maintain her identity in the face of such dehumanizing forces.

In short, Gilead is a state ostensibly based on the principles of Christian fundamentalism. Unfortunately, it is a place where the drive to be literally faithful to the Bible means that compassion and benevolence are lacking in society.[21] It is a society that has lost the meaning of the word love, as Offred explains at one point to her Commander.[22] As far as the religious milieu of the story is concerned, this too is given plausible dimensions which build upon recognizable facets of Christian denominationalism. Thus, the Republic of Gilead is a world in which Quakers are considered dangerous heretics and are actively hunted down for their willingness to defy the state and help those who are persecuted by it to escape to other lands. It is also a world where Baptists take on the role of guerrilla freedom-fighters,[23] the futuristic equivalent of the Zealots of Jesus' day, or the

20. Lacombe (1986: 3-20) offers a fine study along these lines.

21. Cowart (1989: 107) notes: 'Atwood at once satirizes the fundamentalist doctrine of biblical inerrancy and dramatizes the historical horror of sexual slavery'.

22. See Glendinning 1986 and Malak 1987: 15. This is challenged by Miner 1991: 148-65, who discusses the presentation of romantic love in the novel, concentrating on the relationships Offred has with the three main male characters in the story (Luke, her lost husband; the Commander, her master and sexual partner in the Ceremonies; and Nick, the Commander's chauffeur and her illicit lover). Miner notes that structurally the novel presents the Commander and Nick as twin figures, with many striking parallels in terms of attitude and action. Miner (1991: 161-67) goes so far as to suggest that even the salvific role of Nick, who arranges the escape of Offred from Gilead to Canada and presumably is (at some level) responsible for the preservation of her life-story, needs to be taken with a grain of salt. Armitt (2000: 213-15) discusses Miner's ingenious reading of the novel.

23. Kauffman (1989: 239) suggests that this is somewhat ironic given the direction that Southern Baptists have taken in matters involving the inspiration of the Bible and the interpretation of Scripture. She states that Atwood's view of the Southern Baptists (as adduced in the novel) is 'overly optimistic'.

followers of Thomas Muntzer in Martin Luther's. We catch a glimpse of this early on in the story as Offred and Ofglen speak in hushed tones, and with guarded words:

> 'The war is going well, I hear', she says.
> 'Praise be', I reply.
> 'We've been sent good weather'.
> 'Which I receive with joy'.
> 'They've defeated more of the rebels, since yesterday'.
> 'Praise be', I say. I don't ask her how she knows. 'What were they?'
> 'Baptists. They had a stronghold in the Blue Hills. They smoked them out'.
> 'Praise be.' (Atwood 1996: 29).

Another interesting feature of the novel is the way in which the word-game Scrabble is used as a guiding metaphor throughout. Offred and her Commander play the game illicitly when she makes secret assignations to his office under the cover of darkness and away from the watchful gaze of the Commander's wife Serena Joy, a former gospel singer and celebrity now reduced to the status of an unproductive Commander's wife. The gaming activity between Offred and the Commander is deeply subversive, not to say highly dangerous, for Gilead is a society in which reading and writing are outlawed for women. The game of Scrabble between Offred and her Commander becomes highly eroticized, replacing the sexual act itself which has become perfunctory and a matter of mere ritual, evacuated of love and meaning.[24]

The Epilogue of the book provides what Linda Hutcheon has described as a structural irony to the work as a whole, for the interpretation of Offred's story is inextricably bound up with the sexist presuppositions of Professor James Darcy Piexioto as he subjects the story to the detached scrutiny of a historian aiming to make an impression within the world of the academy.[25] At the same time, Hutcheon continues, there is an element of what can be described as a hermeneutic irony, for as she notes, 'the reader has not missed that feminist lesson, even if the male professional

---

24. The importance of the Scrabble-playing is discussed by Turner (1988: 88-89); Andriano (1992–93: 89-96); Jones (1989: 39-40); Miner (1991: 148-49, 165-66); Sage (1992: 166-67); Grace (1994: 196-99) and Armitt (2000: 215-16). The board game is an essential means whereby Offred asserts her identity as a person, capable of independent thought and action.

25. Larson (1989: 34) notes that the Epilogue contains 'the fiction of scholarly neutrality'.

historian has'.[26] Commenting on the ironic 'Historical Notes' section with which the novel concludes, Laurence Coupe similarly remarks that Professor Piexioto

> represents the aridity of *logos*, un-comprehending in the face of *mythos*. Indicatively, he finds the document to be 'in its way eloquent', but 'mute' on important factual matters…Just as Gilead does not know how to read the grand narrative of the Bible without turning it into a handbook of dogma, so the professor does not know how to read the vulnerable and tentative narration before him, this 'Handmaid's tale', without turning it into an object to be explained away (1997: 194).

Ostensibly, Piexioto's keynote lecture is given at an interdisciplinary conference at the University of Denay, Nunavit, in the year 2195. Piexioto, the Director of Twentieth and Twenty-First Century Archives, Cambridge University, England, is offering an interpretation of certain aspects of life in the Republic of Gilead based upon the thirty or so cassette tapes containing Offred's testimony, which survived and were discovered in what was Bangor, Maine. However, it is clear that Atwood is constructing an elaborate satire within the Epilogue, including the pun involving the name of the university—Deny None of It.[27] The Epilogue is thus a fitting conclusion to the novel as a whole, picking up and elaborating some of its most telling themes and challenging prevailing notions about gender roles and the interpretation of history. It sounds the most dismal note in this modern dystopian classic.[28]

Biblical Imagery in The Handmaid's Tale

Above I noted that *The Handmaid's Tale* explores the ways in which women are repressed and silenced within the dystopian society of Gilead. It should not come as a surprise that biblical injunctions to this end are

26. Hutcheon 1991: 24. Lacombe (1986: 5) describes Piexioto's lecture as a 'palimpsest', as he rewrites Offred's life-story in the process of his interpretation of her as a Handmaid from a Gilead now long past. Also see Garrett-Petts 1988: 81-84; Bergmann 1989: 851-54; Cowart 1989: 107-108; Kauffman 1989: 222-31; Ketterer 1989: 212-15; Norris 1990; K.F. Stein 1991–92: 273-74 for more on the Epilogue.

27. Bergmann 1989: 852; Ketterer 1989: 214; Norris 1990: 361.

28. A.E. Davidson (1988: 120) states: '[I]n crucial ways the epilogue is the most pessimistic part of the book'. Foley (1989) offers some interesting comparisons between Atwood's Epilogue and that of George Orwell's *1984*. Atwood (1996: 217) herself notes the parallel between the Epilogue in *The Handmaid's Tale* and the concluding note on Newspeak in *1984*.

invoked within the story. Perhaps the best example of this occurs in Chapter 34, where the notoriously contentious passage from 1 Tim. 2.9-15 is asserted by the Commander as he leads a service at a Prayvaganza, a women's revival meeting designed to evoke loyalty to the state. We read Offred's recollection of the Commander's words, and her assessment of them:

> 'I will that women adorn themselves in modest apparel', he says, 'with shamefacedness and sobriety; not with braided hair, or gold, or pearls, or costly array;
>
> 'But (which becometh women professing godliness) with good works.
>
> 'Let the woman learn in silence with *all* subjection'. Here he looks us over. 'All', he repeats.
>
> 'But I suffer not a woman to teach, nor to usurp authority over the man, but to be in silence.
>
> 'For Adam was first formed, then Eve.
>
> 'And Adam was not deceived, but the woman being deceived was in the transgression.
>
> 'Notwithstanding she shall be saved by childbearing, if they continue in faith and charity and holiness with sobriety'.
>
> Saved by childbearing, I think. What did we suppose would save us, in the time before? (Atwood 1996: 233).

The Handmaid's Tale is perhaps Atwood's most richly textured work, at least as far as its use of biblical materials is concerned. In fact, biblical imagery is scattered throughout the story; there is hardly a chapter which does not illustrate the indebtedness to Scripture at some level.[29] Yet the novel has not often been explored with a view to its reliance upon and allusion to biblical texts.[30] This is somewhat ironic, especially given the title of the work, which sounds as if it is an amalgamation of the Bible and an allusion to the Wife of Bath from Chaucer's *Canterbury Tales* (1380–1400).[31] We would do well to list some of the ways in which both Old and New Testament texts are used within the novel.

The most obvious example of the use of Old Testament imagery within *The Handmaid's Tale* is contained in the first of the three epigraphs with

---

29. Lacombe (1986: 13) speaks of the 'falsification of Biblical texts' in which the literal interpretation of the Bible is used in the language of Gilead which is based upon the phallocentric word made flesh.

30. Larson 1989 is the most comprehensive study along these lines.

31. For more on the reliance upon Chaucer within the novel, see Cowart 1989: 114-16.

which the novel opens.[32] This is the story of Rachel giving her handmaid Bilhah to her husband Jacob, in order that Jacob might sire children by her:

> And when Rachel saw that she bare Jacob no children, Rachel envied her sister; and said unto Jacob, Give me children, or else I die. And Jacob's anger was kindled against Rachel, and he said, Am I in God's stead, who hath withheld from thee the fruit of thy womb? And she said, Behold my maid Bilhah, go in unto her; and she shall bear upon my knees, that I may also have children by her (Genesis 30.1-3) (Atwood 1996: 7).

It is, of course, this evocative image of the handmaid, a familiar one within the Old Testament, that not only provides a partial explanation of the novel's title[33] but also gives the central character a historical backdrop against which to relate her own story.[34] In this case the Commander assumes the role of the patriarch Jacob, while the Commander's wife Serena Joy has the role of Rachel, and Offred takes on the role of the handmaid Bilhah. Nowhere is the Old Testament imagery made more explicit than in the monthly mating rituals between the Handmaids and their Commanders, perhaps the most disturbing image within the work. Here the Handmaids are positioned literally between the legs of their Commander's wife. The same holds true for the actual birth of children of

---

32. Both the epigraphs and the dedication of the novel have been the subject of scholarly inquiry. See Carrington 1987: 127-28; Wagner-Martin 1987: 4; Workman 1989.

33. Atwood (1996: 249) states that the working title of the book was *Offred*, but that the final title comes directly from Genesis 30: 'I think too it was one of those words that puzzled me as a child. 'Hand-maid'. Like 'foot-man'. It's a very odd word'. Kaler (1989: 46) suggests that Atwood's use of the term *handmaid* is deliberately designed to evoke an association with pre-Vatican II Roman Catholic nuns.

34. Ketterer (1989: 210) notes the importance of Gen. 30.1-3 for *The Handmaid's Tale*. He describes the passage as 'the essential seed' of the novel, and goes on to suggest that the description of the ritual coupling between Commander and Handmaid is 'modelled directly on the Genesis passage'. Also see Carrington 1987: 128; Kaler 1989: 46; Kauffman 1989: 225; Freibert 1988: 282-85 and for other interesting comments on the Genesis story as it relates to Atwood's novel. Larson (1989: 38-39) extends the discussion of the Handmaid to include the relationship between Sarah and Hagar in Gen. 16.1-16; 21.9-21, although somewhat strangely the material in Gal. 4.22-31 is not taken into account within the discussison. The Old Testament prophetic literature, notably the books of Amos, Joel and Jeremiah, is also thoroughly explored. The discussion is also extended to include the book of Revelation, notably the passage in ch. 12 recounting the vision of the woman clothed with the sun.

the Handmaids, thus fulfilling literally the unusual phrase from Gen. 30.3 ('she shall bear upon my knees').[35] At one point in the novel these ritual couplings (known as 'the Ceremony') are described in some detail, including how the Commander would read from the Bible before engaging in sexual intercourse with the Handmaid:

> The Commander, as if reluctantly, begins to read. He isn't very good at it. Maybe he's merely bored.
> It's the usual story, the usual stories. God to Adam, God to Noah. *Be fruitful, and multiply, and replenish the earth.* Then comes the mouldy old Rachel and Leah stuff we had drummed into us at the Centre. *Give me children, or else I die. Am I in God's stead, who hath withheld from thee the fruit of the womb? Behold my maid Bilhah. She shall bear upon my knees, that I may also have children by her.* And so on and so forth (Atwood 1996: 99).

The words of Rachel to Jacob ('Give me children, or else I die') are especially important within the novel, appearing not only in the epigraph but twice more within the story-line (1996: 71 and here on page 99 in connection with the initial description of 'the Ceremony'). However, the pleading cry from the heart of Rachel is given a new twist when viewed from the standpoint of Offred the Handmaid. For her, the inability to produce children within three postings as a Handmaid will mean that she will be sent away almost certainly to a premature death in the Colonies, working to help clean up environmental disasters or nuclear accidents. Interestingly, to add further texture to the Old Testament imagery, the name of the Republic of *Gilead* also has an important connection to the patriarch Jacob, for it is in this geographical region that Jacob gathered together stones to mark his pact with his relative Laban and mark the divine promise that he and his family and flocks would be fruitful and multiply (see Gen. 32.20-50 and 37.25).[36] In short, the setting of the story

35. It is interesting to note that the Hebrew words for 'blessing' and 'knee' have the same tri-literal root (ברך). This suggests that the phrase ('she shall bear upon my knees') is a play on words, as if to intimate that Bilhah's giving birth on Rachel's *knees* is a *blessing* for her. The irony in Atwood's re-telling is not to be overlooked or underestimated. There is good evidence to suggest that Atwood is here consciously building upon Puritan customs and practices regarding childbirth, including the use of birthing stools. See Evans 1994: 184 and Howells 1996: 130 for more on this point.

36. Commenting on the use of the Old Testament made by the Republic of Gilead, Howells (1998: 62) interestingly notes: 'One hostile Old Testament reference which Gilead chooses not to use occurs in Hosea 6.8: 'Gilead is a city of wicked men, stained with footprints of blood'.'

within the Republic of *Gilead* reinforces the Jacob motif within the novel, by means of association with the Old Testament texts which bring the patriarch and the geographical place together.

In addition, the significance of the imagery of childbirth within the book of Genesis has an additional manifestation within the story-line. This is based upon Gen. 3.16 where Eve is said to give birth to children in and through much physical pain—a punishment for her part in eating the forbidden fruit from the tree of the knowledge of good and evil in the Garden of Eden. In *The Handmaid's Tale* the verse from Genesis is cited in connection with the birth of the Handmaid Ofwarren's baby (see Evans 1994: 183-84). Here Offred, who anxiously attended the birth, recalls how Aunt Elizabeth, one of the female warders at the aptly-named Rachel and Leah Re-Education Centre (more on this below), explained the contrast between life in former times and life as it is now in the Republic of Gilead:

> Once they drugged women, induced labour, cut them open, sewed them up. No more. No anaesthetics, even. Aunt Elizabeth said it was better for the baby, but also: *I will greatly multiply thy sorrow and thy conception; in sorrow thou shalt bring forth children.* (Atwood 1996: 124).

A further illustration of how the Old Testament is used can be found in the description of the Commander's domestic piety. At one point the Commander concludes the household evening prayers with a verse from 2 Chron. 7.9: 'For the eyes of the Lord run to and fro throughout the whole earth, to know himself strong in the behalf of them whose heart is perfect towards him' (Atwood 1996: 102-103). The passage from 2 Chronicles is likely to be the scriptural source for the idea of the Eyes, the secret police, whose headquarters are in Harvard University and whose task it is to keep watch over all that takes place in the Republic of Gilead. Other sites dotted around the Harvard University campus are given new names and reworked so as to conform to the principles and ideals of Gileadean society. The gymnasium of Harvard University has been turned into the Rachel and Leah Re-Education (Red) Centre, and the wall enclosing Harvard Yard becomes the place of public display for men executed for such offences as rape, performing abortions, and so-called 'Gender Treachery' (homosexuality).[37] Several of the stores around the campus where Offred buys her provisions for the household of her Commander are named after

---

37. It is worth noting that the inspiration for the wall probably reflects the fact that Atwood began writing the novel while living in West Berlin in March–May 1984. Carrington (1987: 130), Nischik (1987: 144) and Cooke (1998: 275-76) all note this.

biblical images or phrases drawn from both the Old and New Testaments. Thus, the grocery store known as 'Milk and Honey' (1996: 34) recalls the familiar Old Testament image of 'the land flowing with milk and honey', used some fifteen times in the Pentateuch as a description of the Promised Land (see Exod. 3.8, for example). Similarly, the butcher's shop, known as 'All Flesh' (1996: 36), is probably an echo of the word of the prophet Isaiah recorded in Isa. 40.6. Meanwhile, the 'Loaves and Fishes' recalls the story of the feeding of the multitudes in Mt. 14.13-21/Mk 6.32-44/Lk. 9.10-17/Jn 6.1-1, while the clothing store, 'Lilies of the Field' (1996: 33), recalls Jesus' words in the Sermon on the Mount in Mt. 6.28. Sometimes the names of the goods themselves are chosen because they evoke biblical images. A good example is Serena Joy's perfume, which is called 'Lily of the Valley' (1996: 90). One other store visited by Offred is also mentioned at several points in the story. This is 'Soul Scrolls', a computerized version of dial-a-prayer, and it is housed in a former lingerie store.

One of the most interesting examples in the novel illustrating the use of prophetic imagery from the Old Testament involves Jer. 8.22. Here the prophet serves as God's mouthpiece of judgment on the people of Judah for their disobedience, proclaiming the desolation which is to fall upon the Promised Land. The extremely fertile area of Gilead is included within this prophecy of judgment, prompting the mournful cry of Jeremiah the prophet, himself a Gileadite: 'Is there no balm in Gilead? Is there no physician there? Why then is not the health of the daughter of my people recovered?'[38] In *The Handmaid's Tale* the old hymn 'There is a Balm in Gilead', which is based upon the provocative image from Jer. 8.22, is sung at one of the Prayvaganzas at which twenty Angels are married to twenty Daughters of the Commanders. The singing of the hymn prompts Offred to recall that her friend Moira used to call the hymn 'There is a Bomb in Gilead' (1996: 218), a suggestive hint of the revolutionary forces brewing just beneath the surface in the repressive Republic of Gilead.

The remark also makes Offred something of a prophetic successor to

---

38. The passage from Jeremiah is discussed by Freibert (1988: 281), D. Jones (1989: 33-34, 39) and Larson (1989: 40-45). Freibert also notes (291) that Atwood may be alluding to Jer. 4.13 and 23.19 by giving the Commander's car the brand name 'Whirlwind': 'The car is a very expensive one, a Whirlwind; better than the Chariot, much better than the chunky, practical Behemoth' (Atwood 1996: 27). The reference to Behemoth alludes to Job 40.15. It may well be that Atwood is also paying tribute here to Edgar Allan Poe, whose influential poem *The Raven* (1854) has the poem's narrator ask the symbolic raven: 'Is there—*is* there balm in Gilead?—tell me—tell me, I implore!'

Jeremiah himself. The imagery inherent in the passage from Jeremiah, involving a healing medicinal balm made from the resin of special trees, is developed further in the novel. We see this, for example, in the form of the butter-pats that the Handmaids secretly steal from the Commander's kitchens, using the butter as an ointment for their dry, chapped hands. It is also worth noting that Offred asks the Commander for a bottle of hand-cream, an equivalent to Gilead's famed medicinal balm, as part of their illicit Scrabble-playing encounters.[39]

Another instance of Old Testament imagery involves the figure of Jezebel, the wife of Ahab, the king of Israel (1 Kgs 16.29-31). Jezebel becomes something of an archetype of an evil and self-possessed woman, with her devotion to the false god Baal and her unscrupulous use of her feminine wiles being focal points of the biblical tirade in 1 and 2 Kings against her (see Ackroyd 1983). In Atwood's novel the Commander of Offred smuggles her into an illegal brothel known as Jezebel's where the upper echelons of society in Gilead are able to indulge their vices.[40] The name 'Jezebel' is also applied to the women who work in the establishment, including Offred's long-standing friend Moira.

Yet another important indication of the Old Testament underpinning of the novel is to be found early on in the story, as the narrator Offred describes to the reader the recollections she has about life within the Rachel and Leah Re-Education Centre (particularly as it involved the Aunts), and about life outside in the larger arena of Gileadean society (particularly as it involved the Marthas). The 'Aunts' were a group of Gileadean drill sergeants, so to speak, whose task was to patrol among the young Handmaids in the training programme at the Rachel and Leah Re-Education Centre and make sure that they toed the line. To force the Handmaids to fulfil their responsibilities, the Aunts were equipped with electric cattle prods, a symbolic instrument of power and control if ever there was one! The 'Marthas' were a servile and domestic group of housekeepers and cleaners named after Martha, one of the followers of Jesus Christ. Martha demonstrated her commitment to her Master primarily through her faithful service as a house-servant, only to be bested by her sister Mary, who was able to detect the higher, spiritual dimension of things (see Lk. 10.38-42 and Jn 11.1; 12.1-3). One is tempted to see the Gileadean Marthas functioning,

39. Commenting on the use made of Jer. 8.22 here, Bartkowski (1989: 152) remarks: 'With this curious detail Atwood is also having fun with her readers'.

40. Ljungberg (1999: 170-71) discusses Atwood's affinity for the Jezebel image within her writing.

with respect to the Handmaids, in precisely the same manner as the Biblical character Martha does to her more spiritually astute sister Mary. Thus, at one level it is the Handmaid Offred who stands at the centre of the discussion, and her connections to the multi-dimensioned character Mary seem obvious. 'Mary' in this instance denotes not only Martha's sister Mary, but also the Virgin Mary, the mother of Jesus, and thirdly, Mary Magdalene, a follower of Jesus whose life (according to tradition) was surrounded by sexual innuendo and controversy thus making her a person with whom it was dangerous to associate, both personally and politically. Indeed, a good case could be made for suggesting that Atwood, by choosing to set up a contrast between the Marthas on the one hand (who represent the structures and order of the Republic of Gilead), and the (potentially) anti-establishment Handmaids on the other (who represent the biblical witness of 'Mary' in all of its three-layered multivalency), is following through a tension within the New Testament documents themselves over the precise relationship between the sisters Martha and Mary. At the same time, the deliberate concentration on the role of the Marthas as *named* characters within *The Handmaid's Tale* makes the relatively less personalized role of the Mary/ Handmaid figure all the more significant as a result. Effectively, this is an ingenious ploy of misdirection, given that the story continually mentions the Martha figures by name (notably Rita and Cora), as well as designating the Aunts by name (Lydia, Elizabeth, etc.), while leaving the names, and therefore the identities, of the Mary/Handmaid characters dependent upon the men they serve.

However, it is in its reworking of some of the words of Jesus of Nazareth that the novel takes its most creative intertextual steps. For example, at one point the words of Jesus recorded in Lk. 17.20-21 are applied to the Republic of Gilead, as a means of emphasizing the Republic's all-pervasiveness, the fact that every aspect of life is watched, regulated and controlled. As Offred goes on her first shopping outing with Ofglen to the centre of the capital city, we have this reflection by the Handmaid:

> This is the heart of Gilead, where the war cannot intrude except on television. Where the edges are we aren't sure, they vary, according to the attacks and counterattacks, but this is the centre, where nothing moves. The Republic of Gilead, said Aunt Lydia, knows no bounds. Gilead is within you (Atwood 1996: 33).

In effect, the Republic of Gilead becomes a parody of the Kingdom of God, for it is the realm of God which is 'within you' according to Jesus.

In addition, several allusions to the words of Jesus as contained in the

Synoptic Gospels are included within the story. One of the first instances of this is a comment by Offred about the teaching she had received at the hands of Aunt Lydia at the Rachel and Leah Re-Education Centre. The imagery used is that of the Parable of the Sower found in Mt. 13.1-9/Mk 4.1-9/Lk. 8.4-8. Offred is learning her way around the estate of her Commander, establishing herself in the daily routine:

> I walk to the corner and wait. I used to be bad at waiting. They also serve who only stand and wait, said Aunt Lydia. She made us memorize it. She also said, Not all of you will make it through. Some of you will fall on dry ground or thorns. Some of you are shallow-rooted. She had a mole on her chin that went up and down when she talked. She said, Think of yourself as seeds, and right then her voice was wheedling, conspiratorial, like the voices of those women who used to teach ballet lessons to children, and we would say, Arms up in the air now; let's pretend we're trees.
> I stand on the corner, pretending I am a tree (Atwood 1996: 28).

Other allusions to the words of Jesus also appear. Frequently it is a mis-quotation, or a misappropriation, of the sayings of Jesus which figures.[41] For example, one day during lunchtime at the Rachel and Leah Re-Education Centre, the Handmaids hear the Aunts drilling into their charges the Gileadean version of Jesus' words at the beginning of the Sermon on the Mount, including an altogether new Beatitude, 'Blessed are the silent'. Offred reflects on these:

> For lunch it was the Beatitudes. Blessed be this, blessed be that. They played it from a disc, the voice was a man's. *Blessed be the poor in spirit, for theirs is the kingdom of heaven. Blessed are the merciful. Blessed are the meek. Blessed are the silent.* I knew they made that up, I knew it was wrong, and they left things out, too, but there was no way of checking. *Blessed be those who mourn, for they shall be comforted.*
> Nobody said when (Atwood 1996: 99-100).

In addition, some other key phrases from Jesus' Beatitudes are alluded to in the course of the story. A good example is a comment by Offred about the teaching she had received at the hands of Aunt Lydia; this time the comment is based on Mt. 5.5 ('Blessed are the meek, for they shall

---

41. Earlier in the novel the phrase 'All flesh is weak' is attributed to Aunt Lydia by Offred in a recollected moment, but the Handmaid somehow recognizes that Aunt Lydia's recitation of Scripture is not right: 'All flesh is grass, I corrected her in my head' (1996: 55). This is a correction which shows that Offred recalls, however distantly, the text of Isa. 40.6, and perhaps 1 Pet. 1.24 (which also alludes to the passage).

inherit the earth'). Offred is contemplating how much she has lost, what she has had to surrender from the past in order to find herself in her present position as a Handmaid. She reminisces:

> I've learned to do without a lot of things. If you have a lot of things, said Aunt Lydia, you get too attached to this material world and you forget about spiritual values. You must cultivate poverty of spirit. Blessed are the meek. She didn't go on to say anything about inheriting the earth (Atwood 1996: 74).

A further allusion is made to the conclusion of the Lord's Prayer in Mt. 6.13: 'For thine is the Kingdom, the power and glory, now and forever. Amen'. In this case Offred throws up a prayer to God which is openly questioning, even if it does make a mockery of the official stance of the Republic of Gilead on such matters:

> I wish I knew what You were up to... I don't believe for an instant that what's going on out there is what You meant... Then there's Kingdom, power, and glory. It takes a lot to believe in those right now. If I were You I'd be fed up. I'd really be sick of it... Oh God. It's no joke (Atwood 1996: 194-195).[42]

Offred also makes other allusions to the Lord's Prayer as recorded in Matthew's Sermon on the Mount (Mt. 6.9-13). Most importantly, there is an extended section in which Offred sits in her room praying as she looks through the window at the empty garden. Again she offers her own prayer to God, basing it on the various petitions contained in the Lord's Prayer.[43]

> My God. Who art in the Kingdom of Heaven, which is within.
> I wish you could tell me Your Name, the real one I mean. But *You* will do as well as anything.
> I wish I knew what You were up to. But whatever it is, help me to get through it, please. Though maybe it's not Your doing; I don't believe for an instant that what's going on out there is what You meant.
> I have enough daily bread, so I won't waste time on that. It isn't the main problem. The problem is getting it down without choking on it.
> Now we come to forgiveness. Don't worry about forgiving me right now. There are more important things. For instance: keep the others safe, if they

---

42.   Walker (1988: 218-19), Larson (1989: 46) and Howells (1996: 132) discuss this passage. Larson (1989: 46-47) goes on to draw out several points of similarity between Offred's life in Gilead and Christ's passion as recorded in the Gospels.

43.   Rooke (1989: 184) calls this Offred's 'deconstruction of the Lord's Prayer'. Keith (1987: 127) also notes how the narrator of the story deconstructs and reconstructs the Lord's Prayer.

are safe. Don't let them suffer too much. If they have to die, let it be fast. You might even provide a Heaven for them. We need You for that. Hell we can make for ourselves.

I suppose I should say I forgive whoever did this, and whatever they're doing now. I'll try, but it isn't easy.

Temptation comes next. At the Centre, temptation was anything much more than eating and sleeping. Knowing was a temptation. What you don't know won't tempt you, Aunt Lydia used to say.

Maybe I don't really want to know what's going on. Maybe I'd rather not know. Maybe I couldn't bear to know. The Fall was a fall from innocence to knowledge.

I think about the chandelier too much, though it's gone now. But you could use a hook, in the closet. I've considered the possibilities. All you'd have to do, after attaching yourself, would be to lean your weight forward and not fight.

Deliver us from evil.

Then there's Kingdom, power, and glory. It takes a lot to believe in those right not. But I'll try it anyway. *In Hope*, as they say on the gravestones (Atwood 1996: 204-205).

At another point Offred recalls the words of Aunt Lydia about the resentment that the Commanders' wives will inevitably feel for the Handmaids. She suggests that the Handmaids are to adopt the same attitude of forgiveness towards them that Jesus did to his executors in Lk. 23.34. Aunt Lydia had said: ' "You should always try to imagine what they must be feeling. Of course they will resent you. It is only natural. Try to feel for them… Try to pity them. Forgive them, for they know not what they do" ' (Atwood 1996: 56).

Occasionally, it is imagery drawn from the New Testament epistles that comes into play. For example, the cushion that Offred has in her room has the word FAITH embroidered upon it, and at one point she speculates idly as to where the companion cushions HOPE and CHARITY have gone (1996: 140). This is an allusion to Paul's words in 1 Cor. 13.13, where we read: 'And now abideth faith, hope, charity, these three; but the greatest of these is charity' (AV). This is a devastatingly sharp, but subtle, criticism of life within the Republic of Gilead, a society which has retained the structure of faith, but lost any notions of hope or charity (love). Indeed, while attending the Salvaging ritual, Offred notes that the cushions upon which she and the other Handmaids kneel have nothing written on them, not even the word FAITH (1996: 51).[44]

44. Kaler (1989: 57) points out that elsewhere in the novel the companion term 'HOPE' is engraved on a gravestone, 'because Offred's only hope is death'.

In many respects *The Handmaid's Tale* is a rather brutal and bloodthirsty novel, containing a number of passages involving bodily mutilation, dismemberment, and shockingly horrific death. What is perhaps most disturbing in this regard is the fact that the violence is very often inflicted by women upon other women.[45] Biblical images are used to legitimate such measures by the authorities, both male *and* female, in the Republic of Gilead. A good example concerns Jesus' words in Mt. 18.8 ('If your hand or your foot offend you...'), which are taken literally. Within the Republic of Gilead the authorities sever the hand of a person caught for a third offence of reading.[46]

A more subtle example of physical violence within the novel is found in the climactic scene involving the 'Salvaging' of the three lawbreakers (Chapter 42). The scene has been likened to the triple executions on Calvary, with Jesus executed between two other malefactors (Cowart 1989: 116). In this case, however, the three people 'Salvaged' are all female instead of male.

Finally, at one significant point a biblical allusion, or to be more precise an *alleged* biblical allusion, to the words of Paul the Apostle, is made. This occurs as one of the Handmaids is in the process of giving birth, and Offred recalls some of the brainwashing words of the Aunts in the Re-education Centre: '*From each*, says the slogan, *according to her ability; to each according to his needs.* We recited that, three times, after dessert. It was from the Bible, or so they said. St Paul again, in Acts'. (Atwood 1996: 117). What is interesting about this passage is the fact that it is a rewriting of a famous phrase from Karl Marx's *Critique of the Gotha Programme* (1875). However, not only is the adage misattributed to Paul the Apostle,[47] but the gender of the pronouns is significantly altered ('from each according to *her* ability; to each according to *his* needs'). This is a way of reinforcing irony within the story-line, especially given the fact that women and men lead lives of such inequality within the Republic of Gilead.[48]

45. This point is well made by Ehrenreich (1986: 34-35).
46. See Larson (1989: 40) for more on this matter.
47. Possibly as an echo of the story of the great Christian communalism of the Jerusalem church, mentioned in passing in Acts 2.44-45 and 4.32-35. Atwood (1991–92: 381) herself describes the misattribution as 'a garbling of Marx'.
48. For more on this intriguing passage, which presumes the reader's ability to recognize the allusion to Marx and detect the irony involved, see Walker 1988: 206-207, 215-16.

Let us turn now to consider two of the artistic adaptations of Atwood's novel which have been produced in recent years.

Dystopia Translates to Radio and Film

Two adaptations of Atwood's novel are worth considering here briefly, the first a film adaptation from 1990, and the second a play for BBC Radio 4 from 2000. Each of these adaptations makes use of the biblical imagery underlying the original novel in its own unique fashion.

Volker Schlöndorff's The Handmaid's Tale *(1990)*
The decision to adapt Atwood's *The Handmaid's Tale* for the cinema prompted a great deal of artistic interest within the film-making industry. A number of directors and actors were involved at various stages of the production, including the actress Sigourney Weaver, who was originally scheduled to take the title role of the Handmaid Offred, but was unavailable due to other contractual obligations. The German film director Volker Schlöndorff was eventually given the directorial assignment, largely on the strength of his faithful adaptation of Günther Grass's *The Tin Drum* (1979). Schlöndorff's *The Handmaid's Tale* (1990) has a star-studded cast, with Natasha Richardson in the title role of the Handmaid, Robert Duvall in the role of the Commander, Faye Dunaway in the role of the Commander's wife Serena Joy, Victoria Tennant as Aunt Lydia, Aidan Quinn as Nick, and Elizabeth McGovern as the Handmaid's rebellious friend Moira. The celebrated playwright Harold Pinter wrote the screen-play for the film, riding the crest of fame for his critically acclaimed screenplay of John Fowles' *The French Lieutenant's Woman* (1981). Filming took place during February–May of 1989 at Duke University in Durham, North Carolina. The film had a budget of $13 million, although only a third or so of this was recovered in box-office receipts.[49]

Most of the memorable features and images of the novel find some sort of expression within the film. The nightmarish premise of a take-over of the United States by right-wing fundamentalists is intact, as is the existence of counter-revolutionary groups, such as peace-loving (but defiant!) Quakers and Baptist guerrilla fighters. Thus, at one point in the film a television news-broadcaster gives a report of a battle:

---

49.   Cooke (1998: 300-302) discusses the film's production.

Good news from the Appalachian Highlands where the Angels of the Apocalypse, 4th Division, are smoking out a pocket of Baptist Guerrillas with air support from the 21st Battalion of the Angels of Light. Enemy casualties are reported as high, where hand-to-hand fighting continues.

It is noticeable that it is specifically *Old Testament* texts and imagery that are invoked within the film. To illustrate the point, the religious minister leading the service for the commissioning of the Handmaids declares as part of his sermon: 'The Old Testament shall be our sole, and only, Constitution'. This emphasis on passages from the Old Testament is carried through at several points in the film. Thus, the Commander and his wife read a section of Gen. 30.1-3 as a prelude to the first Ceremony with Offred, and an abbreviated version of Deut. 22.25 is read out by Aunt Lydia at the beginning of the Particicution ceremony in which the Handmaids rush forwards in a frenzy and tear an alleged 'rapist' to pieces.[50] Clearly Schlöndorff's film presents the Republic of Gilead as a society built solidly on Old Testament foundations. There are no specific allusions to the words of Jesus, no reworkings of the Beatitudes, which I noted as being so central to the message in Atwood's novel. In fact, the only reference to any New Testament passage is a brief allusion to Rev. 17.1-6 when the Handmaid Offred says to her friend Moira: 'You look like the Whore of Babylon'.[51] However, Moira's response quickly takes us back to the familiar ground of the Old Testament when she asks her friend a moment later: 'Do you know what they call this place? Jezebel's!'

Beyond the mention of the 'Whore of Babylon', the closest we get to any further mention of the New Testament or anything traditionally Christian comes in the form of songs that are sung as part of the story-line. In this case, several traditional hymn tunes, favourites of evangelical Christianity, are heard. But although the music is familiar, the lyrics are generally rewritten. Thus, we hear a version of 'Shall We Gather at the River' being sung at the Womens' Salvaging Ceremony, and a version of 'Praise God From Whom All Blessings Flow' is sung by Aunt Lydia at the Rachel and Leah Re-Education Centre. There is also a brief scene in which

---

50. In the film Aunt Lydia announces her text as 'Deuteronomy 25', and then reads: 'If the man forces her and lies with her, then the man that lay with her shall die'. Presumably this is a confusion of the verse number with the chapter number in the book of Deuteronomy.

51. Interestingly, in Atwood's novel (1996: 254) it is Moira who accuses Offred of looking like the 'Whore of Babylon'.

the Commander's wife Serena Joy watches herself singing a rendition of John Newton's classic 'Amazing Grace' on television.

Schlöndorff's film makes several alterations to Atwood's novel that take the story-line in a new direction. For one thing, the central character Offred is given a name, Kate (her Handmaid title is still 'Offred'). This is a huge difference, one that evacuates the story of much of its force given that the mystery surrounding Offred's true name is symbolic of her loss of identity in the story as a whole. Another point of difference is the fact that Kate/Offred is specifically presented as being on her *first* assignment as a Handmaid. This, too, is a departure from the novel which has her assignment to Commander Fred as her *third* assignment as a Handmaid, a point which adds significantly to the dramatic tension of the story. Within the novel she *must* succeed in conceiving a child on this assignment or risk death by getting sent to 'the Colonies'. By having Offred engaged in her first assignment as a Handmaid, the film misses the opportunity of presenting the desperation involved in her situation.

Most significantly, the ending of the film is also drastically altered. There is no attempt to include the novel's clever Epilogue within the film. And instead of having the Handmaid Offred step into the waiting van not knowing whether she is going to freedom or captivity, we have Kate actually kill her Commander, and flee from the oppressive regime of Gilead with the help of her lover Nick. Within the screenplay, the Commander is presented as the Chief of Security for the whole State. So ruthlessly ambitious is he that when it appears that his relationship with Offred is going to cause a scandal, he is ready to sacrifice her without a second thought. His murder by Kate is thus presented as an act of self-defence on her part. She cuts his carotid artery with a knife when he fails to act to help her escape the wrath of Serena Joy, a wrath that threatens to send her to the dreaded Colonies.

As the film closes Kate is safely hidden away in some remote mountain region (presumably the Appalachian Highlands where the Baptist guerrillas are entrenched). She is pregnant with Nick's child, but living alone as he continues to work as an undercover agent for the overthrow of the Republic of Gilead. Given all of these changes, it is not surprising that the film has not been well received.[52]

Sadly, the film seems to have misunderstood the novel's narrative

---

52. Ketterer (1992: 147) describes it as 'disappointing'. Miles (1996: 100) notes that the changes made to the story-line of the novel 'undermine the film's condemnation of repressive gender arrangements'.

complexity, particularly as a vehicle for presenting the establishment of the central character's identity by means of a number of complex story-telling techniques.[53] One of the most effective of these techniques was the use of flashbacks and different narrative voices, features which meant that several time-lines were running throughout the story. There is only one attempt to use the idea of a flashback in the film, and this uses the same basic image three times within the presentation of the story. This involves scenes from the beginning of the film where Kate and her husband Luke take their young daughter Jill and attempt to escape over the border of Gilead into Canada in their car. The escape attempt takes place during the winter and it proves unsuccessful; Luke is killed and Kate and the daughter are captured by soldiers. The flashback episodes show the little girl wearing winter clothing, walking across the snow and plaintively calling out, 'Mommie! Mommie!'[54]

Similarly, the only voice-over within the film occurs at the very end of the story, as Kate offers her thoughts about what has happened to her and what she awaits in the future. As we noted above, she is shown living in a caravan secreted in a desolate countryside, pregnant and anxiously waiting for news from her lover Nick. We hear her concluding thoughts:

> I don't know if this is the end for me, or a new beginning. But I'm safe here in the mountains held by the rebels. They bring me food, and sometimes a message from Nick. And so I wait. I wait for my baby to be born into a different world. I still dream about Jill. About them telling her I don't exist, or that I never existed. But I know we're going to find her. And she will remember me.

The picture of Kate/Offred is, in the end, a confused one. At times she seems true to the character presented in Atwood's novel, and at times she does not. As one reviewer comments upon the aggressive spirit which Pinter's screenplay interjects into the story:

---

53. See Bignell 1993 for more on this. He goes so far as to suggest (82) that 'Schlöndorff's film of the novel disrespects the text by using only parts of it, like the plot, the characters and the setting'. Bignell's overall point is to draw a parallel between Atwood's novel as a multi-voiced work and Canada as a multicultural society. While extremely interesting as a proposal, such comparisons are beyond the scope of our concerns here.

54. Willmott (1995: 167-74) discusses the opening scenes of the film, comparing them to the novel which begins with Offred remembering her time in the Rachel and Leah Re-Education Centre. Also see Clute 1990: 1181.

> Not only is she involved in the violent escape of her fellow Handmaid,
> Moira, but she also deals with the Commander, whom the book leaves to his
> own devices, by taking a knife to his throat. Clumsily and unconvincingly
> staged, this sudden bloodshed implies that she is ready at last to take her
> place among the rebels; but instead the whimpering conclusion leaves the
> heroine stuck on a mountain hoping for the best—an Atwoodesque pose,
> sure enough, but one contradiction too many (Strick 1990: 322).

Similarly, another reviewer comments upon the paradoxical situation in
which Kate finds herself at the end of the film. The Handmaid seems
driven by the very biological destiny which characterized her identity in
the repressive Republic of Gilead:

> The movie tells us that the maternal instinct—not a drive for sexual
> autonomy or self-protection—is what motivates Kate's daring bid for
> freedom. Just like Gilead says: do anything for a baby. Thus the ending of
> *The Handmaid's Tale*, like Gilead, subordinates autonomy to procreation,
> and places Kate in pretty much the same position in which Gilead wanted
> her: alone, in a small room, waiting for her baby, while its father fights for a
> new state (Baughman 1990: 92).

John Dryden's The Handmaid's Tale *(2000)*
John Dryden's adaptation of the novel for BBC Radio 4 was first broadcast
on 9 January 2000. The play was recorded on location in Bedford Hills,
New York, and features Marsha Dietlin as Offred, Leslie Hendrix as Serena
Joy, Marian Seldes as Aunt Lydia, Tasha Lawrence as Moira, Earl Hind-
man as the Commander, and Christopher Burns as Luke. Dryden's play
contains many interesting features which help to ensure that the story holds
together for a radio audience. It uses a documentary-style recording to
convey the notion of the Handmaid's memoirs being preserved on audio-
tape and channelled through a mixture of narrative standpoints, recollections, and flashbacks. To help communicate this complexity of narration
there is a marked difference in the quality of voice reproduction when the
listener is hearing the narrator of the story and when the (supposed) audio-
tape recordings of the Handmaid's voice are heard. In this way, an important feature of the original novel is retained and the 'terrifying realities of
[the Handmaid's] life as a state-controlled breeding machine'[55] communicated. The play also retains the novel's Epilogue, another very significant
structural feature which punches home the novel's message about gender

55. A description taken from the publicity blurb on the BBC Radio Collection
cassettes of the play.

relationships and the stilling of women's voices by a patriarchal establishment. To help set the religious milieu of the story, both Baptist rebels and Quaker resistance fighters figure in the play, as they do within both the novel and the 1990 film.

At one or two points the play appears to demonstrate reliance upon Volker Schlöndorff's film. Perhaps the clearest instance of this involves the opening scenes, where the Handmaid Offred attempts to cross the border into Canada with her husband Luke and their daughter Daisy (a name alteration from the novel). In this regard the play and the film both differ from the novel, for in Atwood's book the reader is introduced to this escape attempt bit by bit, with fragments of Offred's memory of the event surfacing as the story proceeds.

The play has an equivalent declaration to that contained within the film about the biblical basis of Gileadean society, particularly with regard to laws governing marriage and divorce. This occurs in the opening minutes of the play as the Handmaid (she is named only as Offred throughout the play) and Luke, along with their daughter Daisy, attempt to cross the border into New Brunswick. They encounter a border guard who grills them over the propriety of their passport documents:

> Guard: Hi there. How are you doing?
> Luke: We are doing fine. Praise the Lord
> Guard: Praise the Lord. Could you turn your engine off, please?
> Luke: Uh-huh. *[He turns the engine off.]*
> Guard: May I see your passports?
> Luke: *[to Offred]* Honey?
> Guard: Where are you heading, sir?
> Luke: Just over to New Brunswick to see family.
> Guard: How long are you going?
> Luke: I don't know. Just a few days, I guess.
> Guard: You have a lot of luggage for a few days.
> Luke: Yeah, I guess.
> Guard: The child doesn't have a passport?
> Offred: She's only four. She's on my passport. There…you see. Daisy
> Guard. Oh, OK. How long have you been married?
> Offred: Five years.
> Guard: Has your union been blessed in the eyes of the good Lord?
> Luke: Yes.
> Guard: Can I see the certificate?
> Luke: *[to Offred]* Honey?
> Offred: Sure.
> Luke: *[Handing over the certificate.]* Here.
> Guard: This is the *old* certificate. Were you married in the church?

Luke: No. No, but we've since had the marriage blessed.
Guard: Can I see the certificate, sir?
Luke: Honey, we did bring them, didn't we?
Offred: I am sure! I am sure we did.
Luke: Or did we leave that at home?
Offred: I don't know. Um ...
Luke: Officer, I think we... we... We might have left it at home.
Guard: OK.
Luke: Do we have to have it? I can assure you, we are man and wife in the
        eyes of the good Lord!
Guard: That's OK, sir. I just need to ask you a few questions. You got
        married in the bad days, and you now have the marriage blessed. Is
        that correct?
Luke: Uh-huh.
Offred: Yes.
Guard: Have either of you been divorced?
Offred: No.
Guard: Both of you?
Luke and Offred: *[Simultaneously]* No.
Guard: Was the child born before or after your blessing?
Luke: After.
Offred: Before.
Luke: *[His voice rising in volume.]* After, honey.
Offred: Yeah, I think after.
Guard: OK. If you can just pull your car over to the side here, I just need to
        run a check on the computer.
Luke: Why? Is... Is there a problem?
Guard: Just do as I ask, please, sir.
Luke: C'mon, Bud. We've had a long drive. Is there any way we can sort
        this out?
Guard: Sure. Just pull in over here.
Luke: *[With panic in his voice.]* Look...Look, things were different before.
        You know that! You can't just change all the laws overnight!
Guard: Actually, sir, no one has changed the laws. They're in the Good
        Book for all to see. They have been for a long, long time. You just
        failed to observe them.

There are several points at which biblical images and texts are
incorporated within the play. Most of these are drawn directly from the
novel itself, and demonstrate Dryden's close attention to Atwood's text. A
good example is Aunt Lydia reading Gen. 30.1-3 to the Handmaids at the
Rachel and Leah Re-Education Centre (the same passage is read by the
Commander later in the play, just as in Schlöndorff's film where it is read
as a prelude to the first 'Ceremony'). Aunt Lydia also delivers a speech to

the women at the Centre which mentions the image from the Parable of the Sower of the seeds falling on dry or on thorny ground (Mt. 13.4-8/Mk 4.3-8/Lk. 8.5-8). She also cites Jesus' words from Lk. 23.34 ('Forgive them for they know not what they do'), as she gives advice to the Handmaids about how to respond to the wives of the Commanders in their placements, and cites Deut. 22.23-29 as the biblical justification for the execution of a convicted rapist in the Particicution ceremony towards the end of the play. Meanwhile Aunt Elizabeth cites the phrase from Isa. 40.6 and 1 Pet. 1.24 ('All flesh is weak') to the Handmaids as part of their re-education about the attitudes to the seduction of women found in most men. The sequence set in the illicit night-club known as Jezebel's again shows its dependence upon Atwood's novel, with Moira addressing Offred and invoking the imagery from Rev. 17.1-6 ('You look like the Whore of Babylon').[56]

At one point the play interjects a fresh use of biblical imagery, using it to explain why Offred's friend Moira has given up trying to escape from her life as a prostitute in Jezebel's. This involves her dependence on drugs supplied by her employers in the night-club. Safely secluded in the toilets, Moira explains to the shocked Offred that she could never leave Jezebel's, because it would mean and end to her supply of drugs. She is given an hourly hit of snortable powder (suggestive of cocaine) as part of her employment contract; these drugs she describes as 'MFH—Manna from Heaven', alluding to the story of God's provision of manna for the children of Israel in Exod. 16.1-30.

The presentation of the incident when Ofglen and Offred visit the Auto-Church in order to obtain a 'Soul Scroll' is perhaps the most interesting use of biblical texts within Dryden's play, and certainly adds an extra dimension to the story-line of the novel. The Auto-Church is described by the soulless voice of the mechanical assistant as a 'fully automated House of the Lord'. The biblical allusion comes in the form of the words given for Beatitudes in Jesus' Sermon on the Mount. The Beatitudes are voiced-over by Offred's thoughts about them, which is somewhat unfortunate because it means that a couple of the Beatitudes are difficult to make out and thus stand incomplete. However, the seven Beatitudes which can be reasonably made out are as follows:

> Blessed be the poor in spirit, for theirs is the Kingdom of heaven.
> Blessed be those who mourn, for they shall be comforted.

---

56. I noted above that Schlöndorff's film differs from the novel in this respect, reversing the role of the two women in their use of the image from Rev. 17.

Blessed be the silent, for they shall be given strength.
Blessed be those who obey the law, for they will be showered with
    reward.
Blessed be the sober, for they shall be strong.
Blessed be the non-smoker...
Blessed be those who serve their country, for by doing so they will be
    serving their Lord.

Once again, we note how Gileadean society suppresses the ability of women to express themselves, adding to Jesus' words a Beatitude about speech, or the lack of it: 'Blessed be the silent, for they shall be given strength'. At the same time as these new Beatitudes are being read out by the soulless computer-voice of the Auto-Church, Offred offers her observations about the bizarre proceedings:

I knew they'd changed things and left things out, but there was no way of checking. There's a Bible in every home, but locked up. We can be read to from it by the head of our household, we can go to the Auto-Church and get a print-out of the passage, but we cannot read it ourselves. After all, it is an incendiary device. Who knows what we'd make of it if we ever got our hands on one.

Conclusion

Margaret Atwood's novel *The Handmaid's Tale* is destined to become a modern classic, combining as it does a richly textured and varied narrative style with a timely subject matter. Throughout the novel there is an interesting interaction with biblical materials, notably Old Testament texts such as Genesis 1–3 (the stories of Adam and Eve), 30.1-3 (the story of Jacob, Rachel and Bilhah), and Jer. 8.22 (the prophecy of divine judgment on Gilead). At the same time, there are numerous examples where words, phrases and images from the New Testament are employed to fill out the nighmarish world of the Republic of Gilead. Most notable in this regard are some of the sayings of Jesus contained in the Sermon on the Mount, including the Beatitudes (Mt. 5.3-8) and the Lord's Prayer (Mt. 6.9-13). Other words of Jesus are also cited and reworked within the story, including the Parable of the Sower (Mt. 13.1-9/Mk 4.1-9/Lk. 8.4-8, the cryptic statement about the Kingdom of God being 'within you' (Lk. 17.20-21), and Jesus' words from the cross about forgiveness of his persecutors (Luke 23.34). In addition, several key texts from the New Testament epistles are invoked, generally as a means of promoting the idea of the silence of women within the religiously repressive Kingdom of Gilead; most significant in this regard is 1 Tim. 2.9-15.

All of which is to suggest that *The Handmaid's Tale* provides an excellent example of how a dialogue can be set up between the biblical materials and modern literature. Such a dialogue is extended to include other conversation partners, namely those from the worlds of cinema and radio where Atwood's novel has been creatively adapted for fresh audiences. Thus, to help overhear some of this dialogue I have included within the discussion brief forays into Volker Schlöndorff's film from 1990 and John Dryden's play from 2000, both of which attempt to bring Atwood's vision of the future to bear within their chosen art forms. Each of these endeavours also, in its own way, continues the dialogue with the biblical materials, although, as we saw, Schlöndorff's film does so primarily by narrowing the focus so that the patriarchalism of the Old Testament is what dominates.

Chapter 5

'BREAD AND CIRCUSES':
CHRISTIAN HISTORY ACCORDING TO THE WORLD OF *STAR TREK*[*]

The most interesting *Star Trek* episode, at least as far as discussions about the history of early Christianity are concerned, is 'Bread and Circuses'. The screenplay for this episode was written by Gene Roddenberry and Gene L. Coon and was based on a story by John Kneubuhl. The episode was originally aired on 15 March 1968 towards the end of the programme's second season and the contents have made it the occasional subject of comparison with Christianity ever since.

The title of the episode is taken from Juvenal's *Satires*, a humorous, but sharply penetrating criticism of the first-century Roman world by one of its most creative, and enigmatic, poets. Juvenal published his first satires sometime around 100 CE (the exact dates of his birth and death are unknown). He is described by several ancient sources as having been banished by the Emperor Domitian (81–96 CE), which may account for his biting criticism of the Roman political system. In any event, Juvenal was well placed chronologically to observe some of the tensions between the practices of the established Roman state and those of the burgeoning Christian faith. In this sense it is entirely fitting that the *Star Trek* episode which most clearly relates to the historical milieu in which Christianity arose is the one bearing a phrase from Juvenal as its title.

My task within this short chapter is to explore the way in which early Christian history is portrayed within the world of *Star Trek*. I shall be concerned in particular with the way in which the presentation of that history compares with that contained in what is generally regarded as the most historical of the New Testament writings, the two-part work known as Luke–Acts.

---

[*] This study was originally offered at a lecture at the Centre for the Study of Christianity and Culture at Regent's Park College, Oxford on 30 January 1997. See Kreitzer (2001: 207-24).

The phrase 'bread and circuses' (the Latin is *panem et circenses*) has become in modern parlance something of a byword for unrestrained and ill-disciplined pleasure, an all-consuming desire to be entertained, usually at the expense and to the degradation of others. It is especially associated with barbaric displays of physical combat in the Roman amphitheatres, fights to the death between heavily armoured gladiators or maulings of persecuted Christians and unfortunate slaves by wild beasts. One of the most famous descriptions of persecutions of Christians occurs in Tacitus' *Annals* 15.44.2–8. It describes the activities of the notoriously cruel Emperor Nero (54–68 CE) towards his victims:

> Their deaths were made farcical. Dressed in wild animals' skins, they were torn to pieces by dogs, or crucified, or made into torches to be ignited after dark as substitutes for daylight. Nero provided his Gardens for the spectacle, and exhibited displays in the Circus, at which he mingled with the crowd— or stood in a chariot, dressed as a charioteer (Grant 1956: 365-66).

The image is a familiar one to us, depicted in many Hollywood blockbuster films of the 1950s and 1960s. Films such as *The Sign of the Cross* (1932), *Quo Vadis* (1951), *Ben-Hur* (1959), *Spartacus* (1960), *Barabbas* (1962), *Cleopatra* (1963), and especially *The Robe* (1953) and its sequel *Demetrius and the Gladiators* (1954), have all helped to form our mental picture of the clash between Christianity and the Roman Empire in those first formative years following the death and resurrection of Jesus Christ. Indeed, it should hardly come as a surprise that 'Bread and Circuses' used many of the props and costumes of these epic films. After all, Paramount Pictures was the studio responsible for the production of many of them.

Yet we are not without our own contemporary versions of 'bread and circuses', particularly within the mass media. Perhaps the nearest modern equivalent is Sky Television's *WWF Superstars of Wrestling* which is rapidly growing in popularity among less discriminating viewers. Others might point to the sporting gladiatorial contests of Channel 4's *American Football* as another example of popular thirst for the thrill of 'bread and circuses'. Little seems to have changed in human nature in this regard; we have kept the same blood-thirst but simply switched the field of battle to a gymnasium, a sporting ground or a football pitch.

Most people know the Roman roots of Juvenal's phrase, but not many know its source or original context. The original setting of the satire from which it is taken is in itself illuminating. It comes from *Satire* 10, which is an extended discourse on the folly of the unscrupulous pursuit of power and an appeal for the reader to pursue virtue as the only proper goal in life. The immediate context of the crucial phrase (which occurs in line 81) has Juvenal describing the apathy of the Roman people in the aftermath of the fall of Sejanus from a position of power. In the eloquent translation of Peter Green, Juvenal laments the attitude of the people:

> Time was when their plebiscite elected Generals, Heads of State, commanders of legions: but now they've pulled in their horns, and there's only two things that concern them: Bread and the Games (P. Green 1974: 207).

Sejanus was the Prefect of the Praetorian Guard at the ascension of Tiberius to Roman Emperor (14–37 CE), and it is here that we have the first solid, historical connection with Jesus of Nazareth, for it was during the reign of Tiberius that Jesus' public ministry was conducted and it was technically under his imperial authority that Jesus was executed as a political threat. Perhaps the most influential vehicle for a popular knowledge of such matters is the BBC production of Robert Graves' *I, Claudius*.[1] As faithful viewers of the series will recall, Sejanus was a very ambitious man and soon consolidated power to himself, especially after Tiberius's withdrawal from public life to his island retreat on Capri in the bay of Naples. Rumour of the day had it that Sejanus had an eye for the imperial throne, and it took a lengthy missive from Tiberius himself to the Senate in Rome to remove Sejanus from office. Tiberius had been warned about the conspiracy just in the nick of time by Antonia, the widow of his brother Drusus, and took swift action to have Sejanus arrested and tried before the Senate. Sejanus was eventually executed on 18 October 31; he goes down in history as one of the most self-possessed leaders of his time. Juvenal picks out the rise and fall of Sejanus as a particularly apt illustration of the fickleness of fate, noting that had things taken a slightly different turn, Sejanus himself could have easily been Tiberius's successor to the imperial purple.

By a curious twist of circumstance, this character of Sejanus is also an interesting connection to the world of *Star Trek*, for sharp-eyed viewers of *I, Claudius* will recall that the character of Sejanus was played by none other than the accomplished Shakespearean actor Patrick Stewart, now better known as Captain Jean-Luc Picard of the TV series *Star Trek: The Next Generation*. A strange coincidence!

---

1.   The TV production was based on Graves' *I, Claudius* (1934) and *Claudius the God* (1935) and has been shown in America as part of *Masterpiece Theatre* hosted by Alistair Cooke on the Public Broadcasting System (PBS). The BBC released the complete series on videocassette in September 1991.

The Plot of 'Bread and Circuses'

The episode begins with the *Enterprise* encountering space wreckage while on a routine patrol. It is quickly determined that the debris is from the *S.S. Beagle*, a survey vessel under the command of Captain R.M. Merik who was at the Starfleet Academy with Captain Kirk. However, there are no bodies within the wreckage, which has been drifting for six years, and it is assumed that the crew somehow managed to escape before the ship was destroyed. The trajectory of the debris is plotted and course is set for the nearest inhabitable 'M class' planet, Planet No. 4 in System No. 892. The plan is to determine the fate of the Federation crew and ensure that the Prime Directive (that is, the injunction not to interfere with the development or culture of other species) is still in force, assuming that the crew of 47 from the *S.S. Beagle* were fortunate enough to have made it to the planet. In short, this is another of those *Star Trek* episodes which plays with the idea of intervention in other cultures and explores the limits of non-interference in other societies.

What Kirk and his colleagues discover is that Planet No. 4 is remarkably like a twentieth-century Rome. In the words of Kirk's log on board the *Enterprise*, it is 'an amazing example of Hodgkin's law of parallel-planet development. But on this earth Rome never fell. A world ruled by Emperors who can trace their line back 2,000 years to their own Julius and Augustus Caesars'. What links the reference in Juvenal to the story is the fact that this modern Roman world is complete with televised gladiatorial contests which are used to appease the masses—what we have is a TV version of 'bread and circuses'. Unfortunately, Merik and his entire crew have become unwitting pawns in the hands of the unscrupulous leader of the planet and have been forced to do battle in the arena. Merik himself has been given a position of power, 'First Citizen', in charge of the gladiatorial games, but he is really a dupe in the control of another sinister figure, the Proconsul. This power-mad ruler, Claudius Marcus, has his eye on making the crew of the *Enterprise* similar captives—a plot which Kirk must somehow foil without breaking the Prime Directive himself. This dilemma of how to succeed in rescuing survivors without compromise of principle sets up the crisis at the heart of the drama in 'Bread and Circuses'. It is a drama that plays with the fascinating question of what a modern-day Rome would be like, and there are numerous connections with the ancient world built into the story. Let us note what some of these connections are.

First of all, the the inhabitants of the planet have Latin-sounding names reminiscent of those found in ancient Rome. We have slaves by the names of Septimus and Flavius Maximus with prominent places within the story, a gladiator named Achilles, and Captain Merik is known by his Latinized name, Merikus. A slave-girl named Drusilla also appears as the obligatory love interest for Captain Kirk, soon to become one of his many conquests as he sleeps his way around the galaxy. Roman geographical terms are also the norm, including numerous references to a parallel-planet version of 'Rome' itself. The 'Forum Section' of the city is mentioned as the place where dissident slaves are rounded up by the police, recalling the fabled ruins of the (earthly) Eternal City of Rome. Kirk explains to the ex-gladiator Flavius at one point that he is from a distant 'province'—an allusion to the geopolitical make-up of the ancient Roman Empire.

In addition, deliberate parallels to the formal titles of ancient Rome are taken up and used within the episode. Thus Merik is 'First Citizen', echoing the title Princeps chosen by Augustus in 28/27 BCE to express his constitutional position of authority within the Roman world. In addition, the 'baddie' in the story is 'Proconsul' Claudius Maximus, another key title of ancient Rome adopted by a character within the episode. A Senate styled along the lines of the ancient Roman institution exists (at one point the character Septimus describes himself as a former member of it). The imperial military legions even figure briefly, when Flavius assumes, upon first seeing the trio from the *Enterprise*, that their Starfleet uniforms are outfits for some sort of new Praetorian Guard unit. However, more central to our discussion is the presentation of religion within the episode.

'Sun-Worship' and the Brotherhood of Man

The most important religious theme in 'Bread and Circuses' involves those who 'worship the sun' and describe themselves as 'brothers of the sun'. In the story-line, such adherents are invariably slaves within the structures of the parallel Roman society, runaways who have forsaken the brutality of the arena for a different way of life. The first mention of 'sun-worship' occurs when Kirk, McCoy and Spock are captured by a slave, Flavius Maximus, who takes them to meet the leader of the band of runaway slaves to which he belongs, the man named Septimus:

> Septimus: Are you children of the sun?
> McCoy: Well, if you are speaking of a worship of sorts, we represent
>   many beliefs.
> Flavius: There is only one true belief!

Eventually Kirk persuades the slaves of his mission and they agree to have Flavius lead them into the nearby city in order to locate Captain Merik. As the group leave, Septimus blesses the *Enterprise* trio with a benediction, highlighting the religious theme once again: 'May the blessings of the sun be upon you!' However, the group led by Flavius is caught by the Roman police and placed in a prison cell. There they await their fate, presuming their death will be orchestrated in the televised gladiatorial games. While in prison Kirk has a discussion with Flavius which is important for establishing not only the time-scale suggested in the episode, but the nature of the sun-worship which the former gladiator follows.

Kirk:	When the slaves began to worship the sun, they became discontent again. When did all this happen?
Flavius Maximus:	Long ago. Perhaps as long ago as the beginning of the Empire. The message of the sun that all men are brothers was kept from us. Perhaps I am a fool to believe it. It does often seem that man must fight to live.
Kirk:	You go on believing it, Flavius. All men are brothers.

There is a strong pacifist streak within this 'Brotherhood of Sun Worshippers'; they are peaceful and non-violent people. Flavius Maximus illustrates this when he refuses to enter the arena to fight in a gladiatorial contest (very reminiscent of Victor Mature's title character in the film *Demetrius and the Gladiators* mentioned above). At one point Flavius openly declares his commitment to non-violence. The Roman centurion guarding the four prisoners unlocks the cell door and the following exchange takes place:

Centurion:	Flavius! Your friends are waiting for you. You've already been matched for the morning games. Come!
Flavius:	I will not fight. I am a brother of the sun.
Centurion:	Put a sword in your hand and you'll fight! I know you, Flavius! You're as peaceful as a bull.

It is clear up to this point that sun-worship is something quite special within this society. However, we eventually discover within the last moments of the episode (presuming that we had not been able to guess it beforehand) that all of this talk of 'sun-worship' has been deliberately leading us astray. It is up to Lieutenant Uhura, the twenty-third-century equivalent of the women at the tomb, to set the trio (and the viewers) right on this score:

McCoy: Captain, I see on your report Flavius was killed. I am sorry. I liked that huge sun-worshipper.

Spock: I wish I could have examined that belief more closely. It seems illogical for a sun-worshipper to develop a philosophy of total brotherhood. Sun-worship is usually a primitive superstition-religion.

Uhura: I am afraid you have it wrong, Mr. Spock—all of you. I've been monitoring some of their old-style radio waves. The Empire spokesman is trying to ridicule their religion—but he couldn't. Don't you understand? It's not the *sun* up in the sky. It's the *Son* of God.

Kirk: Caesar and Christ! They had them both. And the Word is spreading only now.

McCoy: A philosophy of total love and total brotherhood.

Spock: It will replace their Imperial Rome, but it will happen in their twentieth century.

Kirk: Wouldn't it be something to watch, to be a part of? To see it happen all over again?[2]

In fact, the essential core of the episode is built upon this play on words—the ambiguity of the spoken word 'sun/son'. I have no doubt that it never occurs to many first-time viewers of the episode that it is really about 'Son-worship' from the beginning. Indeed, the director of the episode, Ralph Senensky, has deliberately reinforced our association of 'sun-worship' with what is being said by the actors throughout. The best illustration of this occurs when Septimus pronounces his benediction on the group as they leave the slaves' cave and travel towards the city. Here Senensky deliberately cuts to a shot of the sun shining brightly overhead at the precise point that Septimus says the crucial (ambiguous) word. We may feel, as viewers, that we have been taken for something of a ride on this one, but the surprising revelation of the true nature of the 'Son-worship' certainly makes for dramatic irony and a pleasant twist in the tale. True, we are provided with one hint that things might not be as they first appear in an early exchange between Spock and McCoy on the matter. Speaking of the Roman slaves, they say:

---

2.   Uhura's remark is all the more striking when it is remembered that it is framed by Spock's and McCoy's references to 'total *brother*hood'. In the context of the USA in the late 1960s, a black woman would have been on the margins of much of American society, and Uhura's comment contains a certain amount of irony as a result. Here we have an idealized vision of sexual and social equality in the future trapped in the patriarchalism of the (then) present.

McCoy: Odd that these people should worship the sun.

Spock: Why, Doctor?

McCoy: Because, my dear Spock, it is illogical. Rome had no sun-
worshippers. Why would they parallel Rome in every way except
one?

Yet even this is slightly misleading, for ancient Rome did have sun-worship, not least because it embodied the religious beliefs and traditions of its subject peoples, including the Egyptians—and, as everyone knows, Egyptian religious beliefs included a prominent place for worship of the sun-god Ra. In addition, there is good supporting evidence for the worship of a minor sun-god, named Sol, among Roman peoples themselves. Augustan calendars even set an official date for sacrifice to the god Sol, on 9 August. Nor should we forget the identification of Apollo with Helios early in the ancient Roman world, as witnessed by Horace's *Centennial Hymn*, composed for Augustus's reinstitution of the Saecular Games in 17 BCE. Line 9 of the *Hymn* explicitly addresses Apollo as 'Kind Sun'. Even more striking is the fact that the Roman Emperor Elagabalus (218–222 CE) attempted a reformation of the Roman pantheon with his own local god Sol taking central place (Elagabalus was from Syria, a province renowned for its cultic worship of Sol). A similar move was made by another Roman Emperor, Aurelian (270–275 CE), a generation later. So keen was Elagabalus to promote the worship of Sol, that he identified himself with the god and minted coins bearing inscriptions to that effect. Aurelian did the same and even had a Temple of the Sun built, probably on the Quirinal Hill in Rome. Thus, sun-worship flourished in the Roman Empire up until Constantinian times when it was superseded by Christianity following the Emperor Constantine's conversion to the 'true faith'. Indeed, just to highlight this, it is worth noting that in the year 321 Sunday was declared to be an official day of rest precisely because it was Sun-day.[3] The point is that it would be a brave historian indeed who would categorically assert (as McCoy does) that 'Rome had no sun-worshippers'. Still, the exchange serves its purpose as far as the drama of the *Star Trek* episode is concerned, even if it is historically inaccurate. Clearly the aim is to juxtapose 'sun-worship' and 'Son-worship' within the story.

One final, curious fact is worth remembering here that succeeds in driving home this essential point of contrast ('sun' versus 'Son'), but not

---

3.   This matter of sun-worship is discussed in some detail in Ferguson 1970: 52-56. Ferguson also briefly discusses (237) a Christian mosaic found under St Peter's in Rome which depicts Christ as the sun-god driving his chariot across the sky.

at the expense of historical inaccuracy. It seems that Aurelian's 'Temple of the Sun' was originally dedicated on 25 December, at the winter solstice, as a symbol of the unconquerable sun coming forth once again to increase light. So widespread was the pagan festival associated with Sol and the winter solstice that early in the fourth century the Christian church spiritualized it and transformed it into the Feast of the Nativity of the Son of Righteousness. The first tentative steps were thus taken to the festival we now all know as Christmas.

In short, 'Bread and Circuses' sets out the relationship between 'sun-worship' and 'Son-worship' as a straightforward clash between pagan Rome and the truth of Christianity—and it leaves the impression that Christianity will eventually prevail over the more primitive Roman world. In this sense the episode is very reminiscent of the confrontation between pagan Rome and the Christian church which we see culminate in the legendary words of Emperor Julian II (known as Julian the Apostate, 361–363 CE, who, following his unsuccessful attempt to revive pagan religion at the expense of Christianity, was driven to utter on his deathbed: 'You have conquered, O Galilean!'

However, things are rarely so simple and it is probably nearer the truth to say that historically Christianity prevailed by absorbing, rather than confronting, pagan sun-worship. Let us now turn to consider the way in which the rise of Christianity is explained within both Luke–Acts and 'Bread and Circuses'.

The Historical Framing of the Story

It has long been recognized that Luke's Gospel has a special concern with setting the story of Jesus of Nazareth against its historical background. Indeed, the author (traditionally known as Luke the physician) declares his intention along these lines in the opening paragraph of the work (Lk. 1.1-4):

> Inasmuch as many have undertaken to compile a narrative of the things which have been accomplished among us, just as they were delivered to us by those who from the beginning were eyewitnesses and ministers of the word, it seemed good to me also, having followed all things closely for some time past, to write an orderly account for you, most excellent Theophilus, that you may know the truth concerning the things of which you have been informed.

This same attention to historical detail is echoed throughout Acts, which also opens with a similar declaration made to Luke's patron Theophilus about the life of Jesus (Acts 1.1): 'In the first book, O Theophilus, I have dealt with all that Jesus began to do and teach'.

At several other points in the Gospel narrative the writer provides historical anchors to his account of the life of Jesus of Nazareth. Thus we read in Lk. 2.1-2: 'In those days a decree went out from Emperor Augustus that all the world should be registered. This was the first registration and was taken while Quirinius was governor of Syria'. Or, again in Lk. 3.1-2, Luke's version of the story of John the Baptist, the herald of Jesus' messianic ministry, is opened with these words, filled as they are with references to historical personages:

> In the fifteenth year of the reign of Emperor Tiberius, when Pontius Pilate was governor of Judea, and Herod was ruler of Galilee, and his brother Philip ruler of the region of Ituraea and Trachonitis, and Lysanias ruler of Abilene, during the high priesthood of Annas and Caiaphas, the word of God came to John the son of Zechariah in the wilderness.

The central point here is that Luke clearly gives the story of Jesus of Nazareth an historical context, firmly placing the portrait he wishes to paint within a historical framework. That is not to say that the other Gospel accounts do not contain references to important historical persons or events—they certainly do. However, these are generally incidental to the story of Jesus Christ as they present it and do not have the same theological significance as they do in Luke. When one compares Luke to the Gospel of Matthew, for instance, on this point the difference quickly becomes clear. Matthew opens his account of the life of Jesus with a genealogy (1.1-17), firmly setting forth the Jewish credentials of the Christ with no reference to the historical facts of the contemporary Roman world at all. Indeed, the Roman world is only hinted at in the body of Matthew's Gospel (a Roman military centurion figures in a healing story in 8.5-13 and a version of the debate between Jesus and the Pharisees about paying taxes to Caesar appears in 22.15-22). We have to wait until the trial and crucifixion of Jesus (in Mt. 27) before we have any detailed mention of a Roman citizen, namely Pilate. This stands in stark contrast to Luke, who is making a specific point about Roman history throughout. It is hardly surprising that all four references to the name 'Augustus' contained in the New Testament appear in Luke–Acts (Lk. 2.1; Acts 25.21, 25; 27.1), as does the single New Testament reference to 'Tiberius' (Lk. 3.1), and the two New Testament references to 'Claudius' (Acts 11.28; 18.2). It is as if Luke continually 'drops anchors' into secular Roman history, a style which helps characterize his work. As one New Testament scholar,

Donald Juel, says: 'It is significant that Luke chose history as the medium through which to address his generation' (1983: 121).

Effectively, the *Star Trek* episode does exactly the same thing, spinning out its tale of non-interference in another culture within the context of a defined historical period, that of ancient Rome. Yet what makes 'Bread and Circuses' so effective is that it does not attempt to proceed as a straightforward story about ancient Rome itself. Instead, it updates the story, suggestively setting the whole thing within a futuristic context, bringing into play features of the contemporary world of the 1960s and making us as an audience imagine what a difference they may make in shaping this fictitious Rome. But the key point of contact between Luke's work and 'Bread and Circuses' should not be overlooked—the placing of the story within a concrete historical period, that of imperial Rome.

Three Distinctive Lukan Echoes in the Story

At three particular points, features of Luke's distinctive way of telling the gospel story appear in 'Bread and Circuses'. None of them is immediately obvious (Luke's work is nowhere explicitly quoted, for instance), but when the episode is examined closely they readily appear. Taken together they might be said to demonstrate how much 'Bread and Circuses' relies, perhaps even unconsciously, upon Luke's special contribution to the New Testament.

First, Luke's account of the annunciation of the birth of Jesus is alluded to in a curious way early in the episode. Shortly after Kirk, McCoy and Spock beam down to the planet in order to search for their lost comrades from the *S.S. Beagle*, Dr McCoy remarks: 'Once, just once, I would like to be able to land someplace and say, "Behold, I am the archangel Gabriel" '. This is a fascinating parallel to Luke 1–2, where the archangel Gabriel is instrumental in announcing the births of John the Baptist and Jesus. In fact, Gabriel is mentioned by name only twice in the New Testament, both instances in connection with these annunciations (Lk. 1.19, 26).[4] Secondly, Luke's distinctive description of Jesus' ascension seems to underlie a comment made by Septimus to Captain Kirk while the two are in the confines of the slaves' hideaway cave. Kirk, seeking information concerning the whereabouts of the crew of the *S.S. Beagle*, yet conscious of the need to

---

4. The other Gospel account of the annunciation of Jesus' birth, Mt. 1.18-25, does not mention the angel Gabriel by name.

obey the Prime Directive and maintain secrecy, puts a suitably phrased question of the slave leader, who replies:

> Septimus: No, Captain. I am sure I would have heard of the arrival of other men like you.
> Kirk: Perhaps you have heard, let's say, an impossible story, or a rumour, of men who came from the sky? Or from other worlds?
> Septimus: There are no other worlds.
> Kirk: The stars…
> Septimus: Lights shining through from heaven. It is where the sun is. Blessed be the sun.

It all seems innocent enough—until we remember that it is only in the writings of Luke that we encounter within the New Testament any description of Jesus' ascension from earth into the heavens following his resurrection from the dead. Luke explicitly gives us two declarations of this (Lk. 24.51 and Acts 1.9-11) and alludes to it in a third case (Lk. 9.51), while the rest of the New Testament documents leave Jesus' present heavenly residence an inference at best. The crucial point is that it is only in Luke that Jesus is explicitly said to have ascended into heaven—it is only in Luke's writings that the Son's movement to heaven is described in any detail. The comment of Septimus in 'Bread and Circuses' presumes precisely what Luke describes to us. As Leslie Houlden, commenting on the ascension theme within this New Testament document, has rightly noted: 'This occasion is then the watershed of Luke-Acts and makes sense of the conception of that novel work as a whole, with its wide historical and geographical sweep. In the New Testament it is a unique conception' (1991: 178).

In point of fact, we could legitimately say that the reason why we so often read ascension theology into such descriptions as '[Christ] seated at the right hand of God' (Col. 3.1 drawing upon the messianic passage in Ps. 110.1) when they occur in the New Testament is precisely because Luke at this point has theologically won the day. His description of Jesus Christ's ascension is taken to be normative, setting the tone for our reading of the rest of the New Testament.

Thirdly, there is an explicit polemic against what are perceived as false gods (by the followers of the Sun/Son) within the episode. At one point Spock shows Kirk a magazine entitled *The Gallian* which contains advertisements for a number of consumer goods all being marketed with the names of Roman deities. A Jupiter 8 automobile, Mars toothpaste, and Neptune bath salts are all mentioned. Septimus explains at this point that the names of the products are all 'taken from the names of false gods. When I was a Senator, I worshipped them too. But I heard the words of the sun. I became a brother. For that, they made me a slave'.

The second part of Luke's work, the Acts of the Apostles, describes in several key episodes how the truth of Christianity stands over against pagan belief in false gods. This is especially true in connection with the ministry of the apostle Paul, as he helps spread the message of salvation to the Greek-speaking world. A good example of this occurs in Acts 17.16-33 where Paul confronts the cultured men of Athens about their superstitious belief in false gods. In vv. 22-23 we read these words:

> So Paul, standing up in the middle of the Areopagus, said: 'Men of Athens, I perceive that in every way you are very religious. For as I passed along, and observed the objects of your worship, I found also an altar with this inscription, "To an unknown god". What therefore you worship as unknown, this I proclaim to you'.

This recalls Peter's sermon recorded earlier in Acts in which the particularism of Christian redemption is declared in no uncertain terms. Note the closing words of the sermon (4.12), where, speaking of Jesus Christ, Peter says: 'And there is salvation in no one else, for there is no other name under heaven given among men by which we must be saved.'

Again, it is the implied clash between Roman religion and Christian faith in Jesus Christ which underlies Luke's account. It is precisely this same clash which generates the conflict essential to the dramatic plot of 'Bread and Circuses'. 'Sun-worship' and 'Son-worship' are presented as mutually incompatible and irreconcilably opposed. Remember Flavius Maximus's declaration in the face of McCoy's espousal of religious pluralism (mentioned above): 'There is only *one* true belief!'

Perhaps it is because Luke, more than any other New Testament writer, addresses the Gentile world that this contrast shows up so readily. This is not to say that there is no theological tension within Luke–Acts over the matter; the fact that Luke even discusses the question of the existence of other gods militates against such a simplistic suggestion. But it is to say that for Luke–Acts the final resolution of the matter is in no doubt—Jesus Christ is the sole source of truth and life and the claims of Christianity as a religious faith are absolute. In any event, the attitude expressed by Luke within his work about the pagan religions of the Greco-Roman world is remarkably similar to that of the Son-worshippers on Planet No. 4 and constitutes another point of contact between 'Bread and Circuses' and Luke–Acts. Interestingly, this particularistic attitude also stands in stark contrast to that of the crew members of the *Enterprise*, who are markedly more open and pluralistic in their approach to such religious matters.

Theological Hope or Misplaced Optimism?

Before we get too carried away and make it sound as if 'Bread and Circuses' is nothing more than a popularized version of Luke's account of Christianity dressed up in science-fiction garb, there is one further point of comparison between the two which must not be overlooked. It has to do with the impression left about the future of history. Will Christianity triumph or not? Will the effects of this new religion known as Christianity (or 'Son-worship') be positive or negative? There is little doubt that in 'Bread and Circuses' the viewer is left with a vision of eventual triumph, even over the less desirable aspects of slavery. Spock notes this at one point, remarking on how slavery has evolved into a social institution within this galactic Rome. In short, the story ends on a very optimistic note; some would even say that it crosses the border into naivety. Joyce Tullock hits the nail on the head when, commenting on the world the *Enterprise* crew leave behind, she says:

> Whether or not that world is all that different from ours today, or whether the growth of the worship of 'The Son' will improve conditions in that brutal society, is, in fact, an open question. The 'Son' worshippers are certainly benevolent and morally superior to the decadent Romanlike establishment, so the implication is that the planet's civilization is bound to improve. Let's hope it will. The *Enterprise* leaves it a growing, changing civilization, in accordance with the Prime Directive. But there seems to be something rather naive in the attitude of the crew as they leave the planet. It's as though none of them have ever heard of the Crusades, the Dark Ages, or the witch trials (1980: 96).

However much we may agree with Tullock in her assessment of Christian history (and it is difficult to dismiss it completely), that is not the end of the matter. In one sense this overstated optimism in 'Bread and Circuses' perfectly matches Luke's presentation of Christianity. Luke clearly presents the Christian faith as ultimately triumphant and eventually moving to embrace the whole of the world, spreading to the ends of the earth. Many New Testament scholars have remarked upon the apologetic interest underlying Luke's work, the fact that he wishes to present Christianity in a favourable light to the Roman world of his day, to emphasize its positive features and to downplay the suggestion that the new religion is in any way a threat to the political stability of the Roman world. Others have fastened upon Luke's desire to address the needs of the believing Christian community itself as the motivation for the work. Regardless of what precisely we feel Luke's motivation to have been, it is hard to deny that his work is one of irrepressible hope—Christianity will triumph in the end.

Perhaps *Star Trek's* vision of the future in 'Bread and Circuses' is, as Joyce Tullock suggests, naive in the extreme; but then so was Luke's vision of the progress of Christianity. We could go so far as to say that such optimism is necessary in a rapidly changing world filled with social problems and uncertainty—it is part of the mythic power of both stories. As Juel notes in the conclusion of his helpful little book on Luke–Acts:

> Luke's optimism may be naive. Yet in our time, in a society where Christians have real power or access to power, abandoning creation to the forces of darkness would be a premature surrender. The apocalyptic mentality is more dangerous, perhaps than naive optimism. It is willing to consider the possibility of nuclear holocaust, and its preoccupation with crises of cosmic proportion can conceal the small wounds we regularly inflict upon creation. And even if we possess power, sensing genuine possibilities in our future requires confidence that life makes sense, that the past contains resources for the present, that we can believe in a God who is dependable and can be trusted with our destiny (1983: 123).

CONCLUSION

In his fascinating study entitled *Imaging the Divine: Jesus and Christ-Figures in Film* (1997), Lloyd Baugh explores how the person and ministry of Jesus Christ have been portrayed in various films over the years. He divides his study into two major parts, roughly corresponding to the historical and theological dimensions of the traditional proclamation of the Christian faith. Thus, in the first part, designated 'The Jesus-Film', such films as *King of Kings, The Greatest Story Ever Told, The Gospel According to Saint Matthew, Jesus of Nazareth, The Last Temptation of Christ*, and even *The Life of Brian*, are discussed. In the second part, designated 'The Christ-Figure', such diverse films as *Jesus of Montreal, Babette's Feast, Dead Man Walking, Au Hasard Balthazar* and *Stalker* are addressed. Baugh suggests that film-makers are following in the footsteps of countless generations of artists before them, men and women who have sought to present the Christian message to the world in which they lived. Given that the Roman Catholic faith in particular has such a rich artistic history, it is perhaps not altogether surprising that Baugh himself is based at the Pontifical Gregorian University in Rome, where he now is an Associate Professor of Film Studies and Theology.

The essays within this volume have also been concerned with how some contemporary film-makers have applied their art to works that exhibit theological dimensions. Within these studies, however, the focus has not so much been on the person and ministry of Jesus Christ himself, but on some of the words attributed to him, or on images from the Gospels closely associated with him, and on how these words and images receive cinematic expression. At the same time, I have used well known pieces of literature as additional conversation partners in the discussions. Thus, I began by exploring how the story of the Journey of the Magi (contained in Mt. 2.1-12) was understood by the poet T.S. Eliot as a prefigurement of the passion that the Christ-child was to undergo. The same approach to the story of the Magi can also be seen in several films, notably Pasolini's *The Gospel According to Matthew* and Stevens' *The Greatest Story Ever Told*.

The apocalyptic saying of Jesus contained in Mk 13.14 about 'the abomination of desolation' serves as the entry-point for the discussion of Joseph Conrad's *Heart of Darkness*. In this case the biblical basis for the discussion was expanded to include another image found in apocalyptic literature, namely the Whore of Babylon (Rev. 17.1-6). The apocalyptic imagery of these two texts, along with their concomitant ideas of political oppression, was used as a platform for exploring two films which are based on Conrad's work, Roeg's *Heart of Darkness* and Coppola's *Apocalypse Now*. Meanwhile, the provocative image of Jesus Christ's crucifixion resulting in an apocalyptic 'darkness at noon' was used to examine the Gospel accounts of Jesus' death. Here it was the way in which apocalyptic timetables set up a clash between good and evil that became our focus, and we examined several different films from quite different genres in the course of the discussion, including two versions of the western *High Noon* and the science-fiction adaptation *Outland*.

With the study of Atwood's *The Handmaid's Tale* we returned once again to some of the words of Jesus recorded in the Gospels and noted how creatively these are reworked so as to forge a vision of a dystopian society in the near future. Here it was some of the Beatitudes, for example, which became primary points for discussion, particularly as these are reworked in the various film and radio adaptations of Atwood's novel that have been produced in recent years. Finally, I offered a playful excursus into Gene Roddenberry's fictional universe of *Star Trek* and noted some of the biblical parallels underlying one of the classic episodes of the original television series, an episode entitled 'Bread and Circuses'.

All in all, the essential aim of the volume follows that which I first put forward nearly ten years ago: to allow a dialogue to take place between the biblical text, great works of literature, and that most persuasive of modern art forms, the cinema. There remains so much more to do along these lines; the door is wide open for such interdisciplinary approaches to be developed and refined. My only hope is that the task may not seem too daunting, and that interested explorers will come forward and join in the fray!

BIBLIOGRAPHY

Abercrombie, T.J.
  1985   'Arabia's Frankincense Trail', *National Geographic* 168.4 (October): 474-513.
Ackroyd, P.R.
  1983   'Goddesses, Women and Jezebel', in Averil Cameron and Amélie Kurht (eds.), *Images of Women in Antiquity* (London: Croom Helm): 245-59.
  1984   *T.S. Eliot* (London: Hamish Hamilton).
Adair, G.
  1981   *Hollywood's Vietnam: From* The Green Berets *to* Apocalypse Now (New York: Proteus).
Allison, D.C.
  1987   *The End of the Ages Has Come. An Early Interpretation of the Passion and Resurrection of Jesus* (Edinburgh: T. & T. Clark).
  1993   *The New Moses: A Matthean Typology* (Edinburgh: T. & T. Clark).
Ambrosini, R.
  1991   *Conrad's Fiction as Critical Discourse* (Cambridge: Cambridge University Press)
Amis, K.
  1986   *The Old Devils* (London: Guild Publishing).
Andreas, O.
  1962   *Joseph Conrad: A Study in Non-Conformity* (London: Vision Press).
Andriano, J.
  1992–93   *The Handmaid's Tale* as Scrabble Game', *Essays on Canadian Writing* 48: 89-96.
Aristides, P.A.
  1981   *The Complete Works*. II. *Orations XVII-LIII* (trans. Charles A. Behr; Leiden: E.J. Brill).
Armitt, L.
  2000   *Contemporary Women's Fiction and the Fantastic* (London: Macmillan).
Asimov, I.
  1974   'Pompey and Circumstance', in *The Left Hand of the Electron* (New York: Dell Publishing).
Atwood, M.
  1991–92   'Comment on Allusion', *University of Toronto Quarterly* 61: 382.
  1996   *The Handmaid's Tale* (London: Vintage Books).
Aune, D.E.
  1998   *Revelation 17–22* (WBC, 52C; Nashville, TN: Thomas Nelson Publishers).

Baines, J.
1960   *Joseph Conrad: A Critical Biography* (London: Weidenfeld and Nicolson).
Balabanski, V.
1997   *Eschatology in the Making: Mark, Matthew and the Didache* (SNTSMS, 97;
              Cambridge: Cambridge University Press).
Banerjee, C.
1990   'Alice in Disneyland: Criticism as Commodity in *The Handmaid's Tale*',
              Essays on Canadian Writing 41: 74-92.
Barbour, B.M.
1988   'Poetic Form in "Journey of the Magi" ', *Renascence* 40: 189-96.
Barclay, W.
1976   *The Revelation of John* (DSB; 2 vols.; Philadelphia: Westminster Press,
              1976).
Barnes, T.D.
1968   'The Date of Herod's Death', *JTS* 19: 204-209.
Bartkowski, F.
1989   *Feminist Utopias* (Lincoln: University of Nebraska Press).
Batchelor, J.
1994   *The Life of Joseph Conrad* (Oxford: Blackwell Publishers).
Bauckham, R.
1989   *The Bible in Politics: How to Read the Bible Politically* (London: SPCK).
1991   'The Economic Critique of Rome in Revelation 18', in L. Alexander (ed.),
              Images of Empire (JSOTSup, 122; Sheffield: JSOT Press): 47-90.
1993a   *The Climax of Prophecy: Studies on the Book of Revelation* (Edinburgh: T.
              & T. Clark).
1993b   *The Theology of the Book of Revelation* (Cambridge: Cambridge University
              Press).
Baudrillard, J.
1994   *Simulacra and Simulation* (Ann Arbor: University of Michigan Press).
Baugh, L.
1997   *Imaging the Divine: Jesus and Christ-Figures in Film* (Kansas City: Sheed
              & Ward).
Baughman, C.
1990   'Review of *The Handmaid's Tale*', *Pinter Review: Annual Essays*: 92-96.
Baum, J.
1975   'The 'Real' *Heart of Darkness*', *Conradiana* 7: 183-87.
Beagley, A.J.
1987   *The 'Sitz im Leben' of the Apocalypse with Particular Reference to the Role
              of the Church's Enemies* (BZNW, 50; Berlin: Walter de Gruyter).
Beale, G.K.
1998   *John's Use of the Old Testament in Revelation* (JSNTSup, 166; Sheffield:
              Sheffield Academic Press).
1999   *The Book of Revelation: A Commentary on the Greek Text* (NIGTC; Grand
              Rapids, MI: Eerdmans).
Beare, F.W.
1981   *The Gospel According to Matthew* (Oxford: Blackwell).
Beasley-Murray, G.R.
1956   *Jesus and the Future: An Examination of the Criticism of the Eschatological*

	Discourse, Mark 13 with Special Reference to the Little Apocalypse Theory (London: Macmillan).
1957	*A Commentary on Mark Thirteen* (London: Macmillan).
1978	*The Book of Revelation* (NCB; London: Marshall, Morgan & Scott, rev. edn, 1978).

Beauvery, R.
1983   'Babylone, La Grande Prostituée et Le Sixième Roi Vespasien et La Déesse Rome', *RB* 90: 242-60 + Plate 1.

Behlmer, R.
1989   *Behind the Scenes* (Hollywood: Samuel French).

Benjamin, W.
1968   'The Work of Art in the Age of Mechanical Reproduction', in *Illumination* (trans. Harry Zohn; New York: Schocken Books): 217-51.

Benson, D.R.
1971   '*Heart of Darkness*: The Grounds of Civilization in an Alien Universe', in Kimbrough (ed.) 1971: 210-17.

Bergan, R.
1998   *Francis Coppola* (London: Orion Books).

Bergmann, H.F.
1989   ' "Teaching Them to Read": A Fishing Expedition in *The Handmaid's Tale*', *College English* 51: 847-54.

Bernegger, P.M.
1983   'Affirmation of Herod's Death in 4 B.C.', *JTS* 34: 526-31

Berthoud, J.
1978   *Joseph Conrad: The Major Phase* (Cambridge: Cambridge University Press).

Bignell, J.
1993   'Lost Messages: *The Handmaid's Tale*, Novel and Film', *British Journal of Canadian Studies* 8: 71-84.

Billy, T.
1989   'A Curious Case of Influence: *Nostromo* and *Alien(s)*', *Conradiana* 21: 147-57.

Biskind, P.
1983   *Seeing is Believing: How Hollywood Taught Us to Stop Worrying and Love the Fifties* (New York: Pantheon Books).

Blackburn, W. (ed.)
1958   *Joseph Conrad: Letters to William Blackwood and David S. Meldrum* (Durham, NC: Duke University Press).

Blevins, J.L.
1984   *Revelation* (KPG; Atlanta: John Knox Press).

Bobbin, J.
2000   'It's 'Noon' or Never for Skerritt on TV', *Lexington-Herald Leader*: Bluegrass Edition 37.

Bock, D.L.
1996   *Luke 9.51–24.53* (BECNT, 3B; Grand Rapids, MI: Baker Book House).

Bogue, R.L.
1981   'The Heartless Darkness of *Apocalypse Now*', *Georgia Review* 35: 611-26.

Bond, R.B.
    1992   'Whore of Babylon', in David Lyle Jeffrey (ed.), *A Dictionary of Biblical Tradition in English Literature* (Grand Rapids, MI: Eerdmans): 826-28.
Boring, M.E.
    1989   *Revelation* (IC; Louisville, KY: John Knox Press).
Bourke, M.M.
    1960   'The Literary Genius of Matthew 1–2', *CBQ* 22: 160-75.
Boyle, T.E.
    1971   'Marlow's "Lie"', in Robert Kimbrough (ed.), *Joseph Conrad: Heart of Darkness* (New York: W.W. Norton & Company, rev. edn): 240-44.
Bradbury, M.
    1988   *The Modern World: Ten Great Writers* (London: Penguin Books).
Bradley, I.
    1999   *The Penguin Book of Carols* (London: Penguin Books).
Brantlinger, P.
    1985a   '*Heart of Darkness*: Anti-Imperialism, Racism, or Impressionism?', *Criticism* 27: 363-85.
    1985b   'Victorians and Africans: The Geneaology of the Myth of the Dark Continent', in Henry Louis Gates, Jr (ed.), *'Race', Writing and Difference* (Chicago: University of Chicago Press): 185-222.
Braybrooke, N.
    1967   *T.S. Eliot: A Critical Essay* (Contemporary Writers in Christian Perspective; Grand Rapids: Eerdmans).
Breskin, D.
    1992   *Inner Views: Filmmakers in Conversation* (London: Faber & Faber).
Brodie, S.L.
    1984   'Conrad's Feminine Perspective', *Conradiana* 16: 141-54.
Broes, A.T.
    1966   'T.S. Eliot's *Journey of the Magi*: An Explication', *Xavier University Studies* 5: 129-31.
Brooks, P.
    1996   'An Unreadable Report: Conrad's *Heart of Darkness*', in Elaine Jordan (ed.), *New Casebooks: Joseph Conrad* (London: Macmillan): 67-86.
Bross, A.C.
    1969–70   'The Indistinguishable Light of Belief: Conrad's Attitude Toward Women', *Conradiana* 2: 39-46.
Brown, D.
    1964   'From *Heart of Darkness* to *Nostromo*: An Approach to Conrad', in Boris Ford (ed.), *The Modern Age* (Harmondsworth: Penguin Books, 2nd rev. edn): 119-37.
Brown, R.D.
    1972   'Revelation in T.S. Eliot's "Journey of the Magi"', *Renascence*: 136-40.
Brown, R.E.
    1979   *The Birth of the Messiah: A Commentary on the Infancy Narratives in Matthew and Luke* (Garden City, NY: Image Books).
    1994   *The Death of the Messiah: From Gethsemane to the Grave* (2 vols.; New York: Doubleday).

Bruffee, K.A.
1971   'The Lesser Nightmare', in Robert Kimbrough (ed.), *Joseph Conrad: Heart of Darkness* (New York: W.W. Norton & Co., rev. edn): 233-40.

Bruns, J.E.
1961   'The Magi Episode in Matthew 2', *CBQ* 23: 51-54.
1964   'The Contrasted Women of Apocalypse 12 and 17', *CBQ* 26: 459-63.

Burden, R.
1991   *Heart of Darkness: An Introduction to the Variety of Criticism* (London: Macmillan).

Burgess, E.F.
1984   'T.S. Eliot's "The Journey of the Magi"', *The Explicator* 42.4: 36.

Burrows, E.
1938   *The Oracles of Jacob and Balaam* (London: Burns Oates & Washbourne).

Cahir, L.C.
1992   'Narratological Parallels in Joseph Conrad's *Heart of Darkness* and Francis Ford Coppola's *Apocalypse Now*', *Literature/Film Quarterly* 20: 181-87.

Caird, G.B.
1963   *The Gospel of Saint Luke* (The Pelican New Testament Commentaries; Harmondsworth: Penguin Books).
1966   *The Revelation of St John the Divine* (London: A. & C. Black).
1980   *The Language and Imagery of the Bible* (London: Duckworth).

Callan, M.F.
1993   *Sean Connery: The Untouchable Hero* (London: Virgin Publishing).

Canary, R.A.
1982   *T.S. Eliot: The Poet and his Critics* (Chicago: American Library Association).

Canby, V.
1979a   'The Screen: *Apocalypse Now*', *New York Times* (15 August): C.15.
1979b   '*Apocalypse Now* is "Extremely Misty"', *New York Times* (19 August): Section 2.1, 1, 15.

Carringer, R.L.
1985   *The Making of Citizen Kane* (Berkeley: University of California Press).

Carrington, I.D.P.
1987   'A Swiftian Sermon', *Essays on Canadian Writing* 34: 127-32.

Chadwick, H.
1953   *Origen: Contra Celsum: Translated with an Introduction and Notes* (Cambridge: Cambridge University Press).

Chance, J.B.
1988   *Jerusalem, the Temple, and the New Age in Luke–Acts* (Macon, GA: Mercer University Press).

Chatman, S.
1997   '2½ Film Versions of Heart of Darkness', in Gene M. Moore (ed.), *Conrad on Film* (Cambridge: Cambridge University Press): 207-23.

Chaucer, G.
1951   *Canterbury Tales* (London: Penguin Books).

Chesterton, G.K.
1933   'The Ballad of the White Horse', *The Collected Poems of G.K. Chesterton* (London: Methuen Press, 3rd edn).

Church, A.
    1987   'Conrad's *Heart of Darkness*', *The Explicator* 45: 35-37.
Clark, D.H., with John H. Parkinson and F. Richard Stephenson
    1977   'An Astronomical Re-Appraisal of the Star of Bethlehem—A Nova in 5 BC',
                Quarterly Journal of the Royal Astronomical Society 18: 443-49.
Cleary, T.R., and Terry G. Sherwood
    1984   'Women in Conrad's Ironical Epic: Virgil, Dante and *Heart of Darkness*',
                Conradiana 16: 183-94.
Clute, J.
    1990   'Review of *The Handmaid's Tale* (film)', *Times Literary Supplement*: 1181.
Cohen, H.
    1972   'The *Heart of Darkness* in *Citizen Kane*', *Cinema Journal* 12: 11-25.
Coleridge, S.T.
    1944   *The Rime of the Ancient Mariner* (London: Corevinus Press).
Collins, A.Y.
    1980   'Revelation 18: Taunt-Song or Dirge?', in J. Lambrecht (ed.), *L'Apocalypse
                johannique et l'Apocalyptique dans le Nouveau Testament* (BETL, 53;
                Leuven: Leuven University Press): 185-204.
    1984   *Crisis and Catharsis: The Power of the Apocalypse* (Philadelphia: West-
                minster Press).
Collins, H.R.
    1960   'Kurtz, the Cannibals, and the Second-Rate Helmsman', in Leonard F. Dean
                (ed.), *Joseph Conrad's* Heart of Darkness*: Backgrounds and Criticisms*
                (Englewood Cliffs, NJ: Prentice–Hall): 149-59.
Collins, J.J.
    1993   *Daniel* (HC; Minneapolis: Fortress Press).
Combs, R.
    1986   'When the Big Hand is on the Twelve…or 7 Ambiguities of Time', *Monthly
                Film Bulletin* 53: 186-88.
Conrad, J.
    1921   *Tales of Unrest* (London: J.M. Dent & Sons).
    1926   *Last Essays* (J.M. Dent & Sons).
    1973   *Heart of Darkness* (Penguin Classics; Harmondsworth: Penguin Books)
Cooke, N.
    1998   *Margaret Atwood: A Biography* (Toronto: ECW Press).
Coppola, E.
    1995   *Notes: On the Making of* Apocalypse Now (London: Faber & Faber).
Coupe, L.
    1997   *Myth* (London: Routledge).
Court, J.M.
    1979   *Myth and History in the Book of Revelation* (Atlanta: John Knox Press).
    1994   *Revelation* (NTG; Sheffield: Sheffield Academic Press).
Cow, G.
    1970   'Don't Throw Them Away: Richard Fleischer Talks about Psychology, Life
                and Fiction', *Films and Filming* 17: 20-25.
Cowart, D.
    1989   *History of the Contemporary Novel* (Carbondale, IL: Southern Illinois
                University Press).

Cowie, P.
  1989   *Coppola* (London: Faber & Faber).
Cox, G.B.
  1974   *Joseph Conrad: The Modern Imagination* (London: J.M. Dent).
  1977   *Writers and their Work: Joseph Conrad* (Harlow: Longman).
  1981   'Introduction', in G.B. Cox (ed.), *Conrad:* Heart of Darkness, Nostromo *and*
                Under Western Eyes: *A Selection of Critical Essays* (London: Macmillan):
                11-20.
Crawford, R.
  1987   *The Savage and the City in the Work of T.S. Eliot* (Oxford: Clarendon Press).
Creed, J.M.
  1960   *The Gospel According to St Luke* (London: Macmillan & Co.).
Crews, F.
  1975   *Out of My System: Psychoanalysis, Idealogy, and Critical Methodology*
                (Oxford: Oxford University Press).
Cullen, C.
  1979   'Can We Find the Star of Bethlehem in Far Eastern Records?', *Quarterly
                Journal of the Royal Astronomical Society* 20: 153-59.
Cunningham, J.W.
  1947   'The Tin Star', *Colliers*.
Daleski, H.M.
  1977   *Joseph Conrad: The Way of Dispossession* (London: Faber & Faber).
Danker, F.W.
  1988   *Jesus and the New Age: A Commentary on St Luke's Gospel* (Philadelphia:
                Fortress Press, rev. edn).
Dante, A.
  1949   *The Inferno* (London: Penguin Books).
Darby, W. (and Jack du Bois)
  1990   *American Film Music: Major Composers, Techniques, Trends, 1915–1990*
                (Jefferson, NC: McFarland & Co.).
Daube, D.
  1956   *The New Testament and Rabbinic Judaism* (London: Athlone Press).
Davidson, A.E.
  1988   'Future Tense: Making History in *The Handmaid's Tale*', in Kathryn
                VanSpanckeren and Jan Garden Castro (eds.), *Margaret Atwood: Vision and
                Forms* (Carbondale, IL: Southern Illinois University Press): 113-21.
Davidson, C.N.
  1986   'A Feminist *1984*', *Ms.*: 24-26.
Davies, M.
  1993   *Matthew* (Readings; Sheffield: Sheffield Academic Press).
Davies, W.D., and Dale C. Allison
  1988   *A Critical and Exegetical Commentary on the Gospel according to Saint
                Matthew*, I (ICC; Edinburgh: T. & T. Clark).
Dean, L.F.
  1960   'Conrad, Stanley, and the Scramble for Africa', in Leonard F. Dean (ed.),
                Joseph Conrad's Heart of Darkness: *Backgrounds and Criticisms*
                (Englewood Cliffs, NJ: Prentice–Hall): 76-78.

Dean, M.
1979   'Eliot's "Journey of the Magi, 24-25" ', *The Explicator* 37.4: 9-10.
Dearmer, P., with R. Vaughan Williams and Martin Shaw
1964   *The Oxford Book of Carols* (Oxford: Oxford University Press).
DeBona, G.
1994   'Into Africa: Orson Welles and *Heart of Darkness*', *Cinema Journal* 33: 16-34.
Deer, G.
1992   'Rhetorical Strategies in *The Handmaid's Tale*: Dystopia and the Paradoxes of Power', *English Studies in Canada* 18: 215-33.
DeFuria, R.D.
1980   '*Apocalypse Now*: The Ritual Murder of Art', *Western Humanities Review* 34: 85-89.
Dempsey, M.
1979–80   '*Apocalypse Now*', *Sight and Sound* 49: 5-9.
Derrett, J.D.M.
1975   'Further Light on the Narratives of the Nativity', *NovT* 17: 81-108.
Detweiler, R.
1996   *Uncivil Rites: American Fiction, Religion and the Public Sphere* (Urbana: University of Illinois Press).
Dickins, H.
1970   *The Films of Gary Cooper* (Secaucus, NJ: Citadel Books).
Dietrich, A.
1902   'Die Weisen aus dem Morgenlande', *ZNW* 3: 1-14.
Dilworth, T.
1987   'Listeners and Lies in *Heart of Darkness*', *Review of English Studies* 38: 510-22.
Dodd, C.H.
1947   'The Fall of Jerusalem and the "Abomination of Desolation" ', *JRS* 37: 47-53.
Donohue, W.
1996   'A Little Tea, A Little Chat', in John Boorman and Walter Donohue (eds.), *Projections 5: Film-Makers and Film-Making* (London: Faber & Faber): 168-75.
Dorall, E.N.
1988   'Conrad and Coppola: Different Centres of Darkness', in Kimbrough (ed.): 301-311.
Dowden, W.S.
1957   'The Light and the Dark: Imagery and Thematic Development in Conrad's *Heart of Darkness*', *The Rice Institute Pamphlet* 44: 33-51.
Drew, E.
1950   *T.S. Eliot: The Design of his Poetry* (London: Eyre & Spottiswoode).
Driver, G.R.
1965   'Two Problems in the New Testament', *JTS* 16: 327-37.
Drummond, P.
1997   *High Noon* (London: British Film Institute).
Du Bois, J., and William Darby
1990   *American Film Music: Major Composers, Techniques, Trends, 1915–1990* (Jefferson, NC: McFarland & Co.).

Duchesne-Guillemin, J.
1973   'Jesus' Trimorphism and the Differentiation of the Magi', in Eric John
            Sharpe (ed.), *Man and his Salvation: Essays in Memory of S.G.F. Brandon*
            (Manchester: Manchester University Press): 91-98.
Dyer, K.D.
1998   *The Prophecy on the Mount: Mark 13 and the Gathering of the New
            Community* (International Theological Studies, 2; Bern: Peter Lang).
Eagleton, T.
1976   *Criticism and Ideology: A Study in Marxist Literary Theory* (London: Verso).
Edwards, O.
1982   'Herodian Chronology', *PEQ* 114: 29-42.
Ehrenreich, B.
1986   'Feminism's Phantoms', *New Republic* (17 March): 33-35.
Eliot, T.S.
1971   *The Waste Land, Four Quartets and Other Poems* (HarperCollins
            AudioBooks; London: HarperCollins Inc.).
Elliott, D.W.
1985   'Hearing the Darkness: The Narrative Chain in Conrad's *Heart of Darkness*',
            English Literature in Transition 28: 162-81.
Ellis, J.
1976   'Kurtz's Voice: The Intended as "The Horror!"', *English Literature in
            Transition* 19: 105-10.
Ellis, S.
1991   *The English Eliot: Design, Language and Landscape in* Four Quartets
            (London: Routledge).
Ellul, J.
1977   *Apocalypse: The Book of Revelation* (New York: Seabury Press).
Elsaesser, T., and Michael Wedel
1997   'The Hollow Heart of Hollywood: *Apocalypse Now* and the New Sound
            Space', in Gene M. Moore (ed.), *Conrad on Film* (Cambridge: Cambridge
            University Press): 151-75.
Evans, M.
1994   'Versions of History: The Handmaid's Tale and its Dedicatees', in Colin
            Edward Nicholson (ed.), *Margaret Atwood: Writing and Subjectivity: New
            Critical Essays* (Basingstoke: Macmillan): 177-88.
Evans, R.O.
1960   'Conrad's Underworld', in R.W. Stallman (ed.) *The Art of Joseph Conrad: A
            Critical Symposium* (Michigan State University Press): 171-78.
Farrer, A.
1949   *A Rebirth of Images; The Making of St John's Apocalypse* (London: Dacre
            Press).
1964   *The Revelation of St John the Divine* (Oxford: Clarendon Press).
Feder, L.
1960   'Marlow's Descent into Hell', in R.W. Stallman (ed.), *The Art of Joseph
            Conrad: A Critical Symposium* (Michigan State University Press): 162-70.
Fekkes, J.
1994   *Isaiah and Prophetic Traditions in the Book of Revelation: Visionary
            Antecedents and their Development* (JSNTSup, 93; Sheffield: Sheffield
            Academic Press).

Ferguson, J.
1970   *The Religions of the Roman Empire* (Ithaca, NY: Cornell University Press).
Ferns, C.
1989   'The Value/s of Dystopia: *The Handmaid's Tale* and the Anti-Utopian Tradition', *Dalhousie Review* 69: 373-82.
Ferrari-D'Occhieppo, K.
1989   'The Star of the Magi and Babylonian Astronomy', in Vardaman and Yamauchi (eds.) 1989: 41-53.
1978   'The Star of Bethlehem', *Quarterly Journal of the Royal Astronomical Society* 19: 517-20.
Filmer, W.E.
1966   'The Chronology of the Realm of Herod the Great', *JTS* 17: 283-84.
Finegan, J.
1998   *Handbook of Biblical Chronology* (Peabody, MA: Hendrickson, rev. edn).
Fiorenza, E.S.
1985   *The Book of Revelation: Justice and Judgment* (Philadelphia: Fortress Press).
Fitting, P.
1989   'Recent Feminist Utopias: World Building and Strategies for Social Change', in George E. Slusser and Eric S. Rabin (eds.), *Mindscapes: The Geographies of Imagined Worlds* (Carbondale, IL: Southern Illinois University Press): 155-63.
Fitzgerald, F.
1996   '*Apocalypse Now*', in Mark C. Carnes (ed.), *Past Imperfect: History According to the Movies* (London: Cassell): 284-87.
Fitzmyer, J.A.
1985   *The Gospel According to Luke X–XXIV* (AB, 28A; Garden City, NY: Doubleday).
Fleishman, A.
1967   *Conrad's Politics* (Baltimore: Johns Hopkins University Press).
Fleissner, R.F.
1994   'Eliot's "Journey of the Magi" and Black Identity', *English Language Notes* 32: 65-71.
Fogel, A.
1983   'The Mood of Overhearing in Conrad's Fiction', *Conradiana* 15: 127-41.
Foley, M.
1989   'Satirical Intent in the "Historical Notes" Epilogue of Margaret Atwood's *The Handmaid's Tale*', *Commonwealth Essays and Studies* 11: 44-52.
Ford, D.
1979   *The Abomination of Desolation in Biblical Eschatology* (Washington, DC: University Press of America).
Ford, J.M.
1975   *Revelation* (AB, 38; Garden City, NY: Doubleday).
Foreman, C.
1972   '*High Noon* Revisited', *Punch*: 448-50.
1974   'On the Wayne', *Punch*: 240-42.
Foster, G.
1994   'The Women in *High Noon*: A Metanarrative of Difference', 18.3–19.1 (Spring–Fall): 72-81.

Fotheringham, J.K.
1934   'The Evidence of Astronomy and Technical Chronology for the Date of the
            Crucifixion', *JTS* 35: 146-162.
France, R.T.
1979   'Herod and the Children of Bethlehem', *NovT* 21: 98-120.
1980   'The "Massacre of the Innocents"—Fact or Fiction', in E.A. Livingstone
            (ed.), *Studia Biblica 1978, II. Papers on the Gospels: Sixth International
            Congress on Biblical Studies, Oxford, 3–7 April 1978* (JSNTSup, 2;
            Sheffield: JSOT Press): 83-94.
1981   'The Formula-Quotations of Matthew 2 and the Problem of Communication',
            NTS 27: 233-51.
1985   *Matthew* (TNTC; Leicester: IVP).
Franklin, R.
1968   'The Satisfactory Journey of Eliot's Magus', *English Studies* 49: 559-61.
Frazer, Sir James
1993   *The Golden Bough* (Ware, Hertfordshire: Wordsworth Editions [1890–
            1915]).
Freibert, L.M.
1988   'Control and Creativity: The Politics of Risk in Margaret Atwood's *The
            Handmaid's Tale*', in Judith McCombs (ed.), *Critical Essays on Margaret
            Atwood* (Boston: G.K. Hall & Co.): 280-91.
French, K.
1998   *Apocalypse Now* (Bloomsbury Movie Guide, 1; London: Bloomsbury
            Publishing).
French, P.
1977   *Westerns: Aspects of a Movie Genre* (London: Secker & Warburg, rev. edn).
Fullbrook, K.
1990   *Free Women: Ethics and Aesthetics in Twentieth-Century Women's Fiction*
            (Philadelphia: Temple University Press).
Gaechter, P.
1968   'Die Magikerperikope', *ZKT* 90: 257-95.
Gardner, H.
1949   *The Art of T.S. Eliot* (London: The Cresset Press).
Garland, D.E.
1993   *Reading Matthew: A Literary and Theological Commentary on the First
            Gospel* (London: SPCK).
Garrett, P.K.
1969   *Scene and Symbol from George Eliot to James Joyce* (New Haven: Yale
            University Press).
Garrett, S.R.
1992   'Revelation', in Carol A. Newsom and Sharon H. Ringe (eds.), *The Women's
            Bible Commentary* (London: SPCK): 377-82.
Garrett-Petts, W.F.
1988   'Reading, Writing, and the Postmodern Condition: Interpreting Margaret
            Atwood's *The Handmaid's Tale*', *Open Letter, 7th Series* 1: 74-92.
Gaston, L.
1970   *No Stone on Another: Studies in the Significance of the Fall of Jerusalem in
            the Synoptic Gospels* (NovTSup, 23; Leiden: E.J. Brill).

Geng, V.
1979   'Mistuh Kurtz—He Dead', *New Yorker*: 70-72.
Giannetti, L.D.
1981   *Masters of the American Cinema* (Englewood Cliffs, NJ: Prentice–Hall).
Gibson, A.
1997   'Ethics and Unrepresentability in *Heart of Darkness*', *The Conradian* 22: 113-37.
Gilbert, A.G.
1996   *Magi: The Quest for a Secret Tradition* (London: Bloomsbury).
Gillespie, G.
1985   'Savage Places Revisited: Conrad's *Heart of Darkness* and Coppola's *Apocalypse Now*', *The Comparatist* 9: 69-88.
Givner, J.
1992   'Names, Faces and Signatures in Margaret Atwood's "Cat's Eye" and "The Handmaid's Tale" ', *Canadian Literature* 133: 56-75.
Glendinning, V.
1986   '*Lady Oracle*', *Saturday Night* (January): 39-41.
Glenn, I.
1987   'Conrad's *Heart of Darkness*: A Sociological Reading', *Literature and History* 13: 238-56.
Godshalk, W.L.
1969   'Kurtz as Diabolical Christ', *Discourse* 12: 100-107.
Goethe, J.W. von
1959   *Faust* (London: Penguin Books).
Goldberg, M.
1992   'Magi', in David Lyle Jeffrey (ed.), *A Dictionary of Biblical Tradition in English Literature* (Grand Rapids: Eerdmans): 472-73.
Goodheart, E.
1991   *Desire and its Discontents* (New York: Columbia University Press).
Gordon, L.
1985   'Conversion', in Harold Bloom (ed.), *Modern Critical Views: T.S. Eliot* (New York: Chelsea House Publishers): 77-94.
1998   *T.S. Eliot: An Imperfect Life* (London: Vintage Books).
Grace, S.
1994   'Gender as Genre: Atwood's Autobiographical "I" ', in Colin Edward Nicholson (ed.), *Margaret Atwood: Writing and Subjectivity: New Critical Essays* (Basingstoke: Macmillan): 189-203.
Grández, R.M.
1989   'Las Tinieblas en la Muerte de Jesús: Historia de la Exégesis de Lc 23,44-45a (Mt 27,45; Mk 15,33)', *EstBib* 47: 199-200.
Grant, M. (trans.)
1956   *Tacitus' The Annals of Imperial Rome* (London: Penguin Classics).
Graves, R.
1979   *I, Claudius* (London: Marshall Cavendish).
Grayston, K.
1952   'The Darkness of the Cosmic Sea', *Theology* 55: 122-27.
Green, J.B.
1988   *The Death of Jesus: Tradition and Interpretation in the Passion Narrative* (WUNT, 2.33; Tübingen: J.C.B. Mohr [Paul Siebeck]).

1994 'The Demise of the Temple as 'Culture Center' in Luke–Acts: An Explanation of the Rending of the Temple Veil (Luke 23.44-49)', *RB* 101: 495-515.
Green, P.
1974 *Juvenal's The Sixteen Satires* (London: Penguin Classics).
Greiff, L.K.
1992 'Soldier, Sailor, Surfer, Chef: Conrad's Ethics and the Margins of
Apocalypse Now', *Literature/Film Quarterly* 20: 188-98.
Grenier, R.
1979 'Coppola's Folly', *Commentary* 68: 67-73.
Guerard, A.J.
1958 *Conrad the Novelist* (Cambridge, MA: Harvard University Press).
Guetti, J.
1965 '*Heart of Darkness* and the Failure of the Imagination', *Sewanee Review* 73:
488-504.
Gundry, R.H.
1994 *Matthew: A Commentary on his Handbook for a Mixed Church under
Persecution* (Grand Rapids: Eerdmans, 2nd edn).
Günther, J.J.
1973 'The Fate of the Jerusalem Church: The Flight to Pella', *TZ* 29: 81-94.
Hagen, W.M.
1983 '*Apocalypse Now* (1979): Joseph Conrad and the Television War', in Peter
C. Rollins (ed.), *Hollywood as Historian: American Film in a Cultural
Context* (Lexington, KY: University Press of Kentucky): 230-45.
1988 '*Heart of Darkness* and the Process of *Apocalypse Now*', in Kimbrough (ed.)
1988: 293-301.
Hagner, D.A.
1993 *Matthew 1–13* (WBC, 33A; Dallas: Word Books).
1995 *Matthew 14–28* (WBC, 33B; Dallas: Word Books).
Hammer, S.B.
1990 'The World As It Will Be? Female Satire and the Technology of Power in
The Handmaid's Tale', *Modern Language Studies* 20: 39-49.
Hampson, R.
1990 '*Heart of Darkness* and "The Speech That Cannot Be Silenced"', *English*
39: 15-32.
1992 *Joseph Conrad: Betrayal and Identity* (New York: St Martin's Press).
Harland, P.A.
2000 'Honouring the Emperor or Assailing the Beast: Participating in Civic Life
among Associations (Jewish, Christian and Other) in Asia Minor and the
Apocalypse of John', *JSNT* 77: 99-121.
Harris, W.
1981 'The Frontier on which *Heart of Darkness* Stands', *Research in African
Literature* 12: 86-93.
Hawkins, H.
1979 'Conrad's Critique of Imperialism in *Heart of Darkness*', *PMLA* 94: 286-99.
1981 'Conrad and Congolese Exploitation', *Conradiana* 13: 94-99.
1982 'The Issue of Racism in *Heart of Darkness*', *Conradiana* 14: 163-71.
Hawthorne, J.
1990 *Joseph Conrad: Narrative Technique and Ideological Commitment* (London:
Edward Arnold).

Hawthorne, N.
  1986   *The Scarlet Letter* (London: Penguin Books [1850]).
Hay, E.K.
  1963   *The Political Novels of Joseph Conrad: A Critical Study* (Chicago: University of Chicago Press).
Hellmann, J.
  1984   'Vietnam and the Hollywood Genre Film: Inversions of American Mythology in *The Deer Hunter* and *Apocalypse Now*', *American Quarterly* 34: 418-39.
Hengel, M.
  1985   *Studies in the Gospel of Mark* (London: SCM Press).
Hengen, S.
  1993   *Margaret Atwood's Power: Mirrors, Reflections and Images in Selected Fiction and Poetry* (Toronto: Second Story Press).
Herr, M.
  1978   *Dispatches* (London: Pan Books).
Herzog, T.C.
  1992   *Vietnam War Stories: Innocence Lost* (London: Routledge).
Higham, C.
  1985   *Orson Welles: The Rise and Fall of an American Genius* (London: Guild Publishing).
Hill, D.
  1972   *The Gospel of Matthew* (NCB; London: Marshall, Morgan & Scott).
Hochschild, A.
  1999   *King Leopold's Ghost: A Study of Greed, Terror, and Heroism in Colonial Africa* (London: Macmillan).
Hoehner, H.H.
  1989   'The Date of the Death of Herod the Great', in Vardaman and Yamauchi (eds.) 1989: 101-111.
Hoeppner, E.H.
  1988   '*Heart of Darkness*: An Archeology of the Lie', *Conradiana* 20: 137-46.
Hoffman, S. de Voren
  1965   'The Hole in the Bottom of the Pail: Comedy and Theme in *Heart of Darkness*', *Studies in Short Fiction* 2: 113-23.
Holladay, J.S., Jr
  1968   'The Day(s) the *Moon* Stood Still', *JBL* 87: 166-78.
Hollingworth, A.M.
  1955   'Freud, Conrad, and the Future of an Illusion', *Literature and Psychology* 5: 78-83.
Holtsmark, E.B.
  1991   'The *katabasis* Theme in Modern Cinema', in Martin M. Winkler (ed.), *Classics and Cinema* (Lewisburg, PA: Bucknell University Press): 60-80.
Houlden, L.
  1991   'Beyond Belief: Preaching the Ascension (II)', *Theology* 94: 173-80.
How, W.W., and J. Wells
  1928   *A Commentary on Herodotus, with Introduction and Appendixes*, II (Oxford: Clarendon Press).
Howard, R.E., L. Sprague de Camp and Lin Carter
  1967   *Conan* (New York: Lancer Books).

Howells, C.A.
  1996   *Margaret Atwood* (London: Macmillan).
  1998   *Margaret Atwood's* The Handmaid's Tale (York Notes; London: York Press).
Hughes, D.
  1976   'The Star of Bethlehem', *Nature* 264: 513-17.
  1979   *The Star of Bethlehem Mystery* (London: J.M. Dent & Sons).
Humphrey, E.M.
  1995   *The Ladies and the Cities: Transformation and Apocalyptic Identity in Joseph of Asenath, 4 Ezra, the Apocalypse and The Shepherd of Hermas* (JSPSup, 17; Sheffield: Sheffield Academic Press).
Humphreys, C.J., and W.G. Waddington
  1983   'Dating the Crucifixion', *Nature* 306: 743-46.
  1989   'Astronomy and the Date of the Crucifixion', in Vardaman and Yamauchi (eds.) 1989: 165-81.
Hunter, A.
  1983   *Joseph Conrad and the Ethics of Darwinism: The Challenges of Science* (London: Croom Helm).
Hunzinger, C.-H.
  1965   'Babylon als Deckname für Rom und die Datierung des 1. Petrusbriefes', in Henning Graf Reventlow (ed.), *Gottes Wort und Gottes Land: Hans-Wilhelm Hertzberg zum 70. Geburtstag am 16 Januar 1965, dargebracht von Kollegen, Freunden und Schülern* (Göttingen: Vandenhoeck & Ruprecht): 67-77.
Hutcheon, L.
  1988   *The Canadian Postmodern: A Study of Contemporary English-Canadian Fiction* (Toronto: Oxford University Press).
  1991   *Splitting Images: Contemporary Canadian Ironies* (Oxford: Oxford University Press).
Huxley, A.
  1932   *Brave New World* (London: Chatto & Windus).
Hyland, P.
  1988   'The Little Woman in the Heart of Darkness', *Conradiana* 20: 3-11.
Jean-Aubry, G.
  1927   *Joseph Conrad: Life and Letters* (2 vols.; London: William Heinemann).
Jeffrey, D.L. (and Lenore Gussin)
  1998   'Nativity of Christ', in *The Great Sayings of Jesus* (Oxford: Lion Books): 194-204.
Jensen, R.M.
  2000   *Understanding Early Christian Art* (London: Routledge).
Johnson, B.
  1985   'Conrad's Impressionism and Watt's "Delayed Decoding"', in Ross C. Murfin (ed.), *Conrad Revisited: Essays for the Eighties* (Tuscaloosa, AL: The University of Alabama Press): 51-70.
Johnson, D.
  1989   '"And They Went Eight Stades toward Herodeion"', in Vardaman and Yamauchi (eds.): 93-99.
Johnston, Sir Harry
  1971   'George Grenfell: A Missionary in the Congo', in Kimbrough (ed.): 90-91.

Jones, D.
    1989   'Not Much Balm in Gilead', *Commonwealth Essays and Studies* 11: 31-43.
Jones, G.
    1964   *Approach to the Purpose: A Study of the Poetry of T.S. Eliot* (London: Hodder & Stoughton).
Jones, I.H.
    1994   *The Gospel of Matthew* (EC; London: Epworth Press).
Jones, S.
    1999   *Conrad and Women* (Oxford English Monographs; Oxford: Clarendon Press).
Juel, D.
    1983   *Luke–Acts* (London: SCM Press).
Just, W.
    1979   'Vietnam: The Camera Lies', *Atlantic*: 63-65.
Kael, P.
    1987   *Taking It All In* (London: Arena Books).
Kahane, C.
    1989   'Seduction and the Voice of the Text: *Heart of Darkness* and *The Good Soldier*', in Dianne Hunter (ed.), *Seduction and Theory: Readings of Gender, Representation, and Rhetoric* (Urbana: University of Illinois Press): 135-53.
Kaler, A.K.
    1989   'A Sister, Dipped in Blood: Satiric Inversion of the Formation Techniques of Women Religious in Margaret Atwood's Novel *The Handmaid's Tale*', *Christianity and Literature* 38: 43-62.
Kane, P.
    1988   'A Woman's Dystopia: Margaret Atwood's *The Handmaid's Tale*', *Notes on Contemporary Literature* 18: 9-10.
Kaplan, R.B. (and Richard J. Wall)
    1960   'Eliot's "Journey of the Magi" ', *The Explicator* 19: 8.
Karl, F.R.
    1960   *A Reader's Guide to Joseph Conrad* (London: Thames & Hudson).
    1968   'Introduction to the *Danse Macabre*: Conrad's *Heart of Darkness*', *Modern Fiction Studies* 14: 143-56.
    1979   *Joseph Conrad: The Three Lives* (London: Faber & Faber).
    1985   'Three Problematical Areas in Conrad Biography', in Ross C. Murfin (ed.), *Conrad Revisited: Essays for the Eighties* (Tuscaloosa, AL: The University of Alabama Press): 13-30.
Kauffman, L.
    1989   'Special Delivery: Twenty-First Century Epistolarity in *The Handmaid's Tale*', in Elizabeth C. Goldsmith (ed.), *Writing the Female Voice: Essays on Epistolary Literature* (Boston: Northeastern University Press): 221-44.
Kauvar, G.B.
    1971   'Marlow as Liar', in Kimbrough (ed.) 1971: 244-47.
Keener, C.S.
    1997   *Matthew* (IVPNTCS; Leicester: IVP).
Keith, W.J.
    1987   'Apocalyptic Imaginations: Notes on Atwood's *The Handmaid's Tale* and Findley's *Not Wanted on the Voyage*', *Essays on Canadian Writing* 35: 123-34.

Kermode, F.
1979   *The Genesis of Secrecy: On the Interpretation of Narrative* (Cambridge, MA: Harvard University Press).
Ketterer, D.
1989   'Margaret Atwood's *The Handmaid's Tale*: A Contextual Dystopia', *Science Fiction Studies* 16: 209-217.
1992   *Canadian Science Fiction and Fantasy* (Bloomington: Indiana University Press).
Kimbrough, R.
1971   'Conrad's Manuscript of *Heart of Darkness*', in Kimbrough (ed.) 1971: 136-39.
Kimbrough, R. (ed.)
1971   *Joseph Conrad:* Heart of Darkness (New York: W.W. Norton & Co., rev. edn).
1988   *Joseph Conrad:* Heart of Darkness (New York: W.W. Norton & Co., 3rd edn).
Kinder, M.
1979–80   'The Power of Adaptation in *Apocalypse Now*', *Film Quarterly* 33: 12-20.
Knapp, B.
1991   *Exile and the Writer: Exoteric and Esoteric Experiences. A Jungian Approach* (University Park: Pennsylvania State University Press).
Knight, D.
1987   'Structuralism I: Narratology: Joseph Conrad, *Heart of Darkness*', in Douglas Tallack (ed.), *Literary Theory at Work: Three Texts* (London: B.T. Batsford): 9-28.
Koestler, A.
1940   *Darkness at Noon* (London: Jonathan Cape).
Kokkinos, N.
1989   'Crucifixion in A.D. 36: The Keystone for Dating the Birth of Jesus', in Vardaman and Yamauchi (eds.) 1989: 133-63.
Kraybill, J.N.
1996   *Imperial Cult and Commerce in John's Apocalypse* (JSNTSup, 132; Sheffield: Sheffield Academic Press).
Kreitzer, L.J.
1993   *The New Testament in Fiction and Film: On Reversing the Hermeneutical Flow* (Bib Sem, 19; Sheffield: Sheffield Academic Press).
1994   *The Old Testament in Fiction and Film: On Reversing the Hermeneutical Flow* (Bib Sem, 24; Sheffield: Sheffield Academic Press).
1996   *Striking New Images: Roman Imperial Coinage and the New Testament World* (JSNTSup, 134: Sheffield: Sheffield Academic Press).
1999   *Pauline Images in Fiction and Film: On Reversing the Hermeneutical Flow* (Bib Sem, 61; Sheffield: Sheffield Academic Press).
2000   ' "Revealing the Affairs of the Heart': Sin, Accusation and Confession in Nathaniel Hawthorne's *The Scarlet Letter*', in Larry J. Kreitzer and Deborah W. Rooke (eds.), *Ciphers in the Sand: Interpretations of the Woman Taken in Adultery (John 7.53–8.11)* (Sheffield: Sheffield Academic Press): 139-213.
2001   'Bread and Circuses: Christian History According to the World of *Star*

Trek', in Paul S. Fiddes (ed.), *Faith in the Centre: Christianity and Culture* (Regent's Study Guides, 9; Oxford: Regent's Park): 207-24.

Krodel, G.A.
1989   *Revelation* (ANTC; Minneapolis, MN: Augsburg).

Kuhn, K.G.
1964   'Βαβυλῶν, *TDNT*: I, 514-17.

LaBrasca, R.
1988   'Two Visions of "The horror!" ', in Kimbrough (ed.) 1988: 288-93.

Lacombe, M.
1986   'The Writing on the Wall: Amputated Speech in Margaret Atwood's *The Handmaid's Tale*', *Wascana Review* 21: 3-30.

Ladd, G.E.
1972   *A Commentary on the Revelation of John* (Grand Rapids, MI: Eerdmans).

Land, S.K.
1984   *Conrad and the Paradox of Plot* (London: Macmillan).

Langdon, S.
1998   *Margaret Atwood's* The Handmaid's Tale (Letts Explore Literature Guide; London: Letts Educational).

Langman, F.
1980   '*Heart of Darkness*: From Conrad to Coppola', *Quadrant* 24: 30-33.

Larsen, M.J.
1988   'Conrad and Coppola on the Struggle for Hearts and Minds', in Mario Curreli (ed.), *The Ugo Mursia Memorial Lectures: Papers for the International Conrad Conference, University of Pisa, September 7th–11th 1983* (Milan: Mursia International): 353-61.

Larson, J.L.
1989   'Margaret Atwood and the Future of Prophecy', *Religion and Literature* 21: 27-61.

Laskowsky, H.J.
1982   '*Heart of Darkness*: A Primer for the Holocaust', *Virginia Quarterly Review* 58: 93-110.

Laws, S.
1988   *In the Light of the Lamb: Imagery, Parody, and Theology in the Apocalypse of John* (GNS, 31; Wilmington, DE: Michael Glazier).

Leavis, F.R.
1993   *The Great Tradition* (repr.; London: Penguin [1948]).

LeBihan, J.
1991   '*The Handmaid's Tale*, *Cat's Eye* and *Interlunar*: Margaret Atwood's Feminist (?) Futures (?)', in Carol Ann Howells and Lynette Hunter (eds.), *Narrative Strategies in Canadian Literature: Feminism and Postcolonialism* (Milton Keynes: Open University Press): 93-107.

Ledbetter, M.
1996   *Victims and the Postmodern Narrative or Doing Violence to the Body: An Ethic of Reading and Writing* (London: Macmillan).

Lester, J.
1988   *Conrad and Religion* (London: Macmillan Press).

Levenson, M.
1985–86   'The Value of Facts in the *Heart of Darkness*', *Nineteenth-Century Fiction* 40: 261-80.

Levy, A.
1998   'Fred Zinnemann: The Last Interview', in John Boorman and Walter Donohue (eds.), *Projections 8: Film-Makers and Film-Making* (London: Faber & Faber): 364-73.

Lewis, J.
1995   *Whom God Wishes to Destroy...: Francis Coppola and the New Hollywood* (London: Athlone Press).

Lewis, R.W.
1971   '*Playboy* Interview: John Wayne', *Playboy* (May): 75-92.

Lincoln, K.R.
1972   'Comic Light in *Heart of Darkness*', *Modern Fiction Studies* 18: 183-97.

Ljungberg, C.
1999   *To Join, to Fit, and to Make: The Creative Craft of Margaret Atwood's Fiction* (Bern: Peter Lang).

Lodge, D.
1984   *Language of Fiction: Essays in Criticism and Verbal Analysis of the English Novel* (London: Routledge & Kegan Paul, 2nd edn).

Lohmeyer, E.
1926   *Die Offenbarung des Johannes* (Tübingen: Mohr/Siebeck).

Lombard, F.
1975   'Conrad and Buddhism', in Claude Thomas (ed.), *Studies in Joseph Conrad* (Montpellier: Université Paul-Valéry): 103-112.

London, B.
1989   'Reading Race and Gender in Conrad's Dark Continent', *Criticism* 31: 235-52.

Lothe, J.
1989   *Conrad's Narrative Method* (Oxford: Clarendon Press).

Luedemann, G.
1989   *Opposition to Paul in Jewish Christianity* (Minneapolis: Fortress Books).

Luz, U.
1990   *Matthew 1-7: A Commentary* (Edinburgh: T. & T. Clark).

Macan, R.W.
1908   *Herodotus: The Seventh, Eighth, and Ninth Books, Volume 1, Part 1* (London: Macmillan and Co.).

Macgregor, N., with Erika Langmuir
2000   *Seeing Salvation: Images of Christ in Art* (London: BBC Worldwide Limited).

Maier, P.L.
1968   'Sejanus, Pilate, and the Date of the Crucifixion', *Church History* 37: 3-13.
1969   'The Episode of the Golden Shields at Jerusalem', *HTR* 62: 109-121.
1989   'The Date of the Nativity and the Chronology of Jesus' Life', in Vardaman and Yamauchi (eds.) 1989: 113-30.

Malak, A.
1987   'Margaret Atwood's 'The Handmaid's Tale' and the Dystopian Tradition', *Canadian Literature* 112: 9-16.

Malina, B.J.
1995   *On the Genre and Message of Revelation: Star Visions and Sky Journeys* (Peabody, MA: Hendrickson).

Manso, P.
1994   *Brando* (London: Weidenfeld & Nicolson).
Manson, T.W.
1957   *The Sayings of Jesus* (London: SCM Press).
Marcus, G.
1979   'Journey Up the River: An Interview with Francis Coppola', *Rolling Stone* (1 November): 51-57.
Marcus, J.
1995   'The Old Testament and the Death of Jesus: The Role of Scripture in the Gospel Passion Narratives', in John T. Carroll and Joel B. Green (eds.), *The Death of Jesus in Early Christianity* (Peabody, MA: Hendrickson): 205-33.
Marshall, I.H.
1978   *Commentary on Luke* (Grand Rapids, MI: Eerdmans).
Martin, D.M.
1975   'The Diabolic Kurtz: The Dual Nature of his Satanism in *Heart of Darkness*', *Conradiana* 7: 175-77.
Martin, E.L.
1989   'The Nativity and Herod's Death', in Vardaman and Yamauchi (eds.) 1989: 85-92.
Martin, G.
1970   'Language and Belief in Eliot's Poetry', in Graham Martin (ed.), *Eliot in Perspective: A Symposium* (London: Macmillan): 112-31.
Matera, F.J.
1985   'The Death of Jesus according to Luke: A Question of Sources', *CBQ* 47: 469-85.
Matthiesson, F.O.
1958   *The Achievement of T.S. Eliot: An Essay on the Nature of Poetry* (Oxford: Oxford University Press, 3rd edn).
Marx, K.
1938   *Critique of the Gotha Programme* (London: Lawrence and Wishart [1875]).
Maud, R.
1971   'The Plain Tale of *Heart of Darkness*', in Kimbrough (ed.) 1971: 205-210.
Maurer, C.
1991   'Translation of the Akhim Fragment', in Wilhelm Schneemelcher (ed.), *New Testament Apocrypha*. I. *Gospels and Related Writings* (Cambridge: James Clarke & Co.): 223-27.
Maxwell, D.E.S.
1952   *The Poetry of T.S. Eliot* (London: Routledge & Kegan Paul).
May, J.R.
1982   'Francis Coppola', in John R. May and Michael Bird (eds.), *Religion in Film* (Knoxville: The University of Tennessee Press): 163-69.
McCarthy, M.
1986   'Breeders, Wives and Unwomen', *The New York Times Book Review* (9 February): 1, 35.
McClure, J.A.
1977   'The Rhetoric of Restraint in *Heart of Darkness*', *Nineteenth-Century Fiction* 32: 310-26.

McConnell, D.J.
1962   ' "The Heart of Darkness" in T.S. Eliot's *The Hollow Men*', *Texas Studies in Literature and Language* 4: 141-53.
McDougal, S.Y.
1985   *Made into Movies: From Literature to Film* (Philadelphia: Harcourt Brace Jovanovich College Publishers).
McInerney, P.
1979–80 'Apocalypse Then: Hollywood Looks Back at Vietnam', *Film Quarterly* 33: 21-32.
McLauchlan, J.
1978   'The 'Something Human' in *Heart of Darkness*', *Conradiana* 10: 115-25.
1983   'The Value and Significance of *Heart of Darkness*', *Conradiana* 15: 3-21.
Meier, J.P.
1980   *Matthew* (NTM, 3; Dublin: Veritas Publications).
Meisel, P.
1987   *The Myth of the Modern: A Study of British Literature and Criticism after 1850* (New Haven: Yale University Press).
Mellen, J.
1978   *Big Bad Wolves: Masculinity in the American Film* (London: Elm Tree Books).
Metzger, B.M.
1963   'Explicit References in the Works of Origen to Variant Readings in the New Testament Manuscripts', in J.N. Birdsall and R.W. Thomson (eds.), *Biblical and Patristic Studies* (New York: Herder, 1963): 78-95.
1970   'Names for the Nameless in the New Testament: A Study in the Growth of Christian Tradition', in Patrick Granfield and Josef A. Jungmann (eds.), *Kyriakon: Festschrift Johannes Quasten, Volume 1* (Münster: Verlag Aschendorff): 79-99.
Meyer, B.
1967   *Joseph Conrad: A Psychoanalytic Biography* (Princeton: Princeton University Press).
Meyers, J.
1991   *Joseph Conrad: A Biography* (London: John Murray).
Michaels, W.B.
1979   'The Road to Vietnam', *Modern Language Notes* 94: 1173-75.
Miles, M.R.
1996   *Seeing and Believing: Religion and Values in the Movies* (Boston: Beacon Press).
Miller, J.H.
1985   '*Heart of Darkness* Revisited', in Ross C. Murfin (ed.), *Conrad Revisited: Essays for the Eighties* (Tuscaloosa, AL: University of Alabama Press): 31-50.
Miller, J.I.
1969   *The Spice Trade of the Roman Empire, 29 B.C to A.D. 461* (Oxford: Clarendon Press).
Milosz, C.
1960   'Joseph Conrad in Polish Eyes', in Joseph Stallman (ed.), *The Art of Joseph Conrad: A Critical Symposium* (Lansing, MI: Michigan State University Press): 35-45.

Milton, J.
1974   *Samson Agonistes* (London: University Tutorial Press [1671]).
Minear, P.S.
1968   *I Saw a New Earth: A Complete New Study and Translation of the Book of Revelation* (Washington, DC: Corpus Books).
Miner, M.
1991   "Trust Me': Reading the Romance Plot in Margaret Atwood's *The Handmaid's Tale*', *Twentieth Century Literature* 37: 148-68.
Mitchell, L.C.
1996   *Westerns: Making the Man in Fiction and Film* (Chicago: University of Chicago Press).
Moore, G.M.
1997   'Introduction', in Gene M. Moore (ed.), *Conrad on Film* (Cambridge: Cambridge University Press): 1-15.
Mongia, P.
1993   'Empire, Narrative, and the Feminine in *Lord Jim* and *Heart of Darkness*', in Keith Carabine, Owen Knowles and Wieslaw Krajka (eds.), *Contexts for Conrad* (East European Monographs, 370; Boulder, CO: East European Monographs): 135-50.
Moody, A.D.
1979   *Thomas Stearns Eliot, Poet* (Cambridge: Cambridge University Press).
Morehouse, A.J.
1978   'The Christmas Star as a Supernova in Aquila', *The Journal of the Royal Astronomical Society of Canada* 72: 65-68.
Morris, L.
1983   *Revelation* (TNTC; Leicester: IVP).
Morrissey, L.J.
1981   'The Tellers in *Heart of Darkness*: Conrad's Chinese Boxes', *Conradiana* 13: 141-48.
Moseley, E.
1962   *Pseudonyms of Christ in the Modern World* (Pittsburgh: University of Pittsburgh Press).
Moser, T.
1957   *Joseph Conrad: Achievement and Decline* (Cambridge, MA: Harvard University Press).
Motyer, S.
1987   'The Rending of the Veil: A Markan Pentecost', *NTS* 33: 155-57.
Moule, C.F.D.
1959   'The Intention of the Evangelists', in A.J.B. Higgins (ed.), *New Testament Essays: Studies in Memory of Thomas Walter Manson* (Manchester: Manchester University Press): 165-79.
Mounce, R.H.
1984   *The Book of Revelation* (NICNT; Grand Rapids, MI: Eerdmans, rev. edn).
Moyise, S.
1995   *The Old Testament in the Book of Revelation* (JSNTSup, 115; Sheffield: Sheffield Academic Press).
Mudrick, M.
1971   'The Originality of Conrad', in Kimbrough (ed.) 1971: 185-88.

Murfin, R.C.
1996a   'Introduction: Biographical and Historical Contexts', in Ross C. Murfin (ed.), *Joseph Conrad:* Heart of Darkness (Case Studies in Contemporary Criticism; Boston: Bedford Books of St. Martin's Press, 2nd edn): 3-16.
1996b   'A Critical History', in Ross C. Murfin (ed.), *Joseph Conrad:* Heart of Darkness (Case Studies in Contemporary Criticism; Boston: Bedford Books of St Martin's Press, 2nd edn): 99-114.

Murphy, F.J.
1998   *Fallen is Babylon: The Revelation to John* (The New Testament in Context; Valley Forge, PA: Trinity Press International).

Murphy, P.D.
1990   'Reducing the Dystopian Distance: Pseudo-Documentary Framing in Near-Future Fiction', *Science Fiction Studies* 17: 25-40.

Murray, D.
1987   'Dialogics: Joseph Conrad, *Heart of Darkness*', in Douglas Tallack (ed.), *Literary Theory at Work: Three Texts* (London: B.T. Batsford): 115-34.

Myers, C.
1990   *Binding the Strong Man: A Political Reading of Mark's Story of Jesus* (Maryknoll, NY: Orbis Books).

Najder, Z.
1983   *Joseph Conrad: A Chronicle* (Cambridge: Cambridge University Press).

Neilsen, R.G.
1987   'Conrad's *Heart of Darkness*', *The Explicator* 45: 41-42.

Niles, D.T.
1962   *As Seeing the Invisible: A Study of the Book of Revelation* (London: SCM Press).

Nischik, R.M.
1987   'Back to the Future: Margaret Atwood's Anti-Utopian Vision in '*The Handmaid's Tale*', *Englisch-Amerikanische Studien* 5: 139-48.

Nolland, J.
1993   *Luke 18.35–24.53* (WBC, 35C; Dallas, TX: Word Books).

Norris, K.
1990   'The University of Denay, Nunavit: The "Historical Notes" in Margaret Atwood's *The Handmaid's Tale*', *The American Review of Canadian Studies* 20: 357-64.

Ober, W.U.
1965   '*Heart of Darkness*: "The Ancient Mariner" a Hundred Years Later', *The Dalhousie Review* 45: 333-37.

O'Keeffe, B.
1993   'An Approach to *The Handmaid's Tale*', *The English Review* 3: 10-13.

Olschki, L.
1951   'The Wise Men of the East in Oriental Traditions', in Walter Joseph Fischel (ed.), *Semitic and Oriental Studies: A Volume presented to William Popper, Professor of Semitic Languages, Emeritus, on the Occasion of his Seventy-Fifth Birthday, October 29, 1949* (Berkeley: University of California Press): 375-95.

Ong, W.
1977   'Truth in Conrad's Darkness', *Mosaic* 2: 151-63.

O'Prey, P.
1973   'Introduction', in Joseph Conrad, *Heart of Darkness* (Harmondsworth: Penguin Books): 7-24.

Orwell, G.
1954   *Nineteen Eighty-Four* (London: Penguin Books [1949]).

Ostwalt, C.
1996   '*Dances With Wolves*: An American *Heart of Darkness*', *Literature/Film Quarterly* 24: 209-16.

Otten, T.
1982   *After Innocence: Visions of the Fall in Modern Literature* (Pittsburgh: University of Pittsburgh Press): 80-96.

Palmer, C.
1990   *The Composer in Hollywood* (London: Boyars).

Palmer, R.B.
1984–85   'Masculinist Reading of Two Western Films: *High Noon* and *Rio Grande*', *Journal of Popular Film and Television* 2.4: 156-62.

Palmer, P.
1989   *Contemporary Women's Fiction: Narrative Practice and Feminist Theory* (New York: Harvester Wheatsheaf).

Palmer, W.J.
1987   *The Films of the Seventies: A Social History* (Metuchen, NJ: The Scarecrow Press).

Parker, J.
1993   *Sean Connery* (London: Victor Gollancz).

Parrinder, P.
1986   'Making Poison', *London Review of Books* 8 (20 March): 20-22.
1992   'Heart of Darkness: Geography as Apocalypse', in John Stokes (ed.), *Fin de Siècle/Fin du Globe: Fears and Fantasies of the Late Nineteenth Century* (Houndmills: Macmillan): 85-102.

Parry, B.
1983   *Conrad and Imperialism: Ideological Boundaries and Visionary Frontiers* (London: Macmillan).

Patella, M.
1999   *The Death of Jesus: The Demonical Force and the Ministering Angel (Luke 23,44-49)* (Cahiers de la *Revue biblique*; Paris: J. Gabalda).

Pecora, V.
1985   '*Heart of Darkness* and the Phenomenology of Voice', *English Literary History* 52: 993-1015.

Phillips, G.D.
1990   *Major Film Directors of the American and British Cinema* (London: Associated Press).
1995   *Conrad and Cinema: The Art of Adaptation* (New York: Peter Lang).

Pinion, F.B.
1986   *A T.S. Eliot Companion: Life and Works* (London: Macmillan).

Pinsker, S.
1981   '*Heart of Darkness* Through Contemporary Eyes, Or What's Wrong with *Apocalypse Now*?', *Conradiana* 13: 55-58.

Pippin, T.
1992 *Death and Desire: The Rhetoric of Gender in the Apocalypse of John* (Louis-ville, KY: Westminster/John Knox).
1992 'The Heroine and the Whore: Fantasy and the Female in the Apocalypse of John', *Semeia* 60: *Fantasy and the Bible*: 67-82.
1999 *Apocalyptic Bodies: The Biblical End of the World in Text and Image* (London: Routledge).

Plummer, A.
1901 *A Critical and Exegetical Commentary on the Gospel According to St Luke* (Edinburgh: T. & T. Clark, 4th edn).

Poe, E.A.
1986 'The Raven', in *The Fall of the House of Usher and Other Writings* (London: Penguin Books).

Prince, S.
1999 'Historical Perspective and the Realist Aesthetic in *High Noon* (1952)', in Arthur Nolletti, Jr (ed.), *The Films of Fred Zinnemann: Critical Perspectives* (Albany: State University of New York Press): 79-92.

Provan, I.
1996 'Foul Spirits, Fornication and Finance: Revelation 18 from an Old Testament Perspective', *JSNT* 64: 81-100.

Purdy, D.H.
1984 *Joseph Conrad's Bible* (Norman, OK: University of Oklahoma Press).

Pym, J.
1979–80 '*Apocalypse Now*: An Errand Boy's Journey', *Sight and Sound* 49: 9-10.

Rabinowitz, P.J.
1996 'Reader Response Reader Responsibility: *Heart of Darkness* and the Politics of Displacement', in Ross C. Murfin (ed.), *Joseph Conrad:* Heart of Darkness (Case Studies in Contemporary Criticism; Boston: Bedford Books of St Martin's Press, 2nd edn): 131-47.

Rajan, B.
1976 *The Overwhelming Question: A Study of the Poetry of T.S. Eliot* (Toronto: University of Toronto Press).

Rapf, J.E.
1990 'Myth, Ideology, and Feminism in *High Noon*', *Journal of Popular Culture* 23: 75-80.

Reeves, C.E.
1985 'A Voice of Unrest: Conrad's Rhetoric of the Unspeakable', *Texas Studies in Literature and Language* 27: 284-310.

Reid, J.H.
1967 'A Man For All Movies: The Films of Fred Zinnemann', *Films and Filming* 13: 5-11.

Reid, S.A.
1966 'The 'Unspeakable Rites' in *Heart of Darkness*', in Marvin Mudrick (ed.), *Conrad: A Collection of Critical Essays* (Englewood Cliffs, NJ: Prentice–Hall): 45-54.

Renner, S.
1976 'Kurtz, Christ and the Darkness of "Heart of Darkness"', *Renascence* 28: 95-104.

Rich, F.
    1979   'The Making of a Quagmire', *Time* (24 August): 50-51.
Ridley, F.H.
    1963   'The Ultimate Meaning of *Heart of Darkness*', *Nineteenth-Century Fiction* 18: 43-53.
Riley, B.
    1979   ' "Heart" Transplant', *Film Comment* 15: 26-27.
Rising, C.
    1990   *Darkness at Heart: Fathers and Sons in Conrad* (New York: Greenwood).
Roberts, R.
    1990   'Post-Modernism and Feminist Science Fiction', *Science Fiction Studies* 17: 136-52.
Robinson, J.A.T.
    1976   *Redating the New Testament* (London: SCM Press).
Rogers, W.N.
    1975   'The Game of Dominoes in *Heart of Darkness*', *English Language Notes*: 42-45.
Rooke, C.
    1989   *Fear of the Open Heart: Essays on Contemporary Canadian Writing* (Toronto: Coach House Press).
Rosenbaum, J.
    1972   'The Voice and the Eye: A Commentary on the *Heart of Darkness* Script', *Film Comment* 8: 24-32.
    1997   *Movies as Politics* (Berkeley: University of California Press).
Rosenberg, R.A.
    1972   'The "Star of the Messiah" Reconsidered', *Bib* 53: 105-109.
Rosmarin, A.
    1989   'Darkening the Reader: Reader-Response Criticism and Heart of Darkness', in Ross C. Murfin (ed.), *Joseph Conrad:* Heart of Darkness (Case Studies in Contemporary Criticism; Boston: Bedford Books of St Martin's Press): 148-71.
Rowland, C.
    1993   *Revelation* (Epworth Commentaries; London: Epworth Press).
    1998   'The Book of Revelation', in Leander E. Keck (ed.), *The New Interpreter's Bible, Volume XII* (Nashville: Abingdon Press): 501-736.
Royalty, R.M., Jr
    1998   *The Streets of Heaven: The Ideology of Wealth in the Apocalypse of John* (Macon, GA: Mercer University Press).
Rubenstein, R.
    1988   'Nature and Nurture in Dystopia: *The Handmaid's Tale*', in Kathryn VanSpanckeren and Jan Garden Castro (eds.), *Margaret Atwood: Vision and Forms* (Carbondale, IL: Southern Illinois University Press): 101-112.
Ruthven, K.K.
    1968   'The Savage God: Conrad and Lawrence', *The Critical Quarterly*: 39-54.
Sage, L.
    1992   *Women in the House of Fiction: Post-War Women Novelists* (London: Macmillan).

Saha, P.K.
    1987   'Conrad's *Heart of Darkness*', *The Explicator* 45: 34-35.

Said, E.A.
    1966   *Joseph Conrad and the Fiction of Autobiography* (Cambridge, MA: Harvard University Press).
    1976   'Conrad and Nietzsche', in Norman Sherry (ed.), *Joseph Conrad: A Commemoration. Papers from the 1974 International Conference on Conrad* (London: Macmillan): 65-76.

Saramago, J.
    1993   *The Gospel According to Jesus Christ* (London: The Harvill Press [orig. Portuguese edn 1991]).

Sarvan, C.P.
    1980   'Racism and the *Heart of Darkness*', *International Fiction Review* 7: 6-10.

Saveson, J.E.
    1970   'Conrad's View of Primitive Peoples in *Lord Jim* and *Heart of Darkness*', *Modern Fiction Studies* 16: 163-83.

Sawyer, J.F.A.
    1972a   'Joshua x.12-14 and the Solar Eclipse of 30th September 1131 B.C.', *PEQ* 104: 139-46.
    1972b   'Why Is a Solar Eclipse Mentioned in the Passion Narrative (Luke XXIII.44-45)?', *JTS* 23: 124-28.

Schumacher, M.
    1999   *Francis Ford Coppola: A Filmmaker's Life* (London: Bloomsbury).

Schürer, E.
    1973   *The History of the Jewish People in the Age of Jesus Christ (175 B.C. A.D. 135)* (rev. and ed. Geza Vermes and Fergus Millar; Edinburgh: T. & T. Clark).

Schweitzer, A.
    1910   *The Quest of the Historical Jesus* (London: A. & C. Black).

Schweizer, E.
    1970   *The Good News According to Mark* (Atlanta: John Knox Press).
    1976   *The Good News According to Matthew* (London: SPCK).

Scofield, M.
    1988   *T.S. Eliot: The Poems* (Cambridge: Cambridge University Press).

Scott, B.B.
    1994   *Hollywood Dreams and Biblical Stories* (Minneapolis: Augsburg–Fortress).

Screech, M.A.
    1978   'The Magi and the Star (Matthew, 2)', in Olivier Fatio and Pierre Fraenkel (eds.), *Histoire de l'exégèse au XVIe siècle: Textes du Colloque International Tenu a Genève en 1976* (Geneva: Librairie Droz S.A.): 385-409.

Seidel, M.
    1985   'Isolation and Narrative Power: A Meditation of Conrad at the Boundaries', *Criticism* 27: 73-95.

Selig, M.
    1993   'Genre, Gender, and the Discourse of War: The A/Historical and Vietnam Films', *Screen* 34: 1-18.

Senior, D.
    1997   *The Gospel of Matthew* (IBT; Nashville: Abingdon Press).

1998   *Matthew* (ANTC; Nashville: Abingdon Press).

Seymour, J., with Michael W. Seymour
1978   'The Historicity of the Gospels and Astronomical Events Concerning the Birth of Christ', *Quarterly Journal of the Royal Astronomical Society* 19: 194-97.

Shakespeare, W.
1965   *Antony and Cleopatra* (Arden Edition; London: Methuen).

Sharpe, T.
1991   *T.S. Eliot: A Literary Life* (London: Macmillan).

Sharrett, C.
1980   'Operation Mind Control: *Apocalypse Now* and the Search for Clarity', *Journal of Popular Film and Television* 8: 34-43.

Shea, J.
1983   'Religious-Imaginative Encounters with Scriptural Stories', in Robert Detweiler (ed.), *Art/Literature/Religion: Life on the Borders* (*JAAR* Studies, 49.2; Chico: Scholars Press): 173-80.

Shelley, M.
1985   *Frankenstein* (London: Penguin Books [1818]).

Sherry, N.
1971   *Conrad's Western World* (Cambridge: Cambridge University Press).
1972   *Conrad* (London: Thames and Hudson).

Sherwood, Y.
2000   *A Biblical Text and its Afterlives: The Survival of Jonah in Western Culture* (Cambridge: Cambridge University Press).

Shetty, S.
1989   '*Heart of Darkness*: Out of Africa Some New Thing Never Comes', *Journal of Modern Literature* 15: 461-74.

Shipman, D.
1985   *A Pictorial History of Science Fiction Films* (Twickenham: Hamlyn).

Showalter, E.
1991   *Sexual Anarchy: Gender and Culture at the Fin de Siècle* (London: Bloomsbury).

Singh, F.B.
1988   'The Colonialistic Bias of *Heart of Darkness*', in Kimbrough (ed.) 1988: 268-90.

Sinyard, N.
1986   *Filming Literature: The Art of Screen Adaptation* (London: Croom Helm).

Slonczewski, J.L.
1986   'A Tale of Two Handmaids', *The Kenyon Review* 8: 120-24.

Smailes, T.A.
1970   'Eliot's "Journey of the Magi" ', *The Explicator* (October): item 18.

Smith, C.R.
1990   'Reclaiming the Social Justice Message of Revelation: Materialism, Imperialism and Divine Judgement in Revelation 18', *Transformation* 7: 28-33.

Smith, G.
1956   *T.S. Eliot's Poetry and Plays: A Study of Sources and Meaning* (Chicago: University of Chicago Press).

Smith, J.M.
1989   ' "Too Beautiful Together": Patriarchal Ideology in *Heart of Darkness*', in

Ross C. Murfin (ed.), Heart of Darkness: *A Case Study in Criticism* (New York: St Martin's Press): 179-95.

Smith, S.
1987 'Marxism and Ideology: Joseph Conrad, *Heart of Darkness*', in Douglas Tallack (ed.), *Literary Theory at Work: Three Texts* (London: B.T. Batsford): 181-200.

Southgate, C.
1999 'Reconsidering Phleba's Fields: Faith in the Life and Work of T.S. Eliot', in Liam Gearon (ed.), *English Literature, Theology and the Curriculum* (London: Cassell): 221-28.

Southam, B.C.
1994 *A Student's Guide to the Selected Poems of T.S. Eliot* (London: Faber and Faber, 6th edn).

Sowers, S.
1970 'The Circumstances and Recollection of the Pella Flight', *TZ* 26: 305-320.

Spadoni, R.
1997 'The Seeing Ear: The Presence of Radio in Welles's *Heart of Darkness*', in Gene M. Moore (ed.), *Conrad on Film* (Cambridge: Cambridge University Press): 78-92.

Stableford, B.
1987 'Is There No Balm in Gilead?: The Woeful Prophecies of "The Handmaid's Tale"', *Foundation* 39: 97-100.

Stampfl, B.
1991 'Marlow's Rhetoric of (Self-) Deception in *Heart of Darkness*', *Modern Fiction Studies* 37: 183-96.

Stanley, H.M.
1960 'Through the Dark Continent: Arrival at Matadi', in Leonard F. Dean (ed.), *Joseph Conrad's* Heart of Darkness: *Backgrounds and Criticisms* (Englewood Cliffs, NJ: Prentice–Hall): 79-88.

Stark, B.R.
1974–75 'Kurtz's Intended: The Heart of *Heart of Darkness*', *Texas Studies in Literature and Language* 16: 535-55.

Staten, H.
1986 'Conrad's Mortal Word', *Critical Inquiry* 12: 720-40.

Stauffer, E.
1955 *Christ and the Caesars* (London: SCM Press).
1970 *Jesus and His Story* (New York: Alfred A. Knopf).

Stein, K.F.
1991–92 'Margaret Atwood's *The Handmaid's Tale*: Scheherazade in Dystopia', *University of Toronto Quarterly* 61: 269-79.

Stein, W.B.
1956–57 'The Lotus Posture and "The Heart of Darkness"', *Modern Fiction Studies* 2: 235-37.
1965 'Conrad's East: Time, History, Action, and *Maya*', *Texas Studies in Literature and Language* 7: 265-83.

Steiner, J.E.
1982–83 'Modern Pharisees and False Apostles: Ironic New Testament Parallels in Conrad's "Heart of Darkness"', *Nineteenth-Century Fiction* 37: 75-96.

Stephenson, F.R.
    1977   'The Date of the Book of Joel', *VT* 19 (1969): 224-29.
Stewart, G.
    1980   'Lying as Dying in Heart of Darkness', *Proceedings of the Modern Language Association* 95: 319-31.
    1980-81   'Coppola's Conrad: The Repetitions of Complicity', *Critical Inquiry* 7: 455-74.
Stewart, J.I.M.
    1968   *Joseph Conrad* (London: Longmans).
Straus, N.P.
    1996   'The Exclusion of the Intended from Secret Sharing', in Elaine Jordan (ed.), *New Casebooks: Joseph Conrad* (London: Macmillan): 48-66.
Strauss, D.F.
    1973   *The Life of Jesus Critically Examined* (London: SCM Press).
Strick, P.
    1990   'Review of *The Handmaid's Tale*', *Monthly Film Bulletin* 57: 321-22.
Such, W.A.
    1999   *The Abomination of Desolation in the Gospel of Mark: Its Historical Reference in Mark 13.14 and its Impact in the Gospel* (Lanham, MD: University Press of America).
Sugg, R.P.
    1975   'The Triadic Structure of *Heart of Darkness*', *Conradiana* 7: 179-82.
Sullivan, Z.T.
    1981   'Enclosure, Darkness, and the Body: Conrad's Landscape', *Centennial Review* 25: 59-79.
Sundelson, D.
    1981   'Danse Macabre', *Conradiana* 13: 41-44.
Sutherland, J.
    1998   *Where Was Rebecca Shot?* (London: Weidenfeld & Nicolson).
Sweet, J.
    1979   *Revelation* (Pelican Commentary; London: SCM Press).
Swete, H.B.
    1909   *The Apocalypse of St. John* (London: Macmillan, 3rd edn).
Sylva, D.D.
    1986   'The Temple Curtain and Jesus' Death in the Gospel of Luke', *JBL* 105: 239-50.
Symonds, A.
    1971   'Every Novel Contains Autobiography', in Kimbrough (ed.) 1971: 157-58.
Tamplin, R.
    1988   *A Preface to T.S. Eliot* (London: Longman).
Tannehill, R.C.
    1996   *Luke* (ANTC; Nashville: Abingdon Press).
Tanner, T.
    1976   ' "Gnawed Bones" and "Artless Tales"—Eating and Narrative in Conrad', in Norman Sherry (ed.), *Joseph Conrad: A Commemoration—Papers from the 1974 International Conference on Conrad* (London: Macmillan Press, 1976): 17-36.

Tessitore, J.
1979   'The Literary Roots of *Apocalypse Now*', *New York Times* (21 October):
            Section 2.21.
Thale, J.
1960   'Marlow's Quest', in R.W. Stallman (ed.), *The Art of Joseph Conrad: A
            Critical Symposium* (Michigan State University Press): 154-61.
Theissen, G.
1992   *The Gospels in Context: Social and Political History in the Synoptic Tradi-
            tion* (Edinburgh: T. & T. Clark).
Thompson, G.
1978   'Conrad's Women', *Nineteenth-Century Fiction* 32: 442-63.
Thompson, L.
1990   *The Book of Revelation: Apocalypse and Empire* (Oxford: Oxford University
            Press).
Thompson, R.
1976   ' "Stoked": John Milius Interviewed by Richard Thompson', *Film Comment*
            12 (July–August): 10-21.
Thomson, I.
1984   'Tissot as a Religious Artist', in Krystyna Matyjaszliewicz (ed.), *James
            Tissot* (London: Phaidon Press and Barbican Art Gallery): 86-93.
Thorburn, D.
1974   *Conrad's Romanticism* (New Haven: Yale University Press).
Thumboo, E.
1981   'Some Plain Reading: Marlow's Lie in *Heart of Darkness*', *Literary
            Criterion* 16: 12-22.
Tinsley, E.J.
1969   *The Gospel According to Luke* (The Cambridge Bible Commentary;
            Cambridge: Cambridge University Press).
Todorov, T.
1989   'Knowledge in the Void: *Heart of Darkness*', *Conradiana* 21: 161-72.
Tomasulo, F.P.
1990   'The Politics of Ambivalence: *Apocalypse Now* as Prowar and Antiwar Film',
            in Linda Dittmar and Gene Michaud (eds.), *From Hanoi to Hollywood: The
            Vietnam War in American Film* (New Brunswick, NJ: Rutgers University
            Press): 145-58.
Trexler, R.C.
1997   *The Journey of the Magi: Meanings in History of a Christian Story* (Prince-
            ton: Princeton University Press).
Trilling, L.
1966   *Beyond Culture* (London: Secker and Warburg).
Tullock, J.
1980   'Bridging the Gap: The Promethean Star Trek', in Walter Irwin and G.B.
            Love (eds.), *The Best of Trek No. 3* (New York: Signet Books): 91-105.
Turner, A.R.
1988   'Atwood's Playing Puritans in *The Handmaid's Tale*', in Mirko Jurak (ed.),
            *Cross-Cultural Studies: American, Canadian and European Literatures
            1945–1985* (Ljubljana: English Department): 85-91.
Twain, M.
1966   *The Adventures of Huckleberry Finn* (London: Penguin Books [1876]).

1986   *The Adventures of Tom Sawyer* (London: Penguin Books [1884]).

Ulansey, D.
1991   'The Heavenly Veil Torn: Mark's Cosmic Inclusio', *JBL* 110: 123-25.

Van Bruggen, J.
1978   'The Year of the Death of Herod the Great', in T. Baarda, A.F.J. Klijn and
            W.C. Van Unnik (eds.), *Miscellanea Neotestamentica* II (Leiden: E.J. Brill):
            1-15.

Vardaman, J.
1989   'Jesus' Life: A New Chronology', in Vardaman and Yamauchi (eds.) 1989:
            55-82.

Vardaman, J., and Edwin M. Yamauchi (eds.)
1989   *Chronos, Kairos, Christos: Nativity and Chronological Studies Presented to
            Jack Finegan* (Winina Lake, IN: Eisenbrauns).

Verleun, J.
1981   'Marlow and the Harlequin', *Conradiana* 13: 195-220.

Vitoux, P.
1975   'Marlow: The Changing Narrator of Conrad's Fiction', in Claude Thomas
            (ed.), *Studies in Joseph Conrad* (Montpellier: Université Paul-Valéry):
            83-102.

Wagner-Martin, L.W.
1987   'Epigraphs to Atwood's *The Handmaid's Tale*', *Notes On Contemporary
            Literature* 17: 4.

Wall, K.
1988   *The Callisto Myth From Ovid to Atwood: Initiation and Rape in Literature*
            (Kingston and Montreal: McGill-Queen's University Press).

Wall, R.W.
1991   *Revelation* (NIBC; Peabody, MA: Hendrickson).

Wallace, L.
1959   *Ben Hur* (London: Pan Books [1888])

Walker, N.
1988   'Ironic Autobiography: From *The Waterfall* to *The Handmaid's Tale*',
            Women's Studies 15: 203-20.

Ward, D.
1973   *T.S. Eliot Between Two Worlds: A Reading of T.S. Eliot's Poetry and Plays*
            (London: Routledge & Kegan Paul).

Ward, M.J.
1998–99   'God and the Novelists: Arthur Koestler', *ExpTim* 110: 133-37.

Warshow, R.
1972   'The Westerner', in Daniel Talbot (ed.), *Film: An Anthology* (Berkeley:
            University of California Press): 148-62.

Watson, W.S.
1981   'Willard as Narrator: A Critique and an Immodest Proposal', *Conradiana*
            13: 35-40.
1997   'Conrad Ironies and the Conrad Films', in Gene M. Moore (ed.), *Conrad on
            Film* (Cambridge: Cambridge University Press): 16-30.

Watt, I.
1976   'Impressionism and Symbolism in Heart of Darkness', in Norman Sherry
            (ed.), *Joseph Conrad: A Commemoration—Papers from the 1974 Interna-
            tional Conference on Conrad* (London: Macmillan Press): 37-53.

1978–79   'Marlow, Henry James, and *Heart of Darkness*', *NCF* 33: 159-74.

1980   *Conrad in the Nineteenth Century* (London: Chatto & Windus).

1996   'Ideological Perspectives: Kurtz and the Fate of Victorian Progress', in Elaine Jordan (ed.), *New Casebooks: Joseph Conrad* (London: Macmillan): 32-47.

Watts, C.

1977   *Conrad's* Heart of Darkness*: A Critical and Contextual Discussion* (Milan: Mursia International).

1983   ' "A Bloody Racist": About Achebe's View of Conrad', *Yearbook of English Studies* 13: 196-209.

1984   *The Deceptive Text: An Introduction to Covert Plots* (Brighton, UK: Harvester; Totowa, NJ: Barnes & Noble).

1993   *A Preface to Conrad* (London: Longman, 2nd edn).

Watts, C. (ed.)

1969   *Joseph Conrad's Letters to R.B. Cunninghamme Graham* (Cambridge: Cambridge University Press).

Weinert, F.D.

1982   'Luke, the Temple, and Jesus' Saying about Jerusalem's Abandoned House (Luke 13.34-35)', *CBQ* 44: 68-76.

Wengst, K.

1987   *Pax Romana and the Peace of Jesus Christ* (London: SCM Press).

Wenham, D.

1984   *The Rediscovery of Jesus' Eschatological Discourse* (Gospel Perspectives, 4; Sheffield: JSOT Press).

1992   'Abomination of Desolation', *ABD* 1: 28-31.

Weston, J.L.

1941   *From Ritual to Romance* (New York: Peter Smith).

Welch, J.

1986   'Review of *The Handmaid's Tale*', *America* (12 July): 16-17.

White, A.

1993   *Joseph Conrad and the Adventure Tradition: Constructing and Deconstructing the Imperial Subject* (Cambridge: Cambridge University Press).

Whitehead, L.M.

1969–70   'Conrad's "Pessimism" Re-Examined', *Conradiana* 2: 25-38.

1975   'The Active Voice and the Passive Eye: *Heart of Darkness* and Nietzsche's *The Birth of Tragedy*', *Conradiana* 7: 121-35.

Wilcox, M.

1975   *The Message of Revelation* (BST; Leicester: IVP).

Wilcox, S.C.

1960   'Conrad's Complicated Presentations of Symbolic Imagery in *Heart of Darkness*', *Philological Quarterly* 39: 1-17.

Williams, G.W.

1963   'The Turn of the Tide in *Heart of Darkness*', *Modern Fiction Studies* 9: 171-73.

Williamson, B.

1979   ' "Apocalypse" Finally', *Playboy* (October): 114-21, 195.

Williamson, G.
1967   *A Reader's Guide to T.S. Eliot: A Poem-By-Poem Analysis* (London: Thames and Hudson, 2nd edn).
Willis, G.
1997   *John Wayne: The Politics of Celebrity* (London: Faber and Faber).
Willmott, G.
1995   ''O Say, Can You See: *The Handmaid's Tale* in Novel and Film', in Lorraine M. York (ed.), *Various Atwoods: Essays on the Later Poems, Short Fiction, and Novels* (Concord, Ontario: House of Anansi Press): 167-90.
Wills, J.H.
1954   'Eliot's "Journey of the Magi" ', *The Explicator* 12: 32.
Willy, T.G.
1978   'The "Shamefully Abandoned" Kurtz', *Conradiana* 10: 99-112.
Wilmington, M.
1988   'Worth the Wait: *Apocalypse Now*', in Kimbrough (ed.) 1988: 285-88.
Wohlpart, A.J
1992   'The Sacrament of Penance in T.S. Eliot's "Journey of the Magi" ', *English Language Notes* 30: 55-60.
Wood, M.
1979   'Bangs and Whimpers', *The New York Review of Books* (11 October): 17-18.
Wood, R.
1996   '*Rio Bravo*', in Jim Hillier and Peter Woller (eds.), *Howard Hawks: American Artist* (London: British Film Industry): 87-102.
Workman, N.V.
1989   'Sufi Mysticism in Margaret Atwood's *The Handmaid's Tale*', *Studies in Canadian Literature* 14: 10-26.
Worthy, K.
1992   'Hearts of Darkness: Making Art, Making History, Making Money, Making "Vietnam" ', *Cinéaste* 19: 24-27.
1996   'Emissaries of Difference: Conrad, Coppola, and *Hearts of Darkness*', *Women's Studies* 25: 153-67.
Yamauchi, E.
1989   'The Episode of the Magi', in Vardaman and Yamauchi (eds.) 1989: 15-39.
Yarrison, B.C.
1975   'The Symbolism of Literary Allusion in *Heart of Darkness*', *Conradiana* 7: 155-64.
Yoder, A.C.
1969–70   'Oral Artistry in Conrad's *Heart of Darkness*: A Study in Oral Aggression', *Conradiana* 2: 65-78.
Young, G.
1989   'Kurtz as Narcissistic Megalomaniac in Joseph Conrad's *Heart of Darkness*', in A. Kakouriotis and R. Parkin-Gounelas (eds.), *Working Papers in Linguistics and Literature* (Thessaloniki: Aristotle University): 255-63.
Yule, A.
1993   *Sean Connery: Neither Shaken Nor Stirred* (London: Little, Brown and Co.).
Zamatkin, E.
1993   *We* (London: Penguin Books).

Zinnemann, F.
    1952   'The Choreography of a Gunfight', *Sight and Sound* 22: 16-17.
    1992   *An Autobiography* (London: Bloomsbury).
Zmijewski, J.
    1990   'βδέλυγμα, ατος, τό', *Exegetical Dictionary of the New Testament* (Grand Rapids, MI: Eerdmans): I, 209-10.

INDEXES

INDEX OF REFERENCES

BIBLE

OTHER ANCIENT REFERENCES

INDEX OF AUTHORS

THE BIBLICAL SEMINAR